INDIA AND PAKISTAN

India and Pakistan

A Political Analysis

HUGH TINKER

FREDERICK A. PRAEGER, *Publisher*
New York

BOOKS THAT MATTER

Published in the United States of America in 1962
by Frederick A. Praeger, Inc., Publisher
64 University Place, New York 3, N.Y.

All rights reserved

Library of Congress Catalog Card Number: 62-17298

INDIA AND PAKISTAN is published in two editions:

A paperback edition (U-526)
A clothbound edition

Printed in the United States of America

FOR ELISABETH

with love

CONTENTS

MAPS

I

TRADITIONAL SOCIETY AND AUTHORITY

NEW nations, and ancient cultures: this is how most people see India and Pakistan today. New, experimental systems of democracy, in which parliament and the ballot box are still under trial, are contrasted with the ancient ritual of Hinduism and Islam, caste and tribalism, the art and architecture of Ajanta and the Red Fort, the literature of the *Bhagavad Gita* and the *Babur-Nama*. Yet the paradox of this new-old land is even more complex: ancient social and religious thought and custom intermingle with the ideologies and social attitudes of the West; while the new politics of the people goes hand in hand with the authoritarian tradition of government bequeathed by the Mughal and the British-Indian Empires.

Society, ideas and modes of government are all in flux; and all interact upon each other. It is not only that parliamentary government is hazarded by social and religious forces; by caste-ism or Muslim fanaticism, for example. It is also sapped by the immemorial view of government itself as a dome of absolute authority, suspended high above ordinary folk; a power which they might supplicate, or might even, possibly, manipulate; but which they never could hope to draw into their own hands. The attainment of a broad-based democracy may come about not so much by the actual functioning of democratic institutions, such as parliament, but more by social and religious change; by the demand of lower caste people for social and economic parity; by the spread of adult education, or the gradual emancipation of women from domestic immolation.

In order to appreciate the impact upon the civilisation of India of nineteenth-century ideas of the political virtues of representative govern-

9

ment and twentieth-century ideas of the right of all peoples to independence, it is necessary to commence with a brief account of the nature of traditional society, and traditional systems of authority and government.

The historic unity of India is a theme which nationalist writers insist upon. It is not an empty dream. The eternal snows of the Himalaya, and the great rivers of Sind (Indus) to the west and Brahmaputra to the east form the legendary boundaries of Mother India, *Bharat Varsa*. This idea is expressed in political terms in the concept of *Çakravartin*, universal emperor, and the ideal has been almost realised in epic periods of Indian history. The vision is realised in socio-religious terms in the grand design of Hinduism. The silent peaks of the Himalaya are the abode of the Hindu pantheon; the great rivers—especially Mother Ganges, descending from the snows, fertilising a thousand miles of the northern plains—are sacred, cleansing, life-giving. From Sind to Brahmaputra, the priestly authority of the Brahmin receives supreme regard; while the despised, subhuman degradation of the untouchable is equally universal.

Yet, the hundred years of British rule formed the only time when India was effectively linked together as an entity. The great rulers who aspired to bring all India under their sway invariably strained their resources to breaking-point—and helped to bring on the disruption of the empires they had created. Geography gives India an overall unity: but geography also provides barriers which, even today, interpose formidable divisions. The first great divide comes between north and south. Peninsular India is separated from the northern plains by the Vindhya mountains, running due west to east. Few are the gaps between these jungle-covered hills, and their chain marks, to a surprising degree, the watershed between the small-boned dark-skinned people of the south and the big-boned lighter-skinned peoples of the north. The second great natural boundary is that of the Great Indian Desert, which spreads north from Kutch for 600 miles towards Delhi and Punjab, Land of the Five Rivers. This desert waste separates the riverine cultivation of the Sind from the rest of India: and provides the frontier between West Pakistan and India. The third barrier is not so physically imposing, but is only slightly less obstructive. The Ganges flows across the northern plains, and the Brahmaputra descends from the Assam valley; their waters come together in Bengal, feeding a dozen wide and sluggish rivers. During the monsoon, these rivers—and, virtually, the eastern half of Bengal—become one vast lagoon. Isolated by its riverways, Bengal has evolved upon its own; away from the mainstream of Indian life.[1]

These are only the most important of the natural divisions which have given India its provincial, regional character. Isolation has brought about linguistic variation; there are some twenty main regional languages, which are subdivided into hundreds of dialects. The northern group are usually called the Aryan languages, being largely derived from Sanskrit. The southern group of Dravidian languages has an entirely different root, though the priestly pre-eminence of Sanskrit has had its influence. There are important regional variations within the fold of Hinduism: southern India is a stronghold of Sivaism. The peninsula has a strong maritime tradition: the Malabar and Coromandel coasts have been important entrepôts since the days when they traded with Rome. The Çola kings of the south conquered Ceylon and penetrated Southeast Asia; even today the most important source of Indian overseas emigration and capital investment is provided by the Tamils.

If southern India looks out across the Arabian Sea and the Bay of Bengal, north-west India looks across the mountains of the Hindu Kush (called by Ibn Batuta, the 'Hindu Killer') to central Asia. Through long periods of history, northern India has been linked with Afghanistan, Persia, and Turkistan. The locus of power has shifted beyond the Hindu Kush, and back to Delhi. From central Asia came the conquering, proselytising apostles of Islam. For five hundred years, the northern plains were subject to Muslim rule. The rulers, governors, lawgivers and soldiers of fortune from central Asia introduced new styles: in social usage, dress, architecture, law, language, and administration. Military conquest, as is usual, carried the prestige of success; many of these innovations were absorbed into Indian culture—more particularly at its upper and urban levels. Jawaharlal Nehru has observed that India's 'peculiar quality is absorption, synthesis'. To some extent, this process of synthesis interacted between the Muslim invaders and Hindu society. Hinduism accepted certain features, notably *purdah* (the seclusion of women), and the Muslims borrowed from Hinduism, more particularly, the marriage ritual. The Muslims, believers in the brotherhood of all mankind (or, at any rate, of all Muslims), even absorbed parts of the caste system. They adopted classification by family, tribe and occupation, and

[1] Because of this isolation, Buddhism (which was overthrown in the rest of India by a Brahmanical revival) lingered on. Bengali rural society lacked the extraordinary resilience and resistance given by caste organisation, and at length Muslim conquerors carried out widespread conversion, producing a large Islamic pocket in eastern India. Elsewhere, Hinduism was generally strong enough to resist large-scale Islamic proselytisation.

restricted marriage accordingly; although they did not accept Hindu taboos upon the eating of food. Upper class Muslims and Hindus in northern India developed a common language—Urdu or Hindustani (which took its grammar from Sanskrit, its vocabulary from Indian tongues, Persian, and Turki, and its script from Arabic). Similarly, their dress had many features in common.[1]

Under the Mughal Emperors, Rajput princes received high command, in the army and as governors of important provinces; Brahmin and Kayastha ministers occupied key posts in the administration, and Hindu poets were encouraged to compose in Persian. More: two of the Mughal emperors were the sons of Hindu mothers. Among the ordinary people there was a certain sharing in religious and social practices, especially on the Bombay side, and in Bengal (where a British writer later described the Muslim cultivators as 'circumcised Hindus'). Both communities would take part in the more public portions of each other's festivals; Hindus often worshipped at the tombs of Muslim saints; some Muslims of the trading castes took a Hindu name, along with their Islamic names. Yet, despite these connexions between the two communities, they never coalesced.

For all its message of the universality of God and the brotherhood of man, Islam is (like Judaism and Christianity) an exclusive religion; regarding non-believers as *kafirs,* infidels. Although many of the Muslim rulers were tolerant towards their Hindu subjects, there was constant recurrence of oppression and forcible conversion. Moreover, the Muslim upper classes were very conscious of their ties of blood and culture with central Asia and the near east. The stock was constantly replenished from these areas, and the Muslim élite remained (like the British later) 'Strangers in India'. To this day, their magnificent mosques, forts, and palaces dominate the cities of northern India: yet these are almost as alien as the Gothic churches and colleges which Victorian Englishmen have left as their legacy to these same cities.

The paradoxes of Hinduism also served to create lines of division. Hinduism sees the omnipotence of God in everything; Hinduism is tolerant, passive; yet absorptive and stifling. Hinduism would have accepted, and assimilated the message of the Prophet Muhammad, as it had absorbed the message of Lord Buddha, as a manifestation of divine truth: yet only a facet of the wider insight of Hinduism. Faced with the

---

[1] The costume which Nehru almost always wears on public occasions; *achkin shilwar,* and *chapli* (buttoned-up frock coat, tight white pyjama, and cross-over sandals), is pure Muslim dress. Nehru insists that his mother tongue is Hindustani, not Hindi. His ancestors were officials of the Mughal court at Delhi.

harsh resolution of the faith of the desert, Hinduism could only draw back—and watch, and wait. The impenetrable defence was the web of caste. In social relations, the exclusiveness of caste—which restricts the circle of intercourse to a narrow, hereditary group—isolated Hindus (especially of the higher castes) from Muslims of the same class and calling. The Hindu emphasis upon ritual cleanliness and purity tended to identify the Muslim with unlawfulness and defilement: the generic term *mleccha*, applied to all non-Hindus, has a definite connotation of uncleanness. And so, throughout India, the two communities dwelt, side by side, yet separate. In most areas, the Muslims were associated with administration or with military service, while they also developed hereditary occupations in which they were pre-eminent, such as metalwork. In consequence, they were mainly town dwellers. Only here and there were they to be found settled on the land; usually as colonies of disbanded soldiers, on the Roman pattern. In Punjab and Bengal, however, the majority of the original cultivators were Muslims; and in these parts it was the Hindu commercial community who formed the majority of the town dwellers. Muslim strength was in the 'Law and Order' or internal security services, and in the military; Hindu strength was specially deployed in the financial departments of administration (including the all-important department which collected the revenue from agricultural land), in commerce, and in the priestly and literary occupations: though Hindus of the warrior castes, such as Rajputs, were well represented in military service. Muslims thought of themselves as the ruling race. Hindus accepted their position as the ruled, under necessity; but they never forgot the golden, legendary age of *Ram Rajya,* when Hinduism reigned supreme.

So far, we have been considering the 'Great Society' of India as a whole; but the context of life for the great majority of ordinary folk was the 'Little Society' of the village. Much has been made of the 'self-sufficient' economy of the village, as well as its political autonomy and solidarity: a famous administrator, Charles Metcalfe, talked about the 'little republics', and his aphorism has been repeated by almost every subsequent writer. It is true that, to the great mass of Indians, both of the past and the present, the village represents everything: home and family, a sense of belonging, security, life itself. But all this does not mean that the Indian village is self-sufficient. Even in centuries past, the village did not subsist upon its own resources. It was linked to surrounding hamlets, to a market town; perhaps, to a place of pilgrimage or an administrative centre. This wider setting had its effect upon village economics. It was even more pervasive in the realm of family relationships: few castes contracted marriages within their own communities. Almost always they would go for their brides to a neighbouring village, and as the Indian family system involves well-defined dealings and contacts between the paternal and maternal clans, each village is involved in a web of relationships with the surrounding countryside. The structure of power is not confined within the village, either. Power is deployed upon a patron-dependent basis. Lowly folk will approach one held in high esteem by the village when they want to undertake almost any transaction—perhaps involving religious sanction, the consent of the village leaders, or a boon from the landlord. The patron assists his dependant in return for a specific *douceur* most probably: but also in order to maintain a fund of loyalty within the village community, so that in any dispute or struggle for power he will be able to mobilise a following which will demonstrate his ascendancy. Similarly, in the relation between the village and its landlord, or the local *raja* or governor, there would be lines of mutual interest. Perhaps a certain village leader would be able to approach a superior because both were members of the same caste, or were linked by some other social or religious bond. The relationship would be founded on the same patron-client basis. The superior would consider giving favours to the village leader in return for the loyalty of the village if he were involved in some wider quarrel. A landlord might expect a whole village community to take to the jungle, leaving standing crops unharvested, if this would assist his struggle with higher authority.

All these relationships were based upon inequality. Within village society, the lower castes could never hope to improve their subordinate status. Strict sumptuary custom kept to a minimum their rights, to domestic possessions, to the village services, and to their share in village produce. The higher castes were quick to discipline any low caste man who was so presumptuous as to eat off metalware, in place of vessels of clay; or a low caste woman who presumed to cover her breasts. The lesson would be sharp enough not to be soon forgotten. Yet all the castes had their appointed place in the hierarchy: none could be dispensed with. At the most intimate moments of birth and death, Brahmins and Rajputs were ritually dependent on the services of the lowest Sudras. The entire village united together in mutual protection against an external adversary. It was no coincidence that the village community developed its strongest spirit of cohesion in Punjab, and in the Delhi territory: the traditional invasion pathway from central Asia into India.

Village solidarity has been supposed to reside in the institution of the *panchayat* or Council of Five. It has become fashionable in India to claim that the panchayat was the source of an indigenous system of village democracy and village co-operative effort. Exact scholarship demonstrates that the panchayat was mainly an institution of government for the caste or trade guild. But in certain areas the panchayat was apparently constituted on a village basis as an institution of judicial inquiry or arbitration. Here is a description of such a panchayat, as found in Oudh in 1850:

> When a man suffers wrong, the wrongdoer is summoned before the elders or most respectable men of his village or clan; and if he denies the charge or refuses redress, he is told to bathe, put his hand upon the peepul tree and declare aloud his innocence. If he refuses, he is commanded to restore what he has taken, or make suitable reparation; and if he refuses to do this, he is punished by the odium of all and his life becomes miserable. A man does not put his hand upon the sacred tree and deny the truth—the gods sit in it and know all things.[1]

This is clearly not a picture of a system of village government. Villages might be controlled by an oligarchy of the principal caste leaders, or by a hereditary village headman (in the south, called the *patel*), or even by an agent of a great landlord. The main political links between the village and the government lay in the obligation to pay taxes—the Mughal Empire demanded payment of land revenue, equivalent to half the crop —and the obligation to contribute forced labour on the roads, *begar*.

Government was a power apart. Its character is illustrated in this analysis of kingship which appears in the *Sukraniti*, a late medieval political treatise:

> The King is the ruler, protector, and benefactor of the people . . . he is lord of this earth because of his deeds in the previous births. . . . The King should make the subjects acquire the habits of performing their duties by the use of his terrible sceptre. . . . The Prince who is virtuous is a part of the gods. . .

To this concept of absolute, semi-divine kingship, the Muslim rulers added certain qualities. François Bernier, who visited the Mughal court in the seventeenth century, commented: 'The Great Mogol is a foreigner in Hindustan. . . . He finds himself in a hostile country, or nearly so; . . . he is under the necessity of keeping up numerous armies, even in the time of peace.' Foreign rule; military rule; this was the core of the Mughal system; Bernier described Delhi as 'a military

---

[1] Quoted in the author's *Foundations of Local Self-Government in India, Pakistan, and Burma*, University of London, The Athlone Press, 1954, p. 20.

encampment'.[1] The administrative hierarchy which the Mughals established was military in form: rank was determined according to seniority. This *mansabdari* system created, in effect, an Imperial civil service, which formed the backbone of the Empire. Three-quarters of these high officials were foreigners (Turks, Afghans, Persians). In theory, there was a dual hierarchy; one chain of officials responsible for law enforcement, the second supervising the collection of revenue. The key officials in the Empire were the governors of provinces (termed *subahdar,* or *nazim*). They exercised control of criminal justice. At their side was the *dewan* or finance minister. Provinces were divided into districts, where this dual pattern was reproduced, and districts were subdivided into units normally corresponding to the old Hindu administrative area, the *pargana.* The foundation of Mughal administration was the revenue inquest (not unlike Domesday) undertaken by the Emperor Akbar's Hindu revenue minister, Raja Todar Mal. Cultivated land throughout the Empire was measured and recorded, and a monetary basis for assessment was substituted for payment in kind. An elaborate revenue staff was employed, with the *patwari* or village accountant at its base. The results of the survey were incorporated into a vast gazetteer, the *Ain-i-Akbari* by a central revenue office, employing hundreds of clerks (mainly Hindus) who laboriously copied details from one register into another, copied and recopied orders, and submitted their work to superintendents for check and counter-signature.

The district system, with the district officer as head of the public services and general factotum or Poo Bah, the erection of an administrative hierarchy upon the basis of land revenue collection, and the development of an involute maze of office procedure, these features of Mughal rule were all accepted as the foundation of British rule; and, indeed, to an astonishing degree, in India and Pakistan today local administration is Mughal in spirit.

By the victories of Plassey and Buxar (1757 and 1764) the East India Company became heir to the Mughal Empire, and in the following half century extended its control over the greater part of the continent. But the Company was extremely reluctant to assume the external attributes of sovereignty. Until 1835, the coinage of the East India Company bore the Mughal superscription; the Emperors were permitted to maintain the pretence of a court at Delhi, and the last of their line, Bahadur Shah, was not deposed until 1858, after the great Sepoy Revolt. As we have noted, the fabric of administration was Mughal, and change was slow to

---

[1] Quotations taken from the author's 'People and Government in Southern Asia', *Transactions of the Royal Historical Society,* 5th Series, Vol. 9.

come. Persian remained the language of the law courts and of administration until the 1830s, and the post of *kazi*, the Muslim judge interpreting the law, was not abolished until 1864.

Amongst the British officials who formulated policy, a long struggle went on between the 'Orientalists' who opposed all change (even, for example, measures against *sati*, the burning of the widow upon her husband's funeral pyre) and the 'Anglicists' who wished to introduce Western ideas into government, social usages, and education: and to transform the Indian mind by employing the English language as the medium of communication for the business of government and in the new colleges. In the reforming mood of the 1830s, the Anglicists largely prevailed. For twenty years the British in India were a band of reformers, assailing traditional ideas and customs, by means of Western education, legal reform, and technological change. Then came the Sepoy Revolt: called the Mutiny in British history-books, and called the First War of Independence by modern Indian nationalist publicists (albeit without much conviction). This revolt was so widespread, and aroused such a volume of bitterness, as to cause the British to reconsider their entire purpose and place in India. On the one hand, British success in suppressing the revolt (despite the total ineptitude shown by all senior military officers) appeared to constitute Divine confirmation of British rule in India as the instrument of the Divine purpose. On the other hand, the violent discontent shown by elements in the army and among the leaders of society appeared to have been a reaction against the activities of the social reformers and the Christian missionaries. The British official attitude became set in opposition to all movements for reform. This attitude is summed up in the following extract from an editorial printed in a Calcutta newspaper in 1873: this journal (*The Friend of India*) had led the movement for reform in the 1830s, but after the Mutiny lost its sense of purpose:

> Avoid change; by removing obstructions rather than by supplying new stimulants, slowly develop, but do not violently upheave native society; leave rich and poor to themselves and their natural relations within the limits that prevent oppression.[1]

These words might serve as a threnody for British rule during its remaining ninety years.

The Indian response to the Westernising, reforming movement of the

[1] Quoted in 'People and Government in Southern Asia', *op. cit.*

early nineteenth century was twofold. There was conservative opposition, expressed in the Mutiny, which was the reaction of almost all privileged groups threatened by the new innovations. This opposition was specially strong among the feudal aristocracy, among religious zealots, both Hindu and Muslim and among those who had enjoyed power and influence in the old Mughal administration and in the quasi-independent princely enclaves. In its first phase, this conservative, traditionalist attitude was negative and defensive; it appeared to have suffered a shattering defeat in the Mutiny. The other response (the other side of the medal, as it were) was an Indian movement for social reform which exhibited all the qualities of absorption and synthesis which Nehru identifies as peculiarly Indian. The Erasmus of this movement was Ram Mohan Ray (1774-1833), a Brahmin of Bengal, who led the demand for English higher education, and pioneered social reform. Yet he was no mere Westernising imitator. Observers as different as Marx and Macaulay anticipated that the British impact upon India would reproduce types and classes which duplicated European models. It was the genius of Ram Mohan to avert a slavish Westernisation by accepting, indeed welcoming Western features into a living Hinduism. At a period when the European, or rather, Anglo-Protestant ethos was predominant, he was constrained to demonstrate that India was not wholly primitive, and obscurantist; as critics like Macaulay declared. He tried to show that social evils like sati were degenerate aberrations, rather than essential attributes of Hinduism. He evolved an ethical system, the *Brahmo Samaj*, which was monotheistic, almost Christian in spirit; yet he also sowed the seed from which has sprung the modern *Vedanta* school of philosophy, to which belong such thinkers as Sri Aurobindo, Vivekananda, and Radhakrishnan. Ram Mohan helped to elevate contemporary Hinduism into a rational religion; his principal work was to translate sacred texts into the vernacular, particularly the *Upanisads,* which he rescued from centuries of oblivion.

The intellectual renascence, which Ram Mohan Ray largely generated, was the forerunner of the political renascence towards the end of the century. The spirit of rationalism, and social reform, and a receptive attitude to Western ideas, prevailed among the majority of Indian political leaders till the end of the nineteenth century. But meanwhile, the conservative element had acquired a new and powerful dynamism. A movement called the *Arya Samaj* was founded in 1875 by a former Sanyasi (or wandering ascetic) known as Dayanand Saraswati. Its creed was militant and puritan, based upon the martial epic of Vedic scripture. One branch of the Arya Samaj was the Theosophical Society of Madame

Blavatskaya and Annie Besant. Here was a complete reversal of values and attitudes! Instead of the decadent East looking to the omnicompetent West for education and reform, the West was turning to the East, to Hinduism and Buddhism as the matrix of religion and enlightenment. While Ram Mohan and his followers regarded British scholars as their friends and teachers, Dayanand Saraswati condemned all Christians and Muslims as mlecchas, and launched a campaign for the reconversion of Indians who had embraced other religions to Hinduism.

This pattern was largely repeated among the Muslims. The final collapse of the Mughal Empire, and the gradual eclipse of Muslim modes of government (particularly, the replacement of an Islamic system of law by Courts subscribing to the English Common Law) left the Muslim educated classes isolated, aloof, and resentful. The Hindu literary castes who had adapted themselves to the Persian communication of the Mughals, equally readily adapted themselves to the English language used by the British administration. But to Muslims, Persian and Arabic were not merely means of communication: they represented their religious and literary heritage. For half a century, the Muslims largely remained outside the new Western institutions of higher education, and to an increasing extent they were unable to enter the higher grades of the administration. Gradually, it became clear to the more forward-looking members of the community that, in consequence of their withdrawal, the Muslims had placed themselves at a crippling disadvantage; that the erstwhile pliant, submissive Hindus of the literary castes were in a fair way towards controlling the new institutions of government; that even if they made a determined effort to recapture lost ground, the Muslims would be at least half a century behind their Hindu counterparts in their capability to manipulate the British administrative machine for their own advantage.

A valid interpretation of the subsequent Muslim separatist movement can be advanced in terms of the attempts by the Muslims to make up their disadvantage; to somehow win back the fifty years' start which the Hindu middle class had gained in the race for political and economic primacy.

The leading spirit in the Muslim revival was Sayyid Ahmad Khan (1817-98), a trusted official in the British service. His campaign to rehabilitate his community followed closely (though not consciously) the approach of Ram Mohan Ray. He reinterpreted Islamic doctrine so as to disarm Christian criticism (as by stressing the predominance of monogamy among Muslims). He attempted a synthesis of Islam with the new scientific rationalism; but he also took a firm stand against the attacks of

Christian controversialists against Islam; he urged a return to the Quran, and he asserted the supremacy of Islam amongst the religions of the world, because God uniquely revealed his purpose through the Quran. In practical applications of his ideas, Sayyid Ahmad, like Ram Mohan, believed that his community could be regenerated by Western education, by the absorption of Western thought into the Islamic cosmorama. He established the Anglo-Oriental College at Aligarh (1877), which eventually became the Muslim University.

As Ram Mohan was followed by Dayanand Saraswati, so Sayyid Ahmad was followed by Islamic thinkers (such as Akbar, of Allahabad) who preached a more reactionary militant creed, hostile to other religions.

To consider these trends in social terms: the influence of the mediating, modernist, Western-looking social reformers was confined entirely to the new professional middle classes. The traditionalist, militant West-rejecting reformers were also mainly middle class, but they did achieve some influence among the masses. The Arya Samaj had a considerable following in Punjab, and the western part of the United Provinces (Uttar Pradesh). The Islamic revivalists, notably the body called *Wahabis*, also had considerable influence, especially in Bengal, where they aroused the semi-Hinduised peasantry to a sense of belonging to the wider Islamic community. Indeed, the consequence of the revivalist movements on both sides was to accentuate the differences between Hindus and Muslims. Sayyid Ahmad talked of 'two races' in India: Hindus and Muslims. But he also called the two communitites the 'two eyes' of India, implying that they were complementary. A rift might open—or be closed.

Any who hoped to find the key to this riddle by looking back into Indian history, would discover only that there were two sides to the medal. At certain periods, the two communities had co-operated, as under Akbar; at other times they had been bitterly at odds, as under Alamgir. There was now a new ingredient in the political brew: nationalism. Would nationalism make for unity (as in France) or disunity (as in Austria-Hungary)?

Nationalist writers have often asserted that British Imperial policy was directed towards separating the two communities: Divide and Rule, this has been called. It is outside the scope of this book to attempt any detailed analysis of British policy (whatever that expression may denote) but it is useful to recall the admonition of *The Friend of India*—'avoid change'. British 'policy' after 1857 was predominantly conservative. In the economic sphere it had a positive, creative content (though care was taken not to upset the social balance), but in the social and political sphere, British policy was almost entirely devoted to maintaining the existing structure. The rise of the new professional middle class was viewed with distinct suspicion by the majority of British officials; themselves an intellectual élite, they had little sympathy for the Indian intellectual élite. Whenever the question was raised of increasing the share of Indians in their own government, the British officials retorted by calling for measures to bring forward the 'natural leaders of society'. These 'natural leaders' were, in effect, the rural leaders; from the rustic yeoman and squire up to the great landlords and princes. Because the new middle class was overwhelmingly composed of Hindus of the literary castes, they suspected that the British were attempting to discriminate against them as Hindus. While the 'natural leaders' included certain Hindus (more especially of the Rajput and other martial classes), prominence was given to those landlords and retired officials who, before 1914, formed the spokesmen of the Muslim community. The Muslims were encouraged, partly because they were landlords; the Hindu politicians were discouraged largely because they were all middle class. At the time, few perceived where this would lead.

This chapter seeks to show how the forces of tradition and conservatism have moulded society, and moulded social attitudes to authority and government. The burden of tradition weighed upon the views of both progressive and militant leaders, right down to 1914. Among both the extremist religious leaders who taught that British rule was sacrilege, and the moderate, Westernised political leaders who ardently desired representative institutions, none went so far as to advocate a direct challenge to British authority. The most they tried to do, was to request the British government to grant boons; they approached authority humbly, as petitioners had approached the Mughal Emperors. It never seems to have occurred to them, as a practical possibility, that they might take over power from the British. Yet, within a decade, the political climate was to be transformed: with the appearance of Mahatma Gandhi.

II

POLITICAL MOVEMENTS AND INDEPENDENCE

It is usual to date the birth of the nationalist movement from 1885, with the first session of the Indian National Congress. Yet, certain forms of proto-nationalism existed long before this date, while the strident, emotional, creed of the nation-state did not arouse political India until the 1914-18 War.

As we have seen, there was from ancient times a vague, mystical sense of the unity of India. There was also a more definite spirit of Hindu resistance to Muslim dominance. This was perpetuated in the epic tales of Privthi Raj, the last Hindu king of Delhi, and was reborn in the struggle of the Maratha prince, Sivaji, against Alamgir's efforts to extend Mughal dominion. On their side, the Muslims nourished legends of heroes and martyrs: for example, Sayyid Ahmad Shahid, who resisted the Sikh kingdom in Punjab, and was killed in battle. Perhaps even more potent than this religious 'nationalism' was regional 'nationalism', founded in memories of resistance against aggression by more powerful neighbours. Thus, to this day, the Assamese honour their king, Chakradhvaj Singha, who fought for independence with the war cry, 'Better death than submit to the Bengalis'.

Finally, there were seeds of modern nationalism in the intellectual renascence of the early nineteenth century. It has been called 'Whiggish', because it fastened upon subjects like the reform of antiquated legal and administrative procedure, freedom of the Press, liberty of the subject, and civil equality. This rational, secular political outlook was reinforced by the inauguration of the universities of Calcutta, Bombay, and Madras in 1857. A quarter of a century later, a retired civil servant Allan Octavian Hume, son of the Radical leader, and convert to Theosophy,

22

appealed to the graduates of the Indian universities to convene a National Congress to debate questions of social and political reform. His call was made at one of the rare moments when there was a reforming Viceroy, Lord Ripon: and he also attempted to open a channel for the aspirations of the emerging middle class by the encouragement of local self-government: by setting up municipalities with an elected element, and by creating district councils for the countryside. Both Hume and Ripon were trying to provide for 'political education'; to train the new Westernised élite to participate in their own government. This concern was contrary to the prevailing British view of the necessity to resuscitate the 'natural leadership' of Indian society, while keeping the new Westernised élite ('the educated natives') in their place.

The lawyers, professors, editors, landlords, who now met together each year (a little self-consciously) as the National Congress, had no ultimate goal: they were concerned only with petty, short-term improvements, such as the larger representation of Indians in the superior civil services, and their admission to commissioned rank in the Indian Army. Aptly enough, the President of the Sixth Congress, Pherozeshah Mehta, quoted (or rather, misquoted) these lines by Newman:

> *Keep thou my feet, I do not ask to see*
> *The distant path—one step enough for me.*

The annual petitions of grievances by the Congress to the British Government yielded almost nothing; the Congress were dismissed as a 'microscopic minority' by Viceroys and Secretaries of State. About 1900, there came a departure from the gradualist, reformist approach.

A Maharashtrian Brahmin, Tilak, called for a return to Hindu orthodoxy, a rejection of British innovations, taking as his model the militant struggle of the Marathas under Sivaji against the mlecchas. In Bengal, a terrorist, anarchist movement evoked the patronage of Kali, the dark Mother Goddess. Both movements rejected constitutional methods— the slow germination of 'political education'—for the weapon of violence.

These cults, harking back to the golden age of Hinduism, served to alarm Muslim leaders still further. Sayyid Ahmad had put his faith in higher education, and in the protection of the British Government; he had enjoined his community to keep out of politics, especially out of the Congress, which he dismissed as a Hindu organisation. But by the early 1900s, Sayyid Ahmad's successors were convinced that they must begin to take an active part in politics. Yet, at the level of political know-how and experience, they were conscious of the half-century lead gained by the Hindu middle class in Western expertise; while as a minority representing one-quarter of the total population of India they believed (with good reason) that they could never secure effective representation under an elective system, whereby the Hindu majority community could exclude the Muslims from any voice in the legislative councils.

The remedy sought by the Muslims was 'communal representation' or the allocation of seats to the community on the basis of its numerical strength. In 1906, a deputation of Muslims, led by the Aga Khan, made a request on these lines to the Viceroy, and were assured of his sympathy. The Viceroy's attitude becomes understandable if the original purpose of the legislatures is recalled. When the original proposals for Indian representation in the legislative councils was under discussion, Sir Bartle Frere wrote (in 1860) of the necessity 'of learning what the natives think of our measures and how the native community will be affected by them'. Frere likened the rôle of the Indian councils to that of the darbar of an Indian prince. The darbar was essentially a sounding-board, whereby the prince could ensure that his will was understood by his subjects; it was also a safety-valve for them to air their grievances against unjust officials. The early legislatures being this kind of channel of communication, it was more important to secure a wide representation of interests than to determine the choice of an electorate which (at the period in question) would necessarily be narrow and unrepresentative. The reforms sponsored by Morley, as Secretary of State, and Minto, as Viceroy, which came into effect in 1909, were intended to provide this wide representation of interests. The great landlords, the universities, commerce—and the Muslims—all received separate seats.[1]

Lord Morley vehemently denied that this measure was intended to lead towards parliamentary government in India. Yet, by embedding communal representation into the legislatures, he inadvertently established a precedent and a principle which could not be rescinded when parliamentary government became the object of British policy.

On the eve of the first World War, three main political groups had emerged. Within the Congress there were the 'Extremists' and the 'Moderates' (to employ contemporary terms). The Extremists were militant, fervent religious revivalists, and advocates of the use of force; the Moderates were constitutionalist, secular, and gradualist. Both groups were predominantly Hindus of the literary Brahmin and Kayastha castes.

---

[1] As an illustration of the Muslim predicament: in Punjab the Muslims were not given separate seats under the Morley-Minto Reforms as they formed a slight majority of the population of the province: yet, at the following elections, they did not secure any of the eight elected seats in the legislature, because of educational and economic backwardness and lack of effective organisation.

The third main group was the Muslim League, founded in 1906 by an aristocratic clique of Nawabs and other hereditary leaders. From left to right of this political array, there was no clear voice calling upon the British to hand power over to Indians. Moreover, though the political leaders were joined together in a National Congress, their horizons were limited to their own provinces (even the great Rabindranath Tagore, when required to indicate his nationality, subscribed himself 'Bengalee'). It is true that the cry of *Swaraj* (Our own Rule) had been raised; but when asked to define *Swaraj*, its exponents usually talked about 'colonial self-government'. Most educated Indians still accepted British rule as a dispensation of Divine Providence—perhaps only as a means towards national regeneration—but still an inevitable phase through which India was destined to pass. This recognition of British rule as providential, was clearly shown in 1914 in the public response to the outbreak of war, when (apart from a few revolutionaries) Indians of all classes hastened to demonstrate their loyalty to the British Crown, and to the British people in their hour of trial. Indian Army divisions, it is often forgotten, formed a sizeable element in the B.E.F. in the autumn and winter of 1914, and helped to stem the German attack, while the new volunteer British armies were still under training. Subsequently, a million Indian volunteers were enlisted, and Indian troops took the brunt of the fighting in the middle east and east Africa. Britain recognised this valiant effort. Two Indians were members of the Imperial War Cabinet; India signed the peace treaty, and became a founder-member of the League of Nations. But before then, the Indian response had suddenly changed key: the loyal acceptance of duties had become the strident assertion of rights.

The first notable development of the war years was the rapprochement between Hindu and Muslim political leaders. This was largely engineered by M. A. Jinnah, a Muslim barrister of Bombay, belonging to the Khoja trading caste, which had traditional Hindu associations. Jinnah was a disciple of G. K. Gokhale, the moderate Congress leader who had organised the 'Servants of India', dedicated to social service. Jinnah was also accepted by the Nawabs of the Muslim League, and he persuaded them to hold their annual session at the same time and place as the Congress; in Bombay in 1915, and at Lucknow in 1916. This spirit of co-existence produced the joint Lucknow Pact of 1916, whereby Congress conceded the principle of separate electorates and seats for Muslims, and agreed upon a formula whereby the Muslims accepted a lower ratio of seats to population in their majority areas, Punjab and Bengal, in return for greatly increased representation in the other provinces where they formed a minority. In the central legislature, the Muslims were to enjoy one-third of the elected seats on a reserved basis. This pact represents the high-water mark of Hindu-Muslim agreement: and also the culmination (as it transpired) of the constitutional approach to nationalism.

During the latter years of the war, the political climate darkened. The mounting drama of Ireland was closely followed in India, and Mrs. Besant founded a Home Rule for India League. The British Cabinet, conscious of the debt of gratitude for the Indian war effort, and also aware of the damage which Indian unrest would cause throughout the world, decided that some special gesture must be made. In August 1917, a statement was issued in Parliament, recognising the immediate need for 'the increasing association of Indians in every branch of the administration and the gradual development of self-governing institutions with a view to the progressive realisation of responsible government in India as an integral part of the British Empire'.

To implement this declaration, the Secretary of State, Edwin Montagu, drafted a scheme of political devolution which became known as Dyarchy. It provided, first, for the transfer of many of the functions of government from the central Government of India to the provinces, along with a modicum of financial autonomy. Among these functions were what was called the 'nation-building departments', such as education, local self-government, public health, and agriculture: these were now placed under Ministers, who were elected members of the provincial legislatures, responsible to those legislatures. Responsibility for the maintenance of law and order, with financial supervision, were retained under persons called Members, who might be either British officials or Indian public men, but who were not responsible to the legislatures. These provincial legislatures now contained a majority of elected members, returned according to the formula agreed under the Lucknow Pact. A minority of nominated non-officials and officials completed these legislatures. At the centre, the administration was still in the hands of the Viceroy and his officials (British and Indian) although the central legislature now contained a large elected element. The authors of this scheme carefully considered the possibility of altering the system of separate Muslim representation: they considered this 'a very serious handicap to the development of the self-governing principle', but they felt unable to change the system—and, indeed, separate constituencies were also created for the Sikhs in Punjab.

These proposals (usually called the Montagu-Chelmsford Reforms) were given effect by an Act of 1919. At first, the response from Indian political leaders was favourable. Then, without warning, the whole situation was plunged into bitter confusion: a state which was to persist right up to independence.

The primary factor was the change in the leadership of Congress, and its transformation into an entirely new kind of political organisation. It happened that death suddenly claimed almost all the senior Congress leaders: Pherozeshah Mehta, Gokhale, and Tilak. Into their place stepped M. K. Gandhi, newly returned from his campaign against racial discrimination in South Africa. There he had developed a technique called *Satyagraha*: literally, 'sacrifice-firmness', but usually translated as 'soul force'. The technique depended on the passive defiance of the law, or civil disobedience, by bands of volunteers.

On his return to India, Gandhi first became one of Gokhale's social service workers. His next important task was an investigation into the grievances of the cultivators of Champaran District in Bihar, who were victimised and exploited by the European indigo planters. This experience gave Gandhi considerable insight into peasant conditions, and also helped him develop a technique of disarming British officialdom by placing them in positions where they felt legally and morally uneasy. However, during the war years, Gandhi's objectives were still limited to moving the British Government to redress injustice, in the accepted manner. He even undertook a recruiting campaign on behalf of the war effort. Like others, his first response to the Montagu-Chelmsford Reforms was favourable.

Then came the Amritsar Massacre.

The aftermath of the war brought a surge of discontent to the Indian continent. The authorities replied by tightening up public order. At Amritsar, in April 1919, mob disorders seemed likely to lead to anarchy. The local military commander imposed martial law, and dispersed a militant demonstration by indiscriminate firing in which 379 Indians were killed. This tragedy probably did more than anything else to embitter racial relations between British and Indians; but the Congress did not immediately abandon the policy of co-operation. However, with the publication of the Treaty of Sèvres, which liquidated the power of the Caliph, a surge of pan-Islamic feeling swept through the Muslims of India, and Congress, led by Gandhi, determined to enter this Khilafat movement to further Muslim-Hindu unity and to challenge British power.

Gandhi's lead was not accepted without a struggle. A large section of the Congress, true to the moderate, gradualist philosophy adhered to constitutional methods. They broke from the Congress, and contested the elections for the new, reformed legislatures; subsequently they formed ministries in several provinces, identifying themselves by the political label of the Liberal Federation. But although the Liberals included some of the most able and idealistic political leaders, they ultimately failed to consolidate their position because they failed to create a solid following. It was Gandhi's particular genius to realise that any truly national movement must be based upon the support of the masses; and to perceive how this support might be mobilised. In the words of Dr. Rajendra Prasad, President of India, he 'shifted politics from the drawing-rooms of the educated and the business men to the huts of the tillers of the soil'.[1] This change came about because Gandhi had learnt to present himself and his message to the people in traditional terms: about 1920 he abandoned Western dress for homespun, *khadi,* and similarly he clothed Western ideas in Hindu guise. He dramatised civil disobedience in a way all could understand: by making salt from brine on the sea shore, in defiance of the salt regulations. Satyagraha was not really a traditional Hindu concept, but as presented by Gandhi it was accepted into the mainstream of Hindu custom. Similarly, *ahimsa,* 'non-violence' was inspired by Tolstoy, Ruskin, and the Sermon on the Mount but Gandhi presented ahimsa as part of the superior ethical philosophy of Hinduism. This was in marked contrast to the teaching of political leaders such as Tilak and Lala Lajpat Rai, who stressed the heroic, challenging, sacrificing, conquering traditions of Hinduism; and in linking his first civil disobedience movement with the militant Khilafat agitation, Gandhi was treading on dangerous ground. Too dangerous, it transpired: at Chauri Chaura in the United Provinces, a Congress mob murdered twenty-two police constables in cold blood, while in south India the Khilafat campaign led to a religious rising by the Moplah tribe, in which hundreds of Hindus were slain. Gandhi called off his civil disobedience campaign, announcing that his followers did not yet understand non-violence.

For several years, the influence of Gandhi was in eclipse. The Khilafat movement collapsed when Ataturk abolished the office of Caliph in March 1924. Hindu-Muslim co-operation dwindled. Further sections of the Congress (known as 'Responsivists') broke away to join the Liberals in trying to work the Dyarchy experiment. Parties appeared as alternatives to the Congress. In Madras, the Justice Party was founded to represent the non-Brahmins: Congress being identified with Brahmin domination, and the Brahmin monopoly of public office. The Justice Party was able to form a ministry and make inroads into Brahmin ex-

[1] Rajendra Prasad, *Autobiography*, Bombay, 1957, p. 131.

clusivism. Punjab politics was aligned on the basis of rural leadership versus urban interests. Fazl-i-Husain (whose political loyalties were, like Jinnah's, both to Congress and the Muslim League) created the Unionist Party which included Muslims, Hindus, and Sikhs. He endeavoured to ameliorate communal rivalries by prescribing fixed percentages, based on population, for the three communities in the public services and in educational institutions. He also launched a programme of rural development and local self-government.

These attempts by the Liberals and others to provide an alternative to the Congress appeal foundered partly because these moderate men were wholeheartedly supported by neither British officialdom nor by the traditionalist, conservative landlords. When elements of the Congress decided to contest the elections, between them and the landlords, the Liberals found themselves 'in the unenviable position of the proverbial earthen pot between two brass vessels'.[1] As the one exception, the Unionist Party continued to dominate Punjab politics until the eve of independence: and the Unionists were consistently supported by the landlords and by the officials.

Gandhi refused to consider entry into the Dyarchy legislatures. At length, his opportunity returned, with the appointment of the Simon Commission—from which Indian representatives were wholly excluded—to report on India's constitutional future. A boycott of the Commission largely frustrated its inquiries, while a successful campaign against the payment of taxes at Bardoli in Bombay Province restored the prestige of civil disobedience. The adherence of Motilal Nehru and his son, Jawaharlal, to Gandhi's point of view gave him added strength.

Motilal Nehru had gradually been moving away from the 'gradualist' position. Speaking in the central legislature of the approaching inquiry into India's constitutional advance, he declared, to the British Government: 'We say we are absolutely fit for self-government, as fit as you are in your own island. This is what we say. Here we are occupying that position and you tell us as you would tell schoolboys: be good boys and you will be promoted to a higher form.'[2]

Political education as an acceptable philosophy for educated Indians was pushed aside: though as we shall see, this belief was to be revived in a later time. But while the British Government still talked about 'the gradual development of self-governing institutions,' the Congress demand had hardened into *Purna Swaraj* or independence.

[1] C. Y. Chintamani and M. R. Masani, *India's Constitution at Work*, Bombay, 1940, p. 7.
[2] Quoted in 'People and Government in Southern Asia', *op. cit.*

As a riposte to the Simon Commission's inquiries, a committee of politicians, with Motilal Nehru as chairman and Jawaharlal as secretary, drafted their own constitutional programme. This 'Nehru Report' demanded Dominion Status, i.e. equality with Canada, Australia, and other self-governing Dominions. The Report rejected separate electorates and weightage for minorities. In reply, M. A. Jinnah, on behalf of the Muslim League, repeated the claim that one-third of the seats in the future central legislature should be reserved for the Muslims. No attention was paid by Congress to this demand, and in the view of one detached Indian historian this 'marked the turning point in the life of Jinnah and in the history of the sub-continent'.[1] Many Muslims who had been loyal members of Congress for a decade or more now transferred their allegiance to the Muslim League. Jinnah, the advocate of compromise, was left to survey the failure of his policy.

The Viceroy during this critical period was Lord Irwin (later Lord Halifax): the only statesman of vision and stature to hold this office between Curzon and Wavell. Irwin attempted to regain Indian confidence by issuing a clear statement that the 'natural issue of India's constitutional progress . . . is the attainment of Dominion status'. This declaration alarmed some British Conservatives without winning over Congress. In this atmosphere of stalemate, Gandhi again brought politics down to the level of the people by launching the civil disobedience campaign of 1930. Lord Irwin was determined to break through the suspicion and hostility of the Congress, and he entered into negotiations with Gandhi whereby the campaign was terminated, and Congress agreed to participate in a Round Table Conference to determine the political future. The significance of this move was the invitation to Indian leaders to help determine the future of their country: no longer was the British Parliament alone to be the arbiter of India's destiny.

Three sessions of the Round Table Conference were held, from 1930 to 1932; the Congress was represented by Gandhi at the second session, but thereafter he withdrew. Discussion was largely occupied by the problem of the Muslim and other minorities, and by the status of the Princely states within a federal constitution. As a sequel to the conference, a reformed constitution was drafted, embodied in the Government of India Act, 1935. This measure was bitterly opposed by the right-wing of the Conservative Party, led by Winston Churchill, as a betrayal of the British mission of Imperial trusteeship. It was equally bitterly denounced by the younger Congress leaders, led by Jawaharlal Nehru, as a 'Satanic' constitution.

[1] S. Gopal, *The Viceroyalty of Lord Irwin*, Oxford U.P., 1957, p. 37.

The purpose of the 1935 Act was to transfer the entire range of government functions at the provincial level to elected ministries; to provide political experience in national politics by introducing the Dyarchy system into the central Government of India; and to bring the Princely states into closer association with British India by the acceptance of common, federal functions.

The first elections for the new provincial legislatures were held in 1936. There was now a total electorate of 41,000,000 (about 18 per cent of total population) as compared with the Dyarchy electorate of 6,000,000 (2.8 per cent of total population). The Dyarchy electorate had been restricted to the middle class; the new electorate took in many of the landed peasantry, small shopkeepers, all persons of any education, and a proportion of the lower castes.

The Congress leaders were again divided over whether or not to contest the elections. The more co-operative element prevailed; and Congress achieved a triumph. In five of the eleven provinces they gained a clear majority of seats, and in three other provinces they emerged as the largest party. There followed an even more furious debate within the Congress high command: the Working Committee of the All-India Congress Committee. Should they continue to denounce the 1935 Act and refuse to operate its provisions? Or should they seize this great opportunity to govern in the interests of the people of India? In March 1937, it was decided to form Congress ministries, but further wrangling prevented these eight ministries taking office until July. Nehru, as President of the Congress, continued to oppose any policy of co-operation under the 1935 Act.

The Muslim League was much less successful; less than a quarter of the reserved Muslim seats were won by Leaguers, and nowhere were they able to form a ministry. In the United Provinces, Congress and the League had fought the election on a common front, in the expectation of forming a coalition ministry. However, Congress was sufficiently successful to be able to dispense with League support in the legislature. Congress demanded as the price of including League representatives in the new ministry, that the Muslim League in U.P. should be dissolved and merged into the Congress. This condition was, of course, unacceptable: and the second major Muslim political grievance against Congress was sealed.

The second purpose of the 1935 Act, the introduction of a federal system, was foiled by the last-minute refusal of the Princes to accede to the new federation. In consequence, no transfer of central subjects from official to ministerial control eventuated. Apart from the setting up of certain federal institutions, such as a Supreme Court, the 1935 Act was, in this respect, a dead letter.

The new Congress ministries included several leaders of stature, and in certain provinces (notably Bombay, Madras, and U.P.) a number of important reforms were introduced. Several Congress governments were accused by the Muslims of adopting a policy prejudicial to the community. There was supposed to be discrimination against Muslims in appointments to the public services; Hindi was encouraged at the expense of Urdu, in the schools and on public occasions; cow slaughter was prohibited (many Muslims eat beef); *Bande Mataram,* 'Hail to the Mother' was introduced as a national anthem, and this invocation to the goddess Kali was idolatrous. These portents were enough to alarm the sensitive Muslim spokesmen, and Jinnah now began to change his technique: he too began to appeal to the masses. Membership of the League was now open on payment of a subscription of two annas (about 2d.) and the cry of 'Islam in Danger' was sounded to rouse the crowd.

At this point, Congress, led by Gandhi, committed what was probably the greatest blunder of its history. When the second World War began in September 1939, the Viceroy, without consulting Indian leaders, announced that India was at war with Germany. This may have shown proper attention to constitutional precedent; it showed an abysmal lack of attention to human nature. The Congress leadership, confused by Gandhi's unique form of pacificism, decided to call on their supporters to resign from office in protest. There was a good deal of hesitation (voiced, especially by C. Rajagopalachari, Chief Minister of Madras) but finally the resignations were submitted in October. In eight provinces, ministerial government was replaced by autocratic administration under the Governor. To those Congress leaders who had found satisfaction in creative work, all had ended in futility. In the long run, the experience gained by ministers, 1937-39, formed the foundation of their post-independence achievements; while the functioning of the legislatures, under Congress leadership, acclimatised this institution of government into the Indian scene, and ensured that Parliament would be accepted as the natural focus of government when independence came at last. But the immediate reaction was one of frustration; once again, the struggle had come to a dead end.

To Jinnah and the League, the Congress withdrawal meant opportunity. When the Congress ministries resigned, the League observed a day of thanksgiving and deliverance. Of the three ministries which remained in office, the Punjab was Unionist, and Sind and Bengal were Muslim. Both the Premier of Punjab (Sikander Hyat Khan) and the

Premier of Bengal (Fazl-ul-Haq) while retaining their local political independence recognised the authority of Jinnah and the League. Later, it became possible to form League ministries in Assam and the North-West Frontier Province. The Congress had dismissed with contempt Jinnah's claim to speak for all the Muslims. Now he began to make his claim good. Simultaneously, a new political objective came into view: Pakistan. For some years, Muslim thinkers had been evolving schemes for a separate Muslim polity. Back in 1930, Iqbal, the poet and philosopher, had advocated a Muslim state in northwest India, and in 1933 an Indian scholar living in England, at Cambridge, had evolved the novel concept of Pakistan. Meeting at Lahore in March 1940, the Muslim League adopted a resolution declaring that 'The North-Western and Eastern zones of India should be grouped to constitute "Independent States" in which the constituent units shall be autonomous and sovereign'. There was a vagueness about the precise meaning of this resolution, and few observers believed that the Muslim League actually wanted the partition of the subcontinent.

Despite the political stalemate India began to play a part in the war which repeated the previous gallant effort. Again, Indian divisions held the line while Britain mobilised. After the fall of France, the Indian Army offered the only source of massive support. Recruitment was accelerated, and eventually two million volunteers were enrolled. Then came Japan's entry into the war, the fall of Malaya and Burma, and the prospect of invasion upon the soil of India. At this point, the British Government attempted to associate Indian political leaders of all parties with the defence of India. Sir Stafford Cripps came to India in March 1942, with authority to offer independence as soon as hostilities ceased, and to afford a full share in the direction of government to political leaders meanwhile. Cripps, an ardent Socialist and anti-colonialist, was expected to have influence upon his friend Nehru and upon the Congress. He laboured arduously to bring the parties together, but the leaders were in no mood to agree. Amid the chorus of counter-claims, Cripps was compelled to restate the British Government's concept of its duty to protect the minorities. This displeased the Congress leaders who demanded that he deal with them alone. They believed that time was on their side, and Gandhi dismissed the Cripps proposals as 'A post-dated cheque on a failing bank'. He returned to Britain having achieved nothing.

In the atmosphere of tense frustration which followed, and with the Japanese army pressing on the border, Gandhi launched the 'Quit India' campaign, calling on the British to leave the country. In August 1942, he issued a call to India, 'Do or Die', and the British authorities replied by declaring Congress an illegal organisation and interning the leaders. Plans had been carefully prepared, and a sabotage campaign followed, designed to set up Congress Raj. Non-violence went by the board. 'Civil disobedience was always treading on the brink of violence,' declares an Indian historian, quoting Nehru's confession to Gandhi: 'For myself, I delight in warfare.'[1] The 1942 rising was warfare. However, within six weeks all was over; Congress had temporarily ceased to exist as a political force. Into this vacuum moved the Muslim League—and the Communist Party. Before the war they had formed a slender, scattered coterie of intellectuals. After Hitler's invasion of Russia they came out in support of the British war effort, declaring that this was a people's war. Free to carry on their propaganda while Congress was impotent, the Communists rapidly increased their membership.

By 1944, the tide of war had turned; victory was in sight. The Congress leaders were released from internment, and the new Viceroy, Lord Wavell, made efforts to break the political log-jam. Politics had simplified down to Congress versus the League. Congress still claimed to speak for all India, and dismissed the League as a British-created faction. Jinnah now demanded a separate Muslim state, and insisted on negotiating on terms of equality. Once the Muslims had been satisfied with one-fourth of the seats in legislatures; then they had required one-third of the representation; now they demanded equality with the Congress. Such was the position of strength they had acquired that this was conceded by the British: and only ineffectively opposed by Congress.

When, in 1945, the Labour Government entered office, one of their first decisions was to hold fresh elections in India. The results, for the central legislature, appeared in December: the Muslim League was successful in every one of the separate Muslim constituencies. In the non-Muslim or General constituencies, Congress was almost equally successful. Each party had a clear mandate to press their conflicting demands. Election for the provincial assemblies followed, and although the League captured a majority of Muslim seats, it found difficulty in forming ministries because of the continuing hold of local groups and parties. In Punjab, the League emerged as by far the largest group, with seventy-nine out of a total of 175 seats. They were prevented from obtaining power by an unholy alliance of Sikh landlords and Congress Hindu lawyers, who combined to put a Muslim Unionist Premier, Khizr Hyat Tiwana, into office. Here was a clear warning to the Muslims of what they might expect under Congress Raj.

In February 1946, the British Government sent out a Cabinet Mission,

[1] Gopal, *op. cit.*, pp. 64 and 94.

made up of three ministers, Lord Pethick Lawrence, Sir Stafford Cripps, and A. V. Alexander. The Cabinet Mission spent over three months in India. It first sought for an agreed solution from among the Indian leaders, but when none was forthcoming, the three ministers evolved their own plan, the so-called 'Three Tier Proposal'. This envisaged a central government with slender powers, and provincial governments with all residuary powers. The provinces were to be given the option to merge into groups: Group A (Madras, Bombay, United Provinces, Bihar, Central Provinces, and Orissa, i.e. the Hindu-majority area), Group B (Punjab, North-West Frontier, and Sind; Muslim majority), and C (Bengal and Assam; weak Muslim majority). Both the League and Congress agreed to accept this proposal; both placed their own interpretations upon its implication, but Nehru went as far as to publicly disavow the grouping formula. Faced by this evidence of bad faith, Jinnah also withdrew support from the plan.

While the British Government was most concerned with the long term problem of evolving an acceptable constitutional formula, the Viceroy, Lord Wavell, was more preoccupied with the short-term problem of forming an interim government, representative of both the major parties. Congress insisted upon nominating a nationalist (Congress) Muslim for a Cabinet post in order to preserve its assertion that it was non-communal in character. Jinnah flatly rejected this claim. Jinnah still preferred the path of negotiation, but he believed that Britain would listen to Congress because of its militant record. He determined to demonstrate the Muslims' capacity for physical action, and he called on his followers to observe August 16, 1946, as 'Direct Action Day'. Whatever Jinnah's intention, the consequence was a chain reaction of violence and destruction, beginning in Calcutta, and spreading to East Bengal and Bihar. Before the tide of violence was spent, Congress had agreed to enter an interim government. The initiative thereby passed to the Congress, and six weeks later Jinnah abandoned Direct Action, and League representatives joined the interim Cabinet. This was the occasion for a Congress manœuvre which boomeranged.[1] Congress had to surrender at least one major portfolio to the League: Foreign Affairs, the Home Department, Defence. Congress refused to hand over any of these. Pressed by the Viceroy, at the suggestion of the tough Sardar Patel, they agreed to hand over Finance to a Leaguer, confident that any Muslim would 'make a fool

[1] See Maulana Abul Kalam Azad, *India Wins Freedom*, Calcutta, 1959, p. 166. This is the only personal memoir by an Indian leader of the front rank yet to appear. Bitter, and prejudiced, it does provide valuable insight into the mentality of the Congress leaders.

of himself'. Liaqat Ali Khan, the new Finance Minister, proceeded to make fools of his Congress colleagues. Under the involute system of the Government of India, every department had to obtain financial sanction for every appointment or proposal. Liaqat utilised his power to further League policy or to delay Congress-inspired measures. Moreover, he introduced a budget aimed at levying swingeing sums from the big Hindu industrialists and financiers who were the principal source of Congress funds. It was not easy for self-declared Socialists like Nehru to oppose this measure.

Lord Wavell still persevered with attempts to rescue the Cabinet Mission's plan. He called upon Congress to accept the plan, without reservations. In reply, on February 13, 1947, Nehru announced the intention of the Congress to withdraw from the government unless the League ministers were dismissed. All alternatives seemed to have been exhausted. Wavell presented the Labour Cabinet with two emergency courses of action: one long-term, one short-term. The long-term plan was to abandon the search for a compromise, accept the task of governing India for a further ten or fifteen years, and immediately build up the British element in the administration and the security services so as to make British rule effective. The second, short-term plan (which he advanced only as a course of desperate political expediency) was to transfer power to provincial governments, beginning with those provinces where Congress control was clearly established (virtually, the Group B of the plan), gradually phasing out elsewhere; British military control being withdrawn in conformity with political withdrawal. Both these proposals were designed to ensure effective continuity of administration; neither could be expected to appear attractive to the Labour Government. The first course would have entailed a slowing down of postwar demobilisation, and already there had been mutinies among the R.A.F. stationed in India in protest against alleged delays. The second course might (it was argued) take on the character of a military rearguard action. The Prime Minister decided that Lord Wavell had outlasted his usefulness, and on February 20 he announced his replacement as Viceroy by Lord Mountbatten. Behind Mr. Attlee's mild demeanour lay an iron nerve, and now he showed his determination to break the Indian deadlock. Also in the statement of February 20, he announced that Britain would withdraw from India, come what may, by June 1948. Thereby, he believed, the Indian leaders would be forced to emerge from their private world of personal enmities and legalistic semantics into the actual world of public responsibility.

The new Viceroy had been Commander-in-Chief of South-East Asia

Command, where he had demonstrated two outstanding qualities as a commander. The first was a flair for personal relations. As the King-Emperor's cousin, he appeared to Indian soldiers (as later to Indian politicians) as a warrior-prince, semi-divine. This aura was confirmed by brilliant personal qualities—'a heart of gold, a lad of life, an imp of fame'. Lord Mountbatten deliberately projected his *persona* at the troops under his command, in order to restore the morale of weary soldiers who had written off their commanders as faceless automatons. Mountbatten's second great military virtue was a capacity for bold and rapid decision. Confronted with difficulties in logistics and shortages of *matériel* which other commanders had found adequate cause for staying put, he took the risk, and cut the Gordian knot. This was the man who agreed to interrupt (though not to terminate) his spectacular naval career in order to take on perhaps the most thankless task of the day.

Arriving in India, he made two rapid decisions. First, the morale of the administration had declined to such a low level that the transfer of power could not be delayed even till June 1948; secondly, there was now no possibility of agreement among the leaders, so that Wavell's emergency plan for the transfer of power to provincial governments must be put into effect without delay. Again, the Gordian knot was to be severed at a stroke.

What would be the Congress reaction to the proposed dismemberment of India? Right to the end of 1946, the language of national unity and national resistance was spoken: 'Our patience is fast reaching the limit,' thundered Nehru, 'if these things continue, a struggle on a large scale is inevitable'. Yet, faced with the British ultimatum, the Congress leaders showed no disposition to renew the struggle. Satyagraha, non-violence, offered no solution; the physical force of 1942 also had failed, and the recent communal killings showed where force would now inevitably lead. So Nehru, the revolutionary, and Gandhi, the visionary seemed helpless.

The situation was retrieved by the constitutional experts, notably Sir Benegal Rau, and V. P. Menon, who were advising the Viceroy. They succeeded in convincing the Congress leaders that partition would be better than the 'Balkanisation' of India. Moreover, Jinnah had talked about division into Pakistan and Hindustan: but how if Pakistan were regarded as hiving off from India (as Burma had done in 1937) with the residual India remaining as the essential continuum? To the arguments of the constitutional advisers were added the persuasiveness of the Viceroy. Gandhi, Nehru, and Sardar Patel acquiesced: moreover, in order to facilitate the transfer, it was agreed that the new states should function as Dominions under the constitutional framework of the 1935 Act. And so, the Congress accepted a solution which had been theirs for the taking, at any time since 1942. Nehru, the revolutionary, at the hour of crisis followed the pattern of the moderates, the Liberal reformers. Jinnah, the advocate of constitutional compromise had triumphed by arousing Islamic fervour, declaring that 'the death of 10,000,000 Muslims is not too great a price to pay for Pakistan'. A price was indeed to be paid: though the size of the bill was not realised until after independence had been formally achieved.

The argument for communal self-determination could be used against the Muslims to tear apart their two main strongholds: Punjab and Bengal. In both these provinces there were huge non-Muslim minorities: they, naturally, demanded that the right of self-determination apply to them.[1] Assam, which the Cabinet plan placed in the Muslim-majority grouping, included only one district with a Muslim majority: Sylhet. And so Jinnah, by his own arguments, was compelled to accept what he himself had christened a 'moth-eaten Pakistan'.

The new plan was announced by the Viceroy on June 2, 1947, and was endorsed by Congress and the League. It was now stated that the actual date of the transfer of power was being advanced to August 1947. Barely two months remained to apportion the assets of the continent between the two new Dominions, and to divide up the Indian Army and the public services according to religious and regional affiliations. At first, Muslims belonging to the area which would fall to the new India, largely opted to stay in its service. Some Sikhs and Hindus whose home was in western Punjab also declared that they would take service with their regional government, Pakistan. Many still believed that the new arrangement would leave the fundamental unity of India intact. A Joint Services organisation, under Field-Marshal Auchinleck, was formed to provide co-ordination between the armed services of the two new Dominions. The Indian Army was the one great supra-communal institution which had evolved, and neither officers nor men could envisage the severing of comradeship fostered in barracks and on Frontier watch and ward, and sealed in blood upon battlefields across the world. It was even hoped that Mountbatten might serve as joint Governor-General of both Dominions: the Congress, led by Nehru, warmly invited him to continue as ceremonial head of the new state. Jinnah held his hand, until the advent of

[1] According to the 1931 Census, in Punjab there were 16,217,242 Muslims and 12,201,577 non-Muslims; in Bengal there were 33,005,434 Muslims and 27,301,091 non-Muslims, Assam contained 3,442,479 Muslims and 6,762,254 non-Muslims (many being non-Hindu Animist hill tribes).

independence, when he revealed that he would become Governor-General, not prime minister as expected.

Would the communal killings of earlier months be repeated at the transfer of power? Warning voices were raised in Punjab, where tension between Muslims and Sikhs was razor-sharp. But it was accepted that conflict could be averted by stationing a special Punjab Boundary Force of 50,000 men across the future border districts. The exact frontier was unknown; a joint Boundary Commission, composed of judges (two Muslims, a Hindu, and a Sikh) had been set up with a British judge, Sir Cyril Radcliffe, as chairman. When the Commission got down to its duties, both sides gave their decisions in terms of marked communal bias; Sir Cyril Radcliffe was compelled to make an award on his sole responsibility; perhaps not surprisingly, his decision included some odd anomalies.

In late July and early August, the princes belatedly came to terms with reality. Bahawalpur, the Frontier chiefs, and the Sind Talpurs acceded to Pakistan; the remaining princes (including many Muslims) accepted the inevitable—Congress Raj—which they had hitherto viewed with such suspicion. Only two major princes held aloof: Kashmir, and Hyderabad. Both dreamed of some form of independence. The Maharaja of Kashmir ruled a polyglot state, whose borders reached towards China and Russia. He was a Hindu, and the majority of his subjects were Muslims. Hyderabad, the premier princely state, whose ruler, the Nizam enjoyed the title of Faithful Ally of the British, was by contrast an overwhelmingly Hindu state under a Muslim ruler. For the time being, both these states and the problems they posed were left pending, by the signing of 'standstill agreements' which left the future unresolved.

And so independence came to India and Pakistan, on August 15, 1947. Already, in the Land of the Five Rivers, Punjab, knives were being sharpened and smoke ascended into the broad sky as villages began to burn. As Jinnah drove from Karachi airport towards the town, he was greeted by rapturously cheering crowds. Then he entered one section where the people stood silent, withdrawn. 'Who are they?' he asked. 'Hindus,' was the reply. People were already beginning to discover that one could be a stranger in the town where one's father and grandfather had been respected citizens. From the dockside, British troopships pulled away, to the strains of Auld Lang Syne, played by Gurkhas, Sikhs, Marathas. They were genuinely sorry to see the Tommies go; though among the famous departing regiments of the line, whose battle honours proudly proclaimed Plassey, Assaye, Sobraon, Lucknow, few gave a damn about the land they were leaving for ever.

Above the public buildings of the continent there waved two brand new flags. One depicted a silvery new moon; the fertile crescent of Islam. On the other was the *charkha*, the spinning wheel, which Gandhi had chosen as the symbol of ancient India reborn through satyagraha and service. Yet, still for a long time, a phantom Union Jack would wave, invisible, yet omnipresent; above the Red Fort at Delhi, above Jamrud Fort guarding the Khyber Pass. The British had departed; yet 2,000,000 of their dead slept in neglected cemeteries throughout the continent, and their ghosts brooded over the new nations which now came laboriously to be born.

III

INDIA: A NATION IN THE MAKING?

AFTER the bloody communal conflict of late 1946 and early 1947, widespread unrest was apprehended at independence. In the event, the greater part of India remained calm.[1] Even in Calcutta, the scene of some of the worst pre-independence clashes, there was little disorder. This was mainly because the 40,000,000 Muslims who were left in India were too numbed to move. Suddenly, they realised that the withdrawal of effective Muslim power into Pakistan had left them naked and defenceless. In a state of shock and misery, they were in no mood to offer provocation to the Hindus; and (in general) the latter were sufficiently intoxicated with the wine of independence not to require the stimulus of communal braggadocio. The exception to this general calm was Punjab and Delhi. Trouble had been expected here; the Punjab Boundary Force had been specially deployed in anticipation; but when it came, the explosion exceeded all expectations.

Partition split the lands of the Sikhs into almost equal parts. But their future was not in doubt: Amritsar, with its Golden Temple, and the historic Sikh heartland lay within the new India. The Sikhs of the rich canal-lands which now fell to Pakistan were reluctant to give up their inheritance, but relations with the Muslims (always uncertain) were degenerating fast. The order went out to pack up and leave. The Sikhs marched out in well-disciplined, well-guarded convoys; nourishing a fierce hate for those who had compelled them to abandon their

[1] In dealing with post-independence events, 'India' means the new Union of India in these pages. In talking of both the new countries, the term 'South Asia' will be generally employed, and occasionally the phrase 'the sub-continent' which was formerly popular, but has now become what the Oxford Dictionary calls *obs.*

carefully nurtured fields. They found their compatriots in India in a bloodthirsty mood. As trains headed for Pakistan, carrying Muslim clerks and artisans, neared Amritsar (the last station before the Pakistan border) so the Akalis, the Sikh fanatics, fell upon them with their cruel swordblades. Trainloads of dead and dying crossed into Pakistan: and the word of fear sped fast. Vengeance was levied upon the Hindu and Sikh minority in West Pakistan. They, in turn, panicked and fled. The horrible toll of retribution mounted, on both sides. The Muslim cultivators of West Punjab were less vigorous, less enterprising than the canal-colony Sikhs. They left their homes without plan, without organisation. They were butchered in their thousands. The incoming Sikhs were the leaders in falling on the Muslims: they had been cheated out of their lands: at least they would strip the accursed Muslims of their fields.

The Sikh refugees surged on, into Delhi. Here they spread tales of Muslim atrocities, and led the local *goondas* or gangsters in attacking the numerous Muslim artisan and middle class population of Delhi. Murders were being committed in the very streets round the Parliament building, and the new Congress leaders looked on, wringing their hands. Nehru proved fearless in moving among the mobs, denouncing their insanity; but it was left to the Governor-General, Lord Mountbatten, to reorganise the forces of order, and to move the miserable Muslims into places of refuge, such as the Purana Qila, the ancient fortress, which looks across at twentieth-century New Delhi. Delhi was engulfed in the madness: but the fever spread little further. The United Provinces (now renamed Uttar Pradesh) extends beyond Delhi; and the Sikh refugees crossed into its western districts; spreading tales of horror, and exhorting the Hindus to fall upon the Muslims who form a significant minority in these districts. However, the administration of the United Provinces had remained intact; unlike the provincial services of Punjab, which had been torn asunder. The U.P. services had a high standard, and had met the full shock of the 1942 Congress rising without flinching. The district magistrate in charge of Dehra Dun (where there was the greatest Sikh incursion) was particularly determined. The rabble-rousers were put down without hesitation. There were a number of ugly incidents in the densely packed cities of the United Provinces, where communalism had always been heated; but there was no repetition of the mass killings, and the mass hatred of the Punjab and Delhi. Neither was there a collapse of the forces of law and order.

So 1947 ended: a year which began in complete uncertainty, went on to yield the prize of independence, and expired in a morass of blood.

With the coming of the cold weather, the emotional heats died down: but one last, and worst murder was still to come. On January 20, 1948, Gandhi was assassinated, while at his prayers, in New Delhi. The murderer was a fanatical Brahmin from Maharashtra; the home of the warrior-prince, Sivaji, the scourge of the Muslims. The motive was a militant Hindu protest against the Mahatma's attitude of conciliation towards the Muslims. Gandhi's martyrdom provided a catharsis. Many were startled into a realisation that they had fallen into the attitude where all Muslims were seen as enemies, or at least mlecchas. There was a deep feeling that the people of India had betrayed the Mahatma; and a revulsion against the Hindu fanatics followed. In dying, Gandhi had made his greatest service to ahimsa, non-violence, and to the idea of a non-communal India.

In the long-drawn out rites in which, throughout India, the leaders said their farewells to the dead Gandhi, they were symbolically taking their leave of the movement for freedom, and turning to their new rôle of building the new nation.

Among the many tasks confronting the Congress leaders, two were pre-eminent: the unification of the new country and the preparation of a constitution. Unification was mainly carried through by Sardar Patel who, among all the Congress leaders, most approximated to an American party boss; tough, concerned with reality and not theory, he was both Home Minister and Minister for the former princely states. Within the borders of the new India were 560 principalities; some were larger than major European countries, others were petty anachronisms (the smallest prince was said to have dominion over a well). Some states (notably Mysore) had outpaced British India in social and political progress; others were medieval monstrosities, where the ruler looked on every female subject as an adjunct to his harem, and every male as a potential candidate for his dungeons. The British had supervised this patchwork of princes through the Political Service, whose influence had contributed to perpetuating the whole galanty show of elephant parades, darbars, tiger shoots, diamenté Rolls Royces, and Riviera orgies.

The deluded princes had been encouraged to regard themselves as actual factors in the tussle for political power. Sardar Patel rapidly disillusioned these *rois fainéants*. Almost in every case, pressure to accede to India was accepted (Travancore, for example, with its ancient maritime tradition, played with the idea of separate sovereignty: but not for long). Only three rulers remained stubborn: Kashmir, Junagadh, and Hyderabad.

The polyglot princely state of Kashmir consisted of the Kashmir valley (population, 1.6 million, mainly Muslim), Jammu (mainly Hindu), Poonch (Muslim), the remote dependencies of Gilgit and Baltistan (Muslim) and the isolated province of Ladakh, or 'Little Tibet' (Buddhist). This heterogeneous polity had been grossly misgoverned by its Dogra-Hindu Maharajas. Just before independence, a democratic movement, the Kashmir National Conference, headed by the popular Sheikh Abdullah had launched a campaign to eject the Maharaja; to this Nehru gave his active support. Kashmir was pressed to join both India and Pakistan: as more than three-quarters of the population was Muslim, and the main communications linked with Pakistan, the latter appeared most probable. The Maharaja hoped to avoid commitment to either country, and signed 'standstill agreements' with both. Then Muslim Poonch (which had provided many soldiers for the old Indian Army) threw off the Maharaja's yoke, proclaiming an *Azad* (Free) Kashmir Government. The Poonch leaders made contact with the Pathan tribes of the Frontier, and in mid-October, a tribal invasion of Kashmir, across Pakistan, was launched as jihad or holy war. The Pathans pushed rapidly down the vale of Kashmir, and, by October 25, were within a few miles of Srinagar, the capital. The next day the Maharaja notified the Government of India of his desire to accede to the Indian Union, and asked for Indian troops to be sent immediately. Indian planes touched down on Srinagar airfield just in time for the troops to save the capital from occupation by the tribesmen. In accepting the accession of the Maharaja, Lord Mountbatten as Governor-General added the proviso that 'as soon as law and order have been restored in Kashmir and its soil cleared of the invader, the question of the State's accession should be settled by a reference to the people'. The Maharaja now disappeared from the scene; he was first exiled, then deposed in June 1949. Sheikh Abdullah (who had been in a state jail) became prime minister. The subsequent history of the Kashmir problem will be recounted later.[1] For practical purposes, the greater part of the state had become part of India.

The other forced accession, that of Junagadh, was a small affair. This state on the seacoast of Kathiawar was physically within the Indian Union, but its Muslim ruler signified the accession of the state to Pakistan. An agitation was fomented; Indian troops marched in; and a popular referendum decided in favour of accession to India. The *casus foederis* was precisely opposed to that whereby India justified taking over Kashmir. However: in both cases, possession served to comprise nine points of the law.

[1] See pp. 72-3 and pp. 213-16.

The grounds for the occupation of Hyderabad were slightly different again. This prince (reputed the richest man in the world) sought independence; but his state lacked an outlet to the sea. As he showed no sign of coming to terms with India, a total blockade was established around the state, and apart from clandestine air communications with Karachi, Hyderabad was sealed from the outside world. Moderate elements urged the ruler, the Nizam, to negotiate; but increasingly control passed to extremists. Two Hyderabad districts on the border with Madras passed almost completely into the hands of Communist guerrillas, whose avowed aim was a Telugu-speaking state, composed of both the Nizam's and Madras territory. At the state capital, power was being gained by an extremist Islamic para-military movement, the Razakars. At length, in September 1948, the Indian Government issued an ultimatum: the Nizam must either take steps to disband the Razakars, and bring the Communist guerrillas under control, or else hand over to the central government. Without waiting for parley, a mechanised division moved into Hyderabad. The state forces offered resistance, but within a week the 'police action' (as it is euphemistically called) had brought the rule of the Nizam and India's premier princely dynasty, to a close.

The only remaining territorial questions were posed by the French and Portuguese enclaves. The French possessions were transferred to India peacefully. Chandernagore, a suburb of Calcutta, entirely within India, held a referendum which resulted in its transfer in 1951. France made some attempt to retain her other outposts (Pondicherry, Karikal, Mahé, and Yanam) which were all on the coast; however, after protracted negotiations, these all passed to India in 1954. Portugal proved more recalcitrant. In 1951, Goa, Daman, and Diu—all of which had been Portuguese since the early sixteenth century—were given the status of Overseas Provinces; subsequently, any Indian attempts to discuss them were met by the argument that they formed part of Portugal. India received no assistance from the International Court at the Hague (which ruled that Portugal's legal title was good), and in December 1961, India staged another 'police action' whereby Portuguese rule was rapidly liquidated.

To return to the absorption of the princely states: as soon as these had become part of India, Sardar Patel set out to reorganise the 560 states in conformity with the pattern of former British India. First, the smaller states were grouped into seven 'unions'; the larger states with a population of 1,000,000 or more remained as separate units; while those states which had been surrounded by British territory were amalgamated into a province (for example, Rampur and Benares States became regular districts of Uttar Pradesh). The trend was steadily towards absorption, and the creation of larger units. Thus: the union of the Rajput states, Rajasthan, first of all included ten small states only. Then, in March 1949, the four premier Rajput states were incorporated; and finally the enclave of Ajmer-Merwara (formerly a Mughal, then a British watching-post) and the fringe states of Alwar and Karauli were absorbed. Rajasthan was then the second largest State in India.

A distinction remained between the princely states and the former British Provinces (now also called States): the former were listed as Part 'B' States, with more limited powers than the provinces (now Part 'A' States). Certain rulers were appointed heads of Part 'B' States, under the title of *Rajpramukh*; those rulers whose states had lost their identity were pensioned off, and retired into their make-believe world of hunting, and other pursuits. Within two years, Sardar Patel liquidated two thousand years of history; overthrowing dynasties which the British had accepted as sacrosanct. For several years, administration in the former princely states retained some of its peculiar and unique qualities; but quite rapidly law and administration took on an overall uniformity and unity.

While Patel carried out his work of unification by a series of administrative decisions, the formal structure of government was being created by a constitutional assembly. The two giants of the new nation, Nehru and Patel, took only a sporadic part in its deliberations. The assembly was presided over by Dr. Rajendra Prasad, the future President, but the main architects of the new constitution were the Law Minister, Dr. Ambedkar, the leader of the untouchables, and Sir Benegal Rau, the Constitutional Adviser, an experienced public servant and jurist.

The assembly was in session for two and a half years. The first Resolution on Aims and Objectives visualised a loose confederation of states: but this decentralised system was intended to conciliate the Muslims, and lost its purpose when Pakistan was conceded. In its final form, the structure of government largely reproduced the federal system envisaged under the 1935 Government of India Act. Rau had been concerned in drafting the 1935 Act; while India was actually being governed under its provisions immediately after independence; it was not, therefore, surprising that the Act provided the chief model for the new constitution, many paragraphs being reproduced almost verbatim. Such opposition as there was to the adoption of a constitution on Western lines came mainly from orthodox Gandhians. There were proposals (supported by Dr. Prasad) for basing the new order upon the village council, the panchayat. Rau did not favour the idea, and Ambedkar dismissed it with contempt: he declared, 'I hold that these village republics have been the ruination of India. . . . What is the village but a sink of localism, a den of ignorance, narrow-mindedness and communalism?'

The constitution commences with a declaration of fundamental rights, and directive principles of policy. Rau referred to these as 'moral precepts'; another member of the assembly dismissed them as 'solemn promises and pious platitudes'; while Sir Ivor Jennings observed of the directive principles that 'the ghosts of Sidney and Beatrice Webb stalk through the text'. Time has shown that these rights have considerable substance. The Right to Equality, and Cultural and Educational Rights have been weapons which minorities and underprivileged groups have learnt to use with effect.

The 'business' parts of the constitution begin by entrusting the executive to the President and a Council of Ministers. The President was endowed with vast residual powers, but it was clearly intended that sovereignty should vest in Parliament. Parliament, and the state legislatures elect the President; and Parliament alone can amend the constitution. A judiciary was established as an independent branch of government; its independence was jealously guarded; judges might be removed only by an elaborate (and probably unworkable) procedure.

Underneath the central government, stand the States; reproducing the pattern of President-Cabinet-Parliament, in Governor-Cabinet-Legislative Assembly. The functions of the centre and of the States are distinguished by three lists, set out in the constitution (which here follows the 1935 Act): a Union List, a States List, and a concurrent list of subjects for which both Parliament and State Legislatures may assume responsibility (such as criminal law). The constitution observes, of relations between centre and States: 'The executive power of every State shall be so exercised as to ensure compliance with the laws made by parliament . . . and the executive power of the Union shall extend to the giving of such directions to a State as may appear to the Government of India to be necessary for that purpose.' All this seems to afford proof that the central government has a reserve of power over the States. Presidential powers have been invoked in Punjab, Andhra, and Kerala to suspend the State legislature and to substitute gubernatorial autocracy. Constitutional experts have therefore argued that India is not a federal but a 'quasi-federal' government. The present writer at one time subscribed to this view.[1] But recent events have tended to underline the simple truth that in accepting a federal system, the founding fathers of India

[1] See the author's 'Democratic Institutions in India and China' in *Democratic Institutions in the World Today*, ed. W. Burmeister, London, 1958, p. 137.

contributed to establishing a federal system. As we shall discover, the States of the Indian Union are indubitably States: if not, as yet, so clearly identifiable as the States of the American Union.

When the constituent assembly completed its task, many members believed that they had created a centralised machine, contrary to the tenets of Gandhi: one member declared:

> The first and foremost advice which he (Gandhi) gave . . . was that the constitutional structure of this country ought to be broadbased and pyramid-like. It should be built from the bottom and should taper right up to the top. What has been done is just the reverse.

An outside critic, Dr. Sampurnanand, chief minister of Uttar Pradesh, went even further:

> The attempt at centralisation of all power is hardly veiled and provincial governments have been sought to be reduced to the position of agents of the centre. This is bad.
> Our constitution is a miserable failure. The spirit of Indian culture has not breathed on it; the Gandhism by which we swear so vehemently at home and abroad does not inspire it.

Other critics saw in the constitution evidence of the 'slave mentality' which (as is often asserted) those subject to colonial rule imbibe; now that freedom had arrived, these 'slaves' still hankered after the security of British dominion, and so reproduced a British-style system in the constitution; 'it is just like a bird which has lived in a cage all its life: when released it wants to go back to the cage.' But in general, the new constitution was welcomed as a worthy embodiment of the people's will by the moderate, liberal-minded, Anglicised leaders who represented Indian opinion in its first, post-independence phase.

The constitution came into effect on January 26, 1950. Internally the difference in the working of government was negligible. The main break between the old and the new had come at independence, with the transfer of supreme administrative responsibility from a British Viceroy, answerable to the British Government at Westminster, to an Indian Prime Minister, whose authority was based in leadership of the Congress: still, and for years to come, much more than a political party— symbolising the 'Freedom Movement', the political will of India. Lord Mountbatten, as the first Governor-General after independence, had punctiliously observed the constitutional proprieties of his new rôle as representative of the Crown, chosen by the Government of India: he certainly gave a lead at moments when the new ministers quailed before the magnitude of their responsibilities, but strictly within constitutional bounds. The interregnum of C. Rajagopalachari as Governor-General saw the office further formalised. While Dr. Rajendra Prasad as first President was endowed with plenteous powers in reserve, still Dr. Prasad is a man of modesty, diffidence and piety, and he chose to interpret his powers with caution, leaving the leadership of the nation to the towering figure of Nehru.

The principal change wrought by the constitution was external, in the sphere of Commonwealth relations. The Congress party had long been committed to a republican form of government, and many chafed at the continuing titular supremacy of the Crown during the interim Dominion period. Amid the whittling away of the symbols of British control out of which the 'old' British Commonwealth emerged in the 1920s, the unique rôle of the Crown had been preserved, and indeed re-emphasised. If the Indian leaders insisted on establishing a republic, must India cease to be a member of the Commonwealth family? Reluctantly, British statesmen and jurists decided that this was so. Sir Benegal Rau was determined that India ought to remain in the Commonwealth, in which he ardently believed; Nehru also desired to maintain the connexion as a symbol of the reconciliation of the British and Indian people. Rau devised a formula to permit continuing membership; this included the concept of Commonwealth citizenship, and the recognition of the British monarch as Head of the Commonwealth. A conference was called in London to consider these proposals. Menzies of Australia was opposed to any curtailment of the mystic fealty of the Crown. Finally, Sir Stafford Cripps produced a draft which was a conflation of the Indian and the Australian views (the latter emphasised the continuing allegiance of the 'old' Commonwealth nations to the Crown), and this was adopted as the Commonwealth Declaration of April 1949. In this manner, Indian initiative created the basis upon which a new Commonwealth, predominantly composed of Asian and African members, could be preserved (however tenuously) in the 1950s and '60s.

Politics were partially in a condition of suspense during the first three years of independence. A considerable proportion of the energies of well-known politicians was consumed in the labyrinthine debates upon the constitution, which continued until late in 1949. Effective control over the machinery of government was held by Nehru and Patel; forming a powerful though not always concordant duet. Congress still commanded the loyalty of all politically literate elements in the

population. Before independence, commentators continually predicted
that, when it achieved its goal, Congress would split up into three main
groups: the followers of Gandhi, calling 'back to the village and village
industries'; the followers of Nehru, marching towards a Marxist-
Socialist state; and the 'big business' wing (usually associated with Sardar Patel) who wanted a free enterprise economy, and capitalist industrialisation. This division did not, in fact, come about. The Gandhians
were temporarily in eclipse, following the death of their apostle; while
an uneasy compromise endured between Nehru and Patel and their
followers. The years which led up to the first general election therefore
did not see any pronounced shift in politics. However, certain strains
and fissions developed, which foretold the beginning of the end for the
Congress in its monolithic form.

In forming his first Cabinet, Nehru was naturally concerned to reward
the faithful stalwarts of the Congress; but he was not insensitive to the
need to include other national figures, so as to give his Cabinet an 'all-
India' flavour. Of the first Cabinet, the majority belonged to the Congress old guard, but notable outsiders included the Minister of Finance,
Dr. John Matthai, a Christian with an academic background; Dr.
Ambedkar (Law) the untouchables' leader; and Baldev Singh (Defence)
the Sikh ex-Unionist. The solitary Muslim representative was Abu
Kalam Azad (Education) a lonely figure who, despite his eminence in the
national movement, took virtually no part in decision-making after
independence.

Among these first ministers were some outstanding and eminent independents: however, the Prime Minister did not treat them as con-
fidential colleagues. Dr. Matthai tendered his resignation in May 1950,
at the time of the formation of the new National Planning Commission,
on the grounds that this extra-constitutional body trenched upon the
collective responsibility of ministers. Matthai was succeeded as Finance
Minister by an equally independent-minded and gifted man from outside the ranks of politics: C. D. Deshmukh, a former senior civil servant.
The Prime Minister could respect such a colleague: but he could not
give him his full confidence. Increasingly, Nehru surrounded himself
with men who served the function of courtiers. Sardar Patel organised a
team of loyal and efficient henchmen; Nehru largely operated in isolation. He constantly found himself out of sympathy with the old guard
Congress leaders: men with small-town minds, cast in a mould of
religious and political second-hand orthodoxy. Nehru's thought-
processes are formed by scientific rationalism, Theosophical mysticism,
and other Western influences. He sought intellectual companionship

among Westernised intellectuals who were associated with politics, but were not party politicians. The influence exercised by these friends was mainly intangible and indirect. They included Dr. Radhakrishnan, the Oxford philosopher, later elected President of India; Krishna Menon, Theosophist, Bloomsbury Socialist, High Commissioner in London, and later Cabinet Minister; Rajkumari Amrit Kaur, aristocratic English-educated Christian, and Cabinet Minister; and Professor P. C. Mahalanobis, F.R.S., physicist and statistician.

Mahalanobis played a leading rôle in the setting up of the instrument of government which, more than any other, left its mark upon the early phase of independence: the National Planning Commission.

The Commission was established in March 1950 by a Resolution of the Government of India: an administrative *fiat*. It has been defined as 'the Economic Cabinet, not merely for the Union but also for the States'.[1] Its relation to statutory forms of government was indefinite. The Prime Minister became Chairman (a post he retained permanently) and a Minister for Planning, responsible to Parliament, was appointed in September 1951. But for all practical purposes, the Commission is not responsible to the nation. The Deputy Chairman, Sir V. T. Krishnamachari, is a former Dewan of Baroda, who is not an M.P.; while Professor Mahalanobis from the position of Statistical Adviser exercised the authority of an *éminence grise*. The Commission gave birth to a number of ancillary bodies, such as the Programme Evaluation Organisation, the National Development Council, the Committee on Plan Projects, the Statistical Institute, and various technical divisions. Many of these were empowered to investigate and recommend courses of policy which could affect almost every aspect of national life.

The power of the Commission lies in its control over the distribution of economic resources between the States. As the plans for social and economic development began to be implemented, so the ability of the States to finance their planned projects was seen to be inadequate. The central government, with its larger taxation resources and its hold over foreign exchange, loans, and foreign aid held the key to the rate of development and investment. The Planning Commission was charged with allocating subventions. It also assumed the right to dictate the form of individual States' development: which should be given priority for industrialisation, power, or communications. However, the States had a certain capacity to assert their own will: apart from a few major projects directly under central control (mainly dams for power and irrigation on Tennessee Valley lines) the great majority of schemes were to be

[1] Asok Chanda, *Indian Administration*, London, 1958, p. 92.

implemented by the States themselves. The centre might propose: the States could dispose. Many deliberately exceeded the budgets allotted; some by huge amounts (e.g. Bihar).

The Planning Commission symbolised the first phase of government in independent India. Its philosophy was a curious Fabian, New Deal, and Soviet amalgam. Its ramified establishment, and its doctrinaire, theoretical approach to development, reflected traditions of Mughal administration and of Brahmanical ritual procedure. In no other democracy has there been such a powerful excrescence on the body politic (though the Central Intelligence Agency at Washington runs it pretty close). The Commission characterised Nehru's eclectic technique of government; it also typified the extreme and highly personalised centralisation of the first phase; and its collisions with the State governments foreshadowed the emergence of power at the State level which characterises the second phase in India since independence.

The strains and fissions mentioned earlier in Congress internal politics before the first general election signified the gradual crystallisation of Left- and Right-wing attitudes. The Left-wing movement was most pronounced: yet it was largely abortive, because the Socialist Hamlet, Nehru, excluded himself from the cast. Gandhi had been anxious to retain the Socialists within the Congress fold, and he proposed a Socialist for president of the party in 1946. However, in February 1948, the annual session of the Congress adopted a revised constitution which laid down that a Congress member must not also be a member of a party 'which has a separate membership, constitution, and programme'. Faced with merging their identity into that of Congress at large, the Socialists withdrew, to form a democratic opposition party. The larger part of the younger Socialist element seceded, leaving Nehru to affirm that the goal of Congress remained a Socialist state.

If the Right-wing believed that Nehru's authority was thereby diminished, they were soon to be disenchanted. At the 1950 session of Congress, the conservatives achieved the election as president of Purshottamdas Tandon, an orthodox Hindu of the old guard, over the rival candidature of Acharaya Kripalani, a Gandhian-Socialist, favoured by Nehru. During the following months, conservative tactics further harassed the Prime Minister. On August 10, 1951, Nehru replied by resigning from the Working Committee, the high command of Congress. Thereby he demonstrated not that he was vulnerable, but that he was indispensable. The Congress Parliamentary Party gave him a full vote of confidence. Tandon attempted to manœuvre himself round the situation with no success. He tendered his own resignation, and Nehru was invited to take over the presidency. For the next four years, the Prime Minister retained the office, until he relinquished to a nominee of his own choice, U. N. Dhebar. He had demonstrated beyond doubt that he might be able to get on without Congress; but Congress could never get on without him.

Preparations for the general election neared completion. India had to elect 489 members of the House of the People, the *Lok Sabha*, the lower house of the central parliament, and 3,373 members of the State legislatures.[1] This represented broadly one M.P. for 500,000 to 750,000 population for the central legislature, and one M.L.A. (Member of the Legislative Assembly) for every 100,000 population for the State legislatures. The franchise was open to all adults, giving an electorate of about 173,000,000. This unprecedented electoral operation was entrusted to an Election Commission, supported by the whole machinery of administration throughout the districts. The enormous task of registration, voting, and counting the results was successfully carried through because India possessed a civil service which, from its senior administrators down to its junior clerks, was equal to its job. The first great test of democracy was also the greatest test of the bureaucracy.

Over 17,000 candidates came forward for the 3,800 odd seats. They represented fourteen national political parties, and fifty-one regional or State parties; while an enormous number of candidates stood as independents. Congress of course, dominated the scene; but it was not without serious rivals, between the Hindu communal parties, the Socialists, and the Communists. The oldest of the Hindu communal parties, the All-India Hindu Mahasabha (founded 1915) had passed under a cloud after Gandhi's assassination, though his murderer was actually a former member of the terrorist group, Rashtriya Swamyam Sevak Sangh, only loosely connected with the Mahasabha. Just before the election, the president of the Mahasabha, Dr. Syama Prasad Mookerjee, established a new party, the Bharatiya Jan Sangh, and rallied many members of the Mahasabha and R.S.S.S. to his new organisation. The third important Hindu party, and by far the most orthodox, was the Ram Rajya Parishad, founded in 1948.[2] Besides the Socialist Party itself, there were others of a similar complexion. Another party to be given birth just before election time was the Kisan Mazdur Praja Party (Peasants',

[1] The upper house of parliament, the Council of States or *Rajya Sabha*, is elected by the State legislatures, with certain special representatives.

[2] The names of the communal parties are each a combination of a Sanskritic term for 'assembly' (*sabha, sangha, parishad*), linked with an evocative Hindu concept: *Bharatiya Jan*, 'people of Mother India', *Ram Rajya*, 'the rule of God', i.e. a return to the golden age of Hinduism.

Workers', Peoples' Party). Its leader was Acharaya Kripalani, and he attracted a large following of discontented Congressites by calling for a return to Gandhian principles on socialist lines. The party of the untouchables the Scheduled Castes Federation, led by Dr. Ambedkar, as a 'have not' organisation also had a certain socialist flavour. The last major force in national politics was the Communist Party which, after unsuccessfully pursuing the policy of a guerrilla 'People's War' in Telengana and elsewhere, now returned to 'constitutional communism' and began to expand from a cadre to a mass party.

The campaign was, of course, directly waged between Congress and the rest. Congress relied almost entirely on the magic of Nehru: the one leader whom every peasant, however rustic, knew by name. On every hoarding was his face, with its Mona Lisa-like smile; every banner, every loudspeaker blared forth his name. The other parties avoided any direct attack on Nehru. The Hindu parties accused the Congress of 'fixing' the issue of Kashmir with Pakistan; the K.M.P. attacked Congress corruption, and raised the bogey of bloody revolution. Just as in eighteenth-century England, the opposition dared not directly attack His Majesty's Government, and so confined themselves to accusing individual ministers of betraying His Majesty's trust; so, in newly-independent India, the opposition had to argue that they would carry out the work of Gandhi and Nehru better than Congress. As in eighteenth-century England also, the issue was never in doubt: the government, inevitably, won the election hands down.

Out of the 489 seats in parliament (House of the People), Congress won 357 seats: subsequently increased by the accession of independents and dissidents to the party, to 362.[1] Because of the size of this victory, the details of how it was obtained were not closely scrutinised; but they repay examination.

The figures opposite are forcible reminders that representation in parliament does not always accurately reflect the popular support which a party may enjoy. Under an electoral system based upon the simple majority, and contested by a multiplicity of candidates, Congress with its over-all strength and organisation was the principal beneficiary. The Communist Party was astute enough to limit its challenge and to concentrate its attack where prospects seemed good: this policy produced a fair return in electoral gains for a relatively minute vote. The Hindu parties to some extent pursued a similar policy, with similar results.

[1] The careful reader may detect discrepancies between these figures and those quoted in other works: M.P.s 'floated' between parties, and exact totals are not possible.

1952 Election Results

HOUSE OF THE PEOPLE

	Seats won	Percentage of popular vote
Congress	362	45
Communist	23	3·3
Socialist	12	10·6
K.M.P.	9	5·8
Jan Sangh	3	3·1
Ram Rajya Parishad	3	2
Mahasabha	4	·9
Scheduled Castes Federation	2	2·3
Other parties	30	11·2
Independents	41	15·8

The moderate, democratic left-wing parties were hopelessly over-optimistic in their expectations, fielded far too many candidates, and reaped a meagre electoral harvest, despite a fair degree of popular support.

In the State elections, Congress won 2,248 seats out of a total of 3,279 on a minority vote of 42.2 per cent. Congress failed to win a clear majority in Madras, PEPSU (the Sikh states of Punjab), and Travancore-Cochin (later called Kerala). The Communists emerged as the main opposition group in four State assemblies: Madras, Hyderabad, West Bengal, and Travancore-Cochin. The Socialists achieved some success in Bihar and Uttar Pradesh; the K.M.P. formed a solid bloc in Madras. The most disappointed candidates were those of the Scheduled Castes Federation: they contested the 550 seats reserved for their lowly castes, and won only sixteen. The great majority of these 'reserved' seats went to the nominees of Congress: nonentities for the most part, but returned by the magic name of Nehru. At the States' level, sizeable parties emerged based purely on local bonds of loyalty. In Punjab, the militant Sikh organisation, the Akali Dal, won thirty-two seats in the two assemblies (PEPSU and East Punjab) and sent four M.P.s to Delhi. In Orissa, a conservative party organised by the dispossessed rajas, the Ganatantra Parishad, sprang into prominence, while in Rajasthan a confederation of princely 'independents' appeared.

The election was spread over seventeen weeks (mainly because of climatic difficulties, as in the high hills). 88,600,000 people actually voted, comprising 51.15 percent of the electorate. Voting was highest (70 per cent) where education was most advanced, in Travancore-Cochin (Kerala)—and lowest in the areas which, in the Western sense, were most politically illiterate—Rajasthan (20 per cent). The total cost was estimated at £5,250,000; and the district administration was compelled to switch all its energies to election preparations for six months. The President, Dr. Rajendra Prasad described the election as 'an act of faith' between the people and their leaders, and certainly it represented a sublime vindication of democracy. However, some observers debated whether such an elaborate and costly operation to determine the people's will was justified in a poor and backward country like India; thoughts turned to the possibilities of schemes for indirect election, by electoral colleges; such methods being already employed to elect the Upper House, the Rajya Sabha.

Nehru, of course, returned to the task of governing at New Delhi, and in all the States, Congress governments came into office. This was achieved even where the party formed a minority in the local Assembly; thanks to the lobbying and manoeuvring in which Congressites were so experienced; and thanks also to support from the centre. Ability to call upon the loaves and fishes of central patronage was a sizeable factor in Congress successes in the States.

The non-Congress parties realised that in splitting the vote, and in splitting legislative representation, they were making a gift of power to Congress. Attempts were made everywhere to organise pacts and alliances. Many of these were on a local, *ad hoc* basis (such as the alliance in Madras between the Communist, K.M.P. and a heterogeneous group of minor parties to form the United Democratic Front in February 1952) but in the moderate-Left camp, there was a more fundamental union between the Socialist Party and the K.M.P. to form a new Praja Socialist Party (September 1952), with Kripalani as Chairman and Asok Mehta as General Secretary. In subsequent by-elections the new party made small but steady gains, mainly at Congress' expense.

However, even after mergers and pacts, the opposition was weak and fragmented. Many political commentators, schooled in Anglo-American political thought, lamented the absence of a formed opposition, an alternative government, able to put forward an alternative programme for the electorate's consideration. Congress still regarded its mission as that of a national rally, or popular front; early in 1953, Nehru made tentative overtures to the Praja Socialists to gain their co-operation with Congress; these, however, petered out.

Another significant departure from the Western political pattern was the emergence of a social service movement, *Bhoodan*, which operated entirely outside the framework of party organisation and parliamentary activity, but which attracted a significant body of quasi-political support.

The *bhoodan yajna* (land-gift sacrifice) was first enunciated in April 1951 by Vinoba Bhave, a cherished Brahmin disciple of Gandhi, who wished to revive the Gandhian ideal of dedication, service, and the re-integration of corporate village life. Bhave, like Gandhi before, took to the trackways of rural India—a solitary pilgrim, lacking any organisation or finance, but possessed of an idea : the renunciation of materialistic (and, by implication, Westernised) ends, and the regeneration of rural life. He tramped along, calling for *bhoodan*, the gift of land, which was given to the landless, and (as the idea caught on) *gramdan*, the gift of villages (for co-operative community service) and *jivandan*, the gift of one's life to the service of India's poor. The ultimate goal of the movement is the attainment of *sarvodaya* : this is one of the key concepts in modern Indian political thought. Sarvodaya was Gandhi's vision of an ideal social order, based upon social service and non-violence, and creating a casteless, classless society where universal harmony would prevail. There is this much of identity with the Marxian concept of the classless society : that when the ideal is attained the centralised state 'withers away', politics and government become largely superfluous. The most prominent disciple of Vinoba Bhave is Jayaprakash Narayan, the quondam Socialist Party leader; he became a jivandani in 1954, pledging his life towards the achievement of sarvodaya.

These, then, were the main streams and eddies in national politics, but deep down, the strong currents of State politics were flowing. The turning-point came as the climax to the agitation for a separate Telugu-speaking Andhra State : the fast by the Telugu leader, Potti Sriramalu, which ended in his death on December 16, 1952. Rioting and destruction followed; the central government hastily capitulated, announcing the setting up of Andhra State only three days later, thus conceding the principle of the linguistic State. The full story of the politics of language and religion will be recounted in Chapter VI. Meanwhile, the major occasions of tension between the centre and the States can be briefly noted. In Travancore-Cochin, the Congress government was defeated on a motion of 'no confidence' in September 1953. Elections followed, in February 1954, and an electoral pact was concluded between the Socialist Party and extreme Left-wing groups, to fight as a

'Left Front' against Congress. In the new legislature, totalling 117 members, Congress held forty-five seats, the Praja Socialists had nineteen, and the extreme Leftists, forty seats. In this unbalanced situation Congress offered to support a Praja Socialist government! This narrowly-based Socialist government functioned for a year, until Congress withdrew its support and took over power; they, in turn, were defeated; and in this political deadlock the President dissolved the Assembly under his emergency powers and instituted direct gubernatorial rule. In PEPSU (Punjab) also, the Congress government tottered, thanks to defections among its Sikh allies, and Presidential rule was imposed. Here, a second election in 1954 produced a clear Congress majority; largely because Nehru personally conducted a whirlwind campaign through the State. The new State of Andhra commenced with a legislature provided by the representatives of the area who had previously sat in the Madras Assembly. Congress could only muster forty-five out of its 140 members; but once again astute lobbying produced a Congress-led coalition. This fell apart within a year, and the President again stepped in. New elections were notified for February 1955, and this time Congress took no chances. The tough Bombay party boss, S. K. Patil, was imported to give the State organisation a steel frame; while ample funds were made available from the coffers of the party. All this might not have prevailed, had not Congress made a thorough study of local caste tensions and obligations. By exploiting caste politics (as the Communists had previously successfully done) Congress and its allies won 146 out of the total of 196 in the new Assembly. The Communists were reduced to a rump of fifteen.

Despite these undercurrents, the years between the first and second general election were a period of national confidence and expansion: the high noon of early independence. The period saw the successful completion of the First Five Year Plan (1951-6) with target figures fully achieved. The Second Plan (1956-61) was launched with the ambitious aim of providing the industrial strength to achieve the 'take-off into sustained growth' which economists declared was now feasible. This was also the period of the inception of a nation-wide Community Development Programme. Launched in 1952, the programme was designed to make Indian rural society dynamic; to mobilise the energies of the rural millions through *shramdan* ('work-gift'—a Bhavian echo) and to arouse a new consciousness of how social and economic change might be accelerated in the countryside. The phrase 'the revolution of rising expectations', to describe the stirring of newly independent peoples, has become almost a cliché; but it well exemplifies the mood of the Indian people at this time. Above all, this was the era of Nehru's dominance in world affairs: the era when the concept of 'positive neutralism' did seem to offer the best hope of building a bridge across the Cold War barriers.

The second general election found the peoples of India still in this exalted strain. This time, it was possible to compress the whole election process into nineteen days (February-March 1957), although the electorate had now increased to 193,000,000. This time, few doubted the capability of Congress to win again. The opposition parties made no real effort to present a challenge as an alternative government. Whereas, for the House of the People, 481 candidates came forward on the Congress ticket, the Praja Socialists put up only 190 nominees, the Communists 141, and the Jan Sangh only 125 candidates. At the States' level, the disparity was almost the same; only in West Bengal was the opposition given much chance of success, and here a left-wing coalition made a determined attempt to challenge the unimpressive Congress record. The Socialists were in particularly poor form, having sustained the defection of one of their leading figures, Dr. Lohia, together with a sizeable following.

At the centre, expectations were generally fulfilled.

1957 Election Results

HOUSE OF THE PEOPLE

	Seats won	Percentage of popular vote
Congress	366	46·5
Communist	29	9·8
Praja Socialist	18	10·5
'Lohia' Socialist	6	5
Jan Sangh	4	6
Scheduled Castes Federation	7	4
Others	58	18·2

Again, Congress was master of the field; its nearest rival, the Communist Party, was still a pygmy to its giant. The pretensions of the Socialists to provide an alternative government were hopelessly dissipated. Among the Hindu communal parties, only the Jan Sangh made any ground; the orthodox Ram Rajya Parishad failed to win a single seat.

The situation in the States was more ambiguous. Congress won 65 per cent of the seats in the Assemblies, but this was out of all proportion to its popular support. Only in two provinces did Congress poll over 50 per cent of the vote, while in two provinces (Orissa and Kerala) it polled less than 40 per cent. In the Orissa Assembly of 140 members, Congress held fifty-six seats, against fifty-one for the Ganatantra Parishad (the party of the rajas), eleven Praja Socialists, nine Communist, five Jharkand (tribal) members, and eight others. Congress followed its usual course of fixing those politicians who were out for favours, and managed to form a government. Members oscillated between the parties, and by 1959 Congress was floundering. It was compelled to resign, and to join a coalition with the Ganatantra Parishad.

In Kerala, the Congress had actually polled more votes than the Communists (38.2 per cent, to 36.5 per cent Communist) but sixty Communist members were returned to the State Assembly, and only forty-five Congressites. The remainder were eight Praja Socialists (as usual, the party was disappointed), nine Muslim League (representing a small fanatical Muslim pocket), and five independents. Supported by the independents the Communists took office.[1] The Chief Minister, E. M. S. Namboodiripad, was a former Gandhian. After stormy conflicts, inside the legislature and outside, the central government intervened in July 1959, dismissed the government, and promised fresh elections. These followed in February 1960. This time, Congress made an electoral alliance with the Praja Socialists and the Muslim League, to form a United Front. The result was a clear victory for the United Front (Congress, sixty-two; Socialists, twenty; Muslim League, eleven)—yet although the Communists retained only twenty-eight seats, they increased their popular support by more than a million, and their share of the total vote increased from 40 per cent (1957) to 42.5 per cent (1960).

Elsewhere, Congress was able to form governments without serious difficulty, but the opposition was heavily reinforced. In Bombay, in an Assembly of 315, the combined opposition totalled 162; even in Uttar Pradesh, regarded as the stronghold of Congress, there were 139 Praja Socialists, Communists, Jan Sangh, and opposition independents against 290 Congress and supporters. West Bengal elected an Assembly containing 152 Congress, forty-six Communist and supporters, twenty-four Praja Socialists, and thirty independents. Congress was able to rely upon the Bengali rural vote, but the urban voters were hostile. Calcutta voted

[1] Earning 'the unenviable distinction of being the first State in the Commonwealth to have a Communist Government', as Sir Percival Griffiths observed in the *Sunday Times*.

solidly Communist, indeed, one of the political phenomena of the 1950s was the emergence of a hard-core Communist vote among the slum-dwellers of all the great cities.

Congress would have had no reason to feel depressed because of the 1957 election results alone: most political analysts would interpret such figures, after ten hard years in office, as a triumph. Unfortunately, the general election was only the first mile-stone on a hazardous road.

A hint that there was a divergence between the 'image' of a utopian society where all were labouring harmoniously together for the public good, and the reality of an imperfect democracy, with clashes of interests and the pursuit of self-gain, came with the publication of the 'Balvantray Report' on community development in November 1957.[1] This report provided an indictment of the theoretical, formalistic approach of the Planning Commission and the Community Development agencies in the States. The programme had begun by assuming that the village people could be rapidly persuaded to take over responsibility for the new development projects; instead, the officials, high and low, had directed and controlled everything. As a 'people's programme', community development was an illusion.

The Balvantray Report did little more than disturb the complacency of politicians and officials: the Life Insurance scandal (as it was generally known) produced a tremor throughout the whole politically-literate strata of India. The scandal burst into prominence in February 1958, with the publication of the report by Mr. Justice Chagla on the circumstances whereby the government Life Insurance Corporation purchased stock to the value of £1,000,000 from a Marwari promoter, H. D. Mundhra (described in the report as 'a financial adventurer'), at an allegedly inflated price. The report declared that the Minister of Finance, T. T. Krishnamachari, 'must fully and squarely accept responsibility' for this deal. The minister attempted to shift the onus onto his permanent Secretary, and Nehru showed the greatest reluctance to relieve T. T. Krishnamachari of his portfolio. In parliament, the majority of Congress members accepted the special pleading of Nehru and Krishnamachari complaisantly: but a few voices spoke up sharply and Nehru reluctantly accepted the impropriety of retaining the besmirched minister.

Apart from its intrinsic importance, the whole affair had sinister undertones. There was Nehru's aloofness from public happenings and public opinion; his readiness to accept the version of events supplied by his own courtiers; and his reluctance to divest himself of a courtier,

[1] *Report of the Team for the Study of Community Projects and National Extension Service*, 3 vols., New Delhi, 1957.

when discredited. There was also the continuing division between politicians and senior civil servants (the latter still regarded as the instruments of British rule) and a readiness, when things went wrong, to heap the blame on these officials.

Then, gradually, there came the realisation that the Second Plan was not enjoying the same success as its predecessor; partly because of external difficulties, over which India had no control (e.g. adverse movements in international terms of trade), partly because of extra expenditure on military aircraft, to meet Pakistan's strength in jet planes; but also because the Second Plan had been too lavish in its commitment to heavy industry, thereby neglecting the agricultural sector. An attempt was made to redress the balance, by a resolution passed at the annual session of Congress, at Nagpur in January 1959, calling for increased agricultural production by means of joint co-operative farming. This Nagpur resolution clashed with the innate conservatism of most Congress members, whose interests as traders and landholders would be directly affected by the proposed agricultural revolution. Within a year, the resolution had been tacitly abandoned. At the next session of Congress, at Bangalore in January 1960, it was resolved that 'Co-operative farming should be developed wherever it is desired by the farmers themselves'. Nehru still insisted that co-operative farming 'was not only right, but absolutely right': however, the irresistible force had met the immovable object. The clash with Tandon in 1950 showed that Congress could not push Nehru around with impunity; the abandonment of co-operative farming in 1960 demonstrated that Nehru could not push the Congress in a direction it did not wish to go.

These internal strains and stresses were overshadowed by the growing alarm over the border activities of China. The public became generally aware of Chinese aggressiveness late in 1958, with the arrest of an Indian military police patrol on the Ladakh border. Then came the tightening up of Chinese control over Tibet, and the flight of the Dalai Lama, together with thousands of Tibetans, into India in March 1959. This was the signal for China to become even tougher in border affairs. These developments aroused intense emotional feeling among every shade of opinion, from religious organisations, and the Right-wing, over to the Socialists. For a long while, Nehru countered agitation against Chinese incursions by temporising; the reports were unconfirmed; the region concerned was difficult of access. He desired to keep relations with China on the agreeable basis of the Five Principles of Peaceful Co-Existence, *Pancha Shila,* which he regarded as the main plank in the platform of 'positive neutralism'. Public opinion was not prepared to accept Nehru's assurances, and feeling mounted.

Yet the Chinese menace also served to reinforce Nehru's supremacy. Whatever fissiparous tendencies had appeared at the level of State politics, these were secondary to an aroused national awareness of the threat to national security. Nehru's reply to his critics was also largely unanswerable: he pointed out that, in today's circumstances, a military retort to China's military menaces must mean war: 'and conflict between India and China would shake Asia and shake the world'. This reminder of the alternative to the co-existence policy was sobering, though not completely convincing. Critics still insisted that India should stand more firmly on her rights.

Concern at the unreality of Congress policy under Nehru, both at home and abroad, crystallised in 1959 in the emergence of a 'realist' political force, the Swatantra ('Freedom') Party. This was led by C. Rajagopalachari, the former Governor-General, and Minoo Masani, once a Congress Socialist, but now an independent, to the right of Congress. The Swatantra policy was conservative, condemning the drift towards Socialism, and urging abandonment of neutralism, with alignment more towards the West.

The formation of the Swatantra Party was one aspect of a wider public impatience with Nehru's lofty approach to affairs. There was a growing feeling that the Prime Minister must descend from his pulpit, putting aside the rôle of seer and philosopher, in order to provide practical leadership. This implied no desire to see him go; Nehru had only to hint that he wished to resign to plunge the political world into disarray. The question of 'Who will succeed Nehru?' baffled the insiders of Indian politics as much as the outsiders.

If the gathering sense of impatience with political unrealities was manifested in criticism of Nehru's abstracted methods, it was even more generally voiced in growing dissatisfaction with the Anglo-Saxon parliamentary system. Criticism specially fastened upon the schisms in public life, which were alleged to have been accentuated by a system of government by bare majority—what Indians increasingly called 'Fifty-one per cent democracy'.[1] The contrast between the power-monopoly

[1] It is important to remember that the effective working of the Anglo-Saxon parliamentary tradition depends upon a very wide measure of agreement between the parties upon fundamentals. When the parties are divided over basic issues, such as slavery, or Irish Home Rule, or even the total nationalisation of industry, then parliament, or Congress and President, cease to be viable institutions. The consensus which has prevailed in India over basic issues, such as the secular state, national planning, neutralism, will not necessarily continue.

enjoyed by Congress governments, and the relatively slender degree of electoral support for Congress, gave point to this view. So long as Congress was the 'Freedom Movement', its monopoly of power was readily accepted. But as it steadily became identified with the Establishment, the Ins against the Outs, this dominance was increasingly resented. The remedy proposed, was to embrace the principle of unanimity, or Gandhian sarvodaya. This was enjoined by the Speaker of the Lok Sabha, the first parliamentarian:

> In a parliamentary democracy, unanimity must be aimed at; it may not be practicable. But unanimity must be the goal.... My own feeling is, each man whether he is in the opposition or in the government is as much a representative of his constituency as any other man.... Before important matters are brought before parliament, the government must consult the opposition also.... We have to follow a policy which is evolved according to our own pattern and which is consistent with our own historical tradition.

From the Communist benches, the same sentiments were expressed. Here is P. C. Joshi, member of the Central Committee of the C.P.I.:

> I submit the future of parliamentary democracy in India depends on how all patriotic and democratic elements in our country fulfil the tasks facing the Indian nation.... Can we unite and achieve these things?[1]

Apprehension that the power of the executive has increased rather than declined since independence has led many to hark back to the Gandhian ideal of *panchayati raj*, a federation of village republics. Under this system, the village, not the individual would become the unit of political choice. The Assemblies of the State or nation would be composed on the 'functional' basis of the community. The village, and the region would also be entrusted with executive power. Again, this concept stems from sarvodaya, and its most persuasive exponent is Jayaprakash Narayan. From being regarded as something of a political crank, by 1961 Jayaprakash was becoming the focus of a growing body of serious political thought.

These sentiments were largely forgotten as the 1962 Election drew nearer. The campaign was fought, as before, on the basis of support for, or opposition to the Congress government. The multiplicity of rival

[1] Both quotations from *Future of Asian Democracy*, Indian Bureau of Parliamentary Studies, New Delhi, 1959.

parties and candidates showed no sign of the influence of sarvodaya, the quest for unanimity and harmony.

The mechanics of the election were somewhat altered. The period of the election was reduced to ten days: the first election had been spread over seventeen weeks. The reduction obviated any 'snowball' effects being obtained from the earlier results. Two-member seats were abolished. The single-member constituencies which were now the universal rule were sometimes very large; as in North Bombay, with its 800,000 electors. To 'deliver' the vote in such a constituency required considerable organisation. Altogether, the electorate totalled 212,000,000, of whom at least 160,000,000 were illiterate.

At the national level, about thirty parties took the field—a much smaller number than in previous elections, though the actual number of candidates increased. Against 485 Congress candidates for the Lok Sabha, were arrayed 198 Jan Sangh, 172 Swatantra candidates, and a reduced number from the Communist and Socialist camps. Only Congress campaigned on the basis of offering a programme for the next government. All other parties, including Communists and Socialists, confined themselves to the rôle of an opposition by attacking Congress rule; its corruption, inefficiency, and betrayal of the nation by proving 'soft' to Chinese aggression. This tacit acceptance that they could not win, must have had an enormous effect upon the voting inclination of the electorate. Once again, Nehru dominated the election. He travelled hundreds of miles, and is computed to have addressed 10,000,000 people. This was probably the major factor in persuading more electors than ever before to vote for the Congress. A higher proportion actually went to the poll, 53.7 per cent (7 per cent more than in 1957) and once again Kerala produced the highest poll for the Lok Sabha elections: 69 per cent of the electorate. (See Table overleaf.)

Foreign interest was largely focused upon North Bombay, where Krishna Menon was opposed by Acharaya Kripalani as the candidate of a Leftist coalition. The issues involved were somewhat befogged by the pronouncements of participants and commentators. Menon's candidature was upheld by Nehru as a symbol of progressive, all-India, internationalist policies. His opponents accused him of being a crypto-Communist (no Communist candidate was nominated in North Bombay), and blamed him for the humiliation of unchecked Chinese aggression, forecasting that he intended to seize power and rule with army backing when Nehru quitted the political stage. Besides the support of the active Socialist leaders, Kripalani received the benefit of one of Jayaprakash Narayan's rare excursions into party politics in his cause.

1962 Election Results

HOUSE OF THE PEOPLE

	Seats won	Percentage of popular vote
Congress	355	48
Communist	29	10
Praja Socialist	12	7
'Lohia' Socialist	5	6
Jan Sangh	14	6
Swatantra	22*	7
Others	57	16

* Includes 4 Ganatantra Parishad affiliates.

American and British top line journalists solemnly predicted Menon's defeat, thereby contributing a little more to his chances of winning; and when the poll was declared he received a majority vote of 145,358. At Allahabad, Dr. Lohia's challenge to Nehru in a constituency that has returned Panditji for a quarter of a century, met with predictable disaster. Asok Mehta also went down, leaving the Socialists in the Lok Sabha with virtually no leadership. What joy there was to be gained from the results, went to the parties of the Right. Before the election, nine M.P.s had accepted the Swatantra ticket; after the poll, they numbered twenty-two, forming the largest non-Communist opposition group. The question now was whether they would make common cause with Jan Sangh in order to create a more effective Right-wing opposition. The modest Right-wing success was received by Nehru with denunciation. Although the Prime Minister has frequently gone on record in favour of a more effective opposition, it seems that his approval is more theoretical than actual; for whenever any opposition group appears likely to achieve a breakthrough, he is angered by what he regards as a slur upon the Congress and its right to govern.

In the State elections, where the magic of Nehru's name was less directly involved, Congress suffered more considerable setbacks. The factions within the Pradesh Congress Committees had bitterly contested the lists of official Congress candidates. Many who were disappointed in seeking the party ticket stood, anyway, as independent Congress candidates. Amid the confusion, Congress was fortunate to hold on to power in all the States. Their hold was most marginal in Rajasthan, where they won eighty-eight out of a total of 176 seats in the State legislature, and in Madhya Pradesh where they sank from 232 to 142 out of a total of 288. In Andhra their numbers fell from 240 to 176 in a legislature of 240. Even in the Hindi stronghold there were losses; the Uttar Pradesh Congress total declined from 286 to 242, and the Bihar total from 210 to 175. Only in two States did Congress show real vigour. There were no State elections in Orissa, where the previous year the forceful Chief Minister, Bijoyanand Patnaik had halted the party's decline at a mid-term election caused by the dissolution of the State Assembly. He duly doubled the number of Congress Lok Sabha seats, fighting off a strong challenge from the Ganatantra Parishad which was associated with the Swatantra platform. Maharashtra also saw Congress gains, both in Lok Sabha seats and for the State legislature, where the Congress group rose from 137 to 210. Once again, the main cause was an energetic Chief Minister, Y. B. Chavan.

Congress losses were not fatal, because nowhere did a strong, united opposition emerge. As usual, the Communists were the most serious threat: they returned fifty-one members in Andhra, forty-six in West Bengal, fourteen in U.P. and twelve in Bihar. Nowhere could they hope to challenge Congress. The Right-wing achieved most success in the more tradition-minded areas. In Rajasthan, there were thirty-six Swatantra and fifteen Jan Sangh members: however, with thirty independents in the legislature waiting to be wooed, Congress had little difficulty in making sure of a working majority. Madhya Pradesh was the scene of worst confusion. The Chief Minister, the old guard leader K. N. Katju, was defeated by a Jan Sangh candidate, and the Hindu communal parties effected their biggest gains: forty-one seats to Jan Sangh, and ten to Ram Rajya Parishad (Swatantra won only two seats). The Hindi stronghold was not immune from the swing to the Right. In U.P. Jan Sangh achieved their highest score, forty-six seats, with fifteen going to Swatantra; their showing in Bihar was largely reversed, with Swatantra gaining forty-eight seats (their largest total) and the Jan Sangh winning only three. The relative success of the Right-wing parties depends greatly upon how far they are taken up by leaders able to command some local prestige and influence. The good showing of Swatantra in Rajasthan owed a great deal to the championship of the Maharani of Jaipur, who combined the automatic influence of the premier Rajput princely house with undoubted personal *réclame*. The Socialists, the forgotten men of Indian politics, managed to hold on to some of their following in the Hindi areas (U.P., thirty-seven, Bihar, twenty-seven, and Madhya

Pradesh, thirty-two). They also held twenty seats in Mysore, but in the remaining eight States their standing is negligible. Finally, one must note the remarkable success of the Dravida Munnetra Kazhagam in winning fifty seats in the Madras Assembly on a platform of Tamil separatism.

The elections over, the politicians braced themselves for the next phase; the struggle for power and position. At the centre there was no manœuvring of any significance. As the Grand Old Man of Indian politics, Nehru can dispose of his colleagues as he chooses; on and on he goes: a Gladstone untroubled by a Queen Victoria or an Irish problem. Krishna Menon's personal triumph in North Bombay gives him, for the first time, a stature in the Cabinet and in Congress commensurate with his towering intellect. The return of T. T. Krishnamachari to the Cabinet, with a strong animus against capitalists and bureaucrats, gives Menon support in his stand to the Left.

In the States, the necessity to crank up the sputtering Congress machinery for another five year stint has led to much pulling of wires and squeezing of oil cans. The fact that State politics is so involved with politicking need not, necessarily, be a cause for concern. But the absence of dynamism, the absence of new men and new measures in the new Congress governments is disturbing. Among the many diverse trends revealed by the third general election, it must be remembered that the great mass of the ordinary people of India once again demonstrated their faith in the Congress. How long will their faith endure?

IV

PAKISTAN: TRIALS OF DEMOCRACY

WHEN people in India today want to talk about the recent past, they say, 'Since independence . . .' Referring to the same period, Pakistanis invariably say, 'Since partition . . .' In vast areas of the Indian Union, the people were quite unaffected by the division of the sub-continent; but scarcely a district, or even a family of Pakistan was left untouched or unmarked by this upheaval.

The traumatic effect was felt most in West Pakistan: there, before partition, each province had a sizeable non-Muslim population (one and a third million in Sind, one-quarter million in the North-West Frontier, and about two and three-quarter million in West Punjab). Almost all these fled, in the mass migrations; leaving, beside the Muslims, only small Christian colonies, and the urban Parsi business community. This exodus included all the merchants, bankers, and traders, most of the doctors and technical personnel, and a good proportion of teachers of higher education. In their place, there arrived from East Punjab a flood of poor peasants, together with artisans and small shopkeepers from Delhi and other towns. On balance, there was an increase of almost a million out of this forced exchange. But those who came could not contribute anything vital to the economy, while those who were gone represented the whole network of commerce and exchange; the nerves and sinews of the economic system of West Pakistan.

It is not entirely clear how the economy avoided complete, sudden collapse. There remained the British banks, where English and Scots managers somehow scrambled through the work of their departed Hindu clerical staff; and there remained the residue of a fine system of co-operative societies (Punjab had been the leading province in setting up co-operatives providing seed, credit, and marketing facilities). The newly arrived peasants were hastily set to harvest the crops sown by the departed Sikhs; somehow the crop was moved along the railroads, and the economy shuddered and survived.

The government was in similar straits. Somehow, the new central government had to be improvised at Karachi out of nothing. The disjointed provincial governments had to receive, and feed the refugees, and allocate houses and land to them. Somehow, all this was done. Whereas India dispensed with the services of most British officials immediately, having a sizeable cadre of senior Indian administrators, Pakistan took on all British officials who were willing to stay. Three of the four Governors of provinces were British, as were most of the permanent Secretaries to Government. These men of tried experience were mostly 'more Pakistani than the Pakistanis' in their enthusiasm for the new country, and they toiled valiantly. Even more vital was the devoted service of humble officials. Hardbitten, hard-drinking sub-inspectors of police forswore bribes and dedicated themselves to their countrymen; cynical, time-serving office clerks took on social service duties, and lived among squalour and filth. Pakistan survived because enough Pakistanis were determined that it should survive.

Yet, the lands which border the Indus had been impoverished irretrievably by the Hindu and Sikh exodus. India, despite the departure of so many Muslims, retains its cultural richness and diversity: even the legacy of Islam still exercises some influence. West Pakistan was entirely bereft of its former cultural variety; in the towns, most of the life and colour had been provided by the Hindus; in the countryside, the Sikhs had contributed invaluable pioneering drive and enterprise. Now, they were all gone, and only shuttered Hindu temples, and padlocked Sikh *gurudwaras* remained, their empty monuments. A Punjabi Hindu has written a vividly evocative memoir of the old Punjab, and he reflects

> It is strange to think that in all the land between Ravi and Chenab, from Chenab to Jhelum, from Jhelum to Indus, in the foothills and in the plain down to Panjnad, where the five rivers eventually merge, land which had been the homes of our biradaris [brotherhoods] since the dawn of history, there is no one left of our kind.[1]

The social transformation of East Pakistan was not so sudden or complete. There was a considerable efflux of middle-class Hindus (in one

[1] Prakash Tandon, *Punjabi Century*, 1857-1947, London, 1961, p. 249.

up-country university college, a young Muslim assistant lecturer suddenly found himself Dean of the Faculties of Arts, Sciences, Law, and Engineering—a magnificent academic Poo Bah), but even so, about one-third of the population was still Hindu, many being professional and business men. But East Pakistan was crippled in a different way. The West, was, in embryo, a viable economic unit, with a complete railroad system, a fully developed port, and an international airport: even if it entirely lacked an industrial base. The East had formed part of the hinterland of Calcutta; its principal product, jute, was processed and exported from the Hooghley industrial nexus. Now, Calcutta with its mills was in another country. East Pakistan had no means of processing its staple crop, and only a second-rate port (Chittagong) through which to squeeze its exports.

The economic build-up of Pakistan is outside the scope of these pages, but the continuing backwardness of the East was to provide one of the most bitter political grievances of the Bengalis. Within a few years, the West was launched upon an impressive programme of industrialisation. Apart from the expansion of the port of Chittagong, the East received hardly any share in this industrial development: yet East Pakistan jute formed the main asset in the country's accumulation of foreign exchange. As we shall see, a sense of neglect in economic development contributed to the growth of political disharmony between East and West Pakistan.

The constitutional debate in Pakistan was infinitely more protracted than in India: a constitution was not finally adopted until February 1956. Until then, the country was governed under the 1935 Government of India Act, somewhat amended and modified. The long delay was partially caused by adventitious political circumstances, but also by fundamental disagreements on two major questions: the rôle of Islam in the new state, and the relations between the East and West wings, and the central government. In part, the prolongation of the debate was caused by the untimely death of Jinnah in September 1948 within a few months of independence. Jinnah did not have the time to evolve a constitutional formula, and he left no accepted declaration of political faith (as did Gandhi) upon which his followers could build. In consequence, Jinnah's views were rapidly by-passed by those zealots who sought to establish Pakistan as an Arab polity of the kind propounded by the Holy Prophet.

The inaugural speech which Jinnah, as incoming Governor-General, addressed to the Constituent Assembly of Pakistan, appears to the outsider to envisage the creation of a secular state, similar to the new India:

Work together in a spirit that every one of you, no matter
to what community he belongs . . . no matter what is his caste,
colour or creed, is first, second and last a citizen of this state
with equal rights, privileges and obligations. . . . I cannot emphasise it too much. We should begin to work in that spirit
and in course of time all these angularities of the majority
and minority communities . . . will vanish. . . . You may belong
to any religion or caste or creed—that has nothing to do with
the state.

For the brief remainder of his life, Jinnah was an ailing man, driving
himself on by an effort of will. The leaders of the new country had more
than enough to occupy their energies in the struggle for survival. However, yet another problem arose to distract the over-taxed Jinnah and
his ministers and advisers: that of Kashmir.

It is still not clear how far the tribal invasion of Kashmir was encouraged by higher authority in Pakistan, how far merely condoned—
or even whether its launching came as a genuine surprise to all but a
few local officials. The prompt Indian reaction to the invasion came as a
bitter shock. In the case of Junagadh (see p. 44) the revolt of the people
against the decision of the maharaja was the occasion for Indian intervention: in the present case, Indian action appeared entirely to reverse
the Junagadh argument (the Indian Government, of course, based its
intervention on the necessity to rid Kashmir of the tribal invaders).
When Jinnah was given the news of Indian acceptance of the maharaja's
accession, he regarded this as yet another example of Hindu or Congress
perfidy. He immediately ordered the advance of the Pakistan Army into
Kashmir. His Commander-in-Chief, and most of the senior army officers were British; and Jinnah was met with two arguments; first, that
the army was still being sorted into regular units, and could not mount
an invasion; second, that invasion must lead immediately to war with
India, in which case all British officers would be required to quit the
Pakistan service. Reluctantly, Jinnah countermanded his order.

In the following months, the tribal forces were compelled to retreat.
The restricted area of Azad Kashmir seemed likely to disappear completely. In the Spring of 1948, the Pakistan Army was ordered into
Kashmir. During the following months, Pakistan regained some lost
ground, and assumed control over the vast but largely barren terrain of
the northern dependencies of Kashmir which stretch towards the Karakorum mountains. The main object of the unacknowledged contest between the Indian and Pakistan armies was control over the tiny capital
of Poonch. There was always the grave danger that the fighting would

spill over from Kashmir into the territory of India or Pakistan proper. Then, the fiction of the undeclared war could no longer be upheld: war along the whole front must break out.

The Indian Army was by no means content with a situation in which a major part of its forces was committed to an endless struggle fought at the end of tenuous lines of communication, which might be severed by climatic hazard at any time. Informal contacts were still maintained between the Commanders of the Indian and Pakistan armies, both still British officers. In December 1948, they prevailed upon their governments to accept a cease-fire based upon the existing dispositions of their troops. The cease-fire came into effect on January 1, 1949. The military phase was over: the diplomatic and political phase had only just begun.[1]

Meanwhile, the architect of Pakistan had died. His successor as Governor-General was Khwaja Nazimuddin, previously chief minister of East Bengal: an aristocratic Bengali landlord of an amiable and pious disposition. Nobody could take the place of Jinnah: he had been called *Quaid-i-Azam*, Great Leader, and there could be no other. The leadership of the nation now passed to the Prime Minister, Liaqat Ali Khan, Jinnah's trusted lieutenant, whose integrity and impartiality was universally acknowledged. The constitutional balance now approximated to that of India, and the old Dominions, with the Governor-General as ceremonial head of state, and the Prime Minister as the fulcrum of power.

January 1949 brought the first taste of what was to become a commonplace in the years to come: suspension of parliamentary government, and a return to direct gubernatorial rule in West Punjab. The cause of the constitutional breakdown was also ominous: the unsavoury feuding between the leaders of the two factions of the Muslim League, both powerful landlords, and both exposed as self-seekers.

More hopeful was the start made upon the task of formulating a constitution. The constituent assembly comprised those members of the original, all-India assembly who now belonged to Pakistan, together with members nominated to represent the princely states and border areas which had joined Pakistan (these included Bahawalpur and Khairpur states, Baluchistan, Chitral, and Swat). Of the eighty members, twelve represented Congress, one belonged to Ambedkar's Scheduled Castes Federation, one (Shaukat Hyat Khan) was a former Unionist, and one (Khan Abdul Ghafur Khan) was a Congressite 'Red Shirt': but he was in jail. The remainder were all members of the Muslim League.

[1] The further history of the Kashmir dispute is summarised in the Appendix: Kashmir and the Borderlands.

Just as Congress dominated the Indian Constituent Assembly, so the League held unchallengeable sway in Pakistan. In East-West terms, East Pakistan had a small majority of members (forty-four), but as these included the Hindu bloc, the West Pakistan League group was more numerous.

In March 1949, Liaqat Ali introduced a resolution on the 'Aims and Objects of the Constitution'. Later, a learned judge was to dismiss this resolution as 'nothing but a hoax'. Mr. Justice Munir pointed out the inconsistency of its opening words, 'Whereas sovereignty over the entire universe belongs to Allah Almighty alone' with the subsequent affirmation, 'The Constituent Assembly ... have resolved to frame for the sovereign independent State of Pakistan a constitution'.[1] Liaqat Ali laid stress on the undertaking which was included in the resolution to fully observe 'the principles of democracy, freedom, equality, tolerance and social justice as enunciated by Islam'. To this, the Hindu representatives demanded how far non-Muslims could expect to be treated as equals in an explicitly Islamic state? And the more orthodox Leaguers insisted that only true Muslims could be entrusted with leadership and responsibility in the new nation: even the tolerant Liaqat Ali showed an inclination to adopt this attitude when, in 1950, being Chairman of the Muslim League, he declared unequivocally that he regarded himself as responsible to the League rather than to the Constituent Assembly. The historical attitude of Muslim states to those of their subjects who were not believers was to class them as *dhimmis* or *zimmis*: second-class citizens. The attitude of professed democrats in Pakistan was, to say the least, ambiguous on this matter.

How could Islamic principles be incorporated in the constitution? How strong was to be the power of the central government over the provinces? And what safeguards could East Bengal obtain? Inability to find an answer to these and other questions delayed the prospects of any early constitutional settlement. Then, in 1951, the political barometer plunged from Unsettled to Stormy. The first sign of unrest beneath the surface was the Rawalpindi conspiracy case. Without warning, a group of high-ranking military officers were arrested on charges of conspiring

---

[1] *Report of the Court of Inquiry constituted under Punjab Act II of 1954 to enquire into the Punjab disturbances of 1953*, Lahore, 1954. Cited under as 'Munir Report'. The judge declared: 'An Islamic state ... cannot be sovereign, because it will not be competent to abrogate, repeal or do away with any law in the Quran or the *sunna* [recorded tradition].' Thus, he argued, an Islamic state cannot be a democracy: the legislature will not be responsible to the people. These were not juristic niceties; they represent a real dilemma for Muslims who wish to be democrats.

to overthrow the state, involving conspiracy with a foreign power. Those arrested included Major-General Akbar Khan, Brigadier Latif, and Group-Captain Janjua. The trial took place in camera; but it was known that the accused were charged with planning to set up a military dictatorship. They were sentenced to long terms of imprisonment. Politics in the province of Sind had always been corrupt, sinister, and often bloody. Ayub Khuhro had pursued a Borgia-like ministerial career: now, as chief minister, he faced criminal charges. Sind was placed under direct administration, and Khuhro was debarred from office under the Public and Representative Offices (Disqualification) Act—PRODA—promoted by Liaqat Ali in January 1949 in an effort to purify public life. By the time the Sind affair was over, Liaqat Ali was no more. He fell to the bullet of an Afghan assassin in October 1951: the murderer was torn to pieces by the crowd, so his exact motive was never discovered.

Who was to succeed Liaqat Ali? Both Jinnah and Liaqat possessed the invaluable quality of being outside the East-West imbroglio; Jinnah's home was Bombay, and Liaqat's, the United Provinces. Both had been genuinely national leaders, accepted by both East and West. But most of the front-rank Leaguers were identified with one particular province. The man who was believed to be Liaqat's chosen successor was Abdur Rab Nishtar, a jovial but masterful Punjabi landlord, with long political experience stretching back to the days of the Khilafat movement. Since July 1949 he had governed West Punjab, but Liaqat was known to have thought of bringing him into the cabinet as deputy Prime Minister. The cabinet made their choice: and it came as a surprise. Nazimuddin was invited to relinquish the office of Governor-General to become Prime Minister. His place was taken by the Finance Minister, Ghulam Mohammad, a former senior civil servant.

The machiavellian motivation behind this manœuvre was a balancing of the East-West interests. Nazimuddin was a Bengali; Ghulam Mohammad was a Punjabi. Nazimuddin was regarded as weak; therefore the Punjabis discounted him, while his Bengali confrères expected to mould him to their will. Ghulam Mohammad was known to be tough and unyielding; but he was a sick man (he had been about to depart as Ambassador to the United States where he hoped to recoup his health), and anyhow the office of Governor-General was surely now only ceremonial? In taking this decision, the Pakistan cabinet unwittingly terminated the parliamentary experiment in their country.

Nazimuddin's premiership lasted eighteen months. It represented a mathematical balance between East and West: three Bengalis and three Punjabis in the cabinet, and thirty-three Bengalis against twenty-seven

Punjabis, Pathans, and other Westerners, in the parliamentary party of
the League. The main activity during this time was a further attempt to
evolve a constitution; in December 1952, the Basic Principles Committee presented its report. Among its proposals was the recommendation that 'the head of the state, who should be a Muslim, should constitute a board of not more than five persons, well-versed in Islamic
laws, to advise the head of the state about the repugnancy of new laws
to the Quran and the sunna'. The religious climate was encouraging
to the bigots, and an agitation was fomented against the Ahmadiyya
community; generally regarded as an Islamic sect, though its relationship might not unfairly be compared to that of the Mormons with
Christianity. During 1953, an agitation built up, fostered by the orthodox Ahrar leaders, directed generally against the Ahmadis, and particularly against Sir Zafrulla Khan, an Ahmadi who was Pakistan's
exceedingly able Foreign Minister. The agitation was encouraged by the
chief minister of West Punjab, Mumtaz Daultana (whose cynical mani-
pulations had contributed to the breakdown of January 1949).
Eventually, agitation led to rioting and the collapse of law and order in
the city of Lahore and other towns. Daultana encouraged the administration and the police to mark time; thereby expecting to exert pressure
on Nazimuddin at Karachi. Nazimuddin was perplexed; piety struggled
with his sense of duty; he prevaricated, and did nothing. As Lahore
burned, the permanent official who was Defence Secretary, Major-
General Iskander Mirza, pressed the Governor-General to take action:
the army, he said, could restore order in Lahore within a few hours.
And so, martial law was promulgated; the army marched into Lahore
city, and reduced anarchy into order within thirty-six hours.

Ghulam Mohammad now decided to dismiss his Prime Minister.
Although Nazimuddin still commanded a majority in the Assembly,
his supporters acquiesced in the substitution of the almost unknown
Muhammad Ali (Bogra), a relatively young Bengali business man, who
was Pakistan's ambassador in the United States.

The Munir Report upon the Lahore riots closed with a veiled recommendation that Pakistan return to a form of Dyarchy, in which the
politicians would not be given responsibility for public order. 'If,' observed the judge, 'democracy means the subordination of law and order
to political ends—then Allah knoweth best, and we end the report.' The
régime of Muhammad Ali (Bogra) proved to be a kind of Dyarchy,
with the watchful Governor-General and his senior officials exerting
control on one hand; and the resentful politicians, especially the Bengali
group, pulling away in the other direction.

The constitutional debates were resumed in September 1953, and the Prime Minister proposed an ingenious formula to assuage the East-West conflict. In a Lower House of 300 members, East Bengal would receive a clear majority of 175; but in the Upper House of fifty, East Bengal would count only as one 'unit', along with the 'units' of Punjab, the North-West Frontier, Sind and Khairpur, Baluchistan, Bahawalpur and Karachi. Like all constitutional devices which try to conceal cleavages by cleverness, this failed to please anyone. Suddenly, the whole basis of Pakistan politics was blown away by the provincial election of March 1954 in East Bengal. The contest was between the official Muslim League, and a curious array of opposition groups, the 'United Front' stretching from extreme Right to extreme Left. In all, 309 seats were to be filled, of which seventy-two were reserved for caste Hindus, Untouchables, Buddhists, Christians, and women. A fantastic relic of the Muslim fear of Hindu dominance remained in the labelling of the thirty Hindu seats as 'General Constituencies', with the 228 Muslim seats grouped among the minorities! The result was a *débâcle* for the League. The former chief minister was overwhelmingly defeated by an eighteen-year-old student, and all the other ministers were unseated. Only ten Leaguers were returned, the other 300 members belonged to the Krishak Sramik (Workers and Peasants) Party led by the aged Fazl-ul Haq, and the Awami League of H. S. Suhrawardy, the last chief minister of undivided Bengal, whose following included Muslims, caste Hindus, and untouchables.

As a result of this *volte-face,* the Prime Minister could no longer claim to speak for Bengal; neither could the Muslim League claim to speak for the nation. In the Assembly, the Prime Minister attempted to prop up his authority by a deal with the politicians which would deprive the high-handed Ghulam Mohammad of power. First, PRODA was repealed; thereby, the politicians imagined they had disarmed the executive from coercing them. Then, the 1935 Act was amended to deprive the Governor-General of powers to dismiss a ministry which still enjoyed the Assembly's confidence. Secure, as he imagined, in this settlement, the Prime Minister left for the United States.

On October 24, 1954, Ghulam Mohammad announced that the constituent assembly was dissolved. The Viceroy had enjoyed the power to dissolve the legislature under Section 19 of the 1935 Act, but this section had been expressly deleted by an ordinance of the Governor-General of 1947. There followed a series of legal arguments, at the end of which the Governor-General secured the support he required from the Supreme Court (Mr. Justice Cornelius dissenting). Clearly, the nature of constitutional authority was becoming cloudy. The constituent assembly had exhausted whatever mandate it had originally received; the Muslim League had ceased to represent any kind of 'Freedom Movement'; and the politicians were, in the eyes of the ordinary public, representatives merely of their own, selfish interests.

In the beginning, Pakistan had survived, because among the leaders and the people there was a spirit of high dedication. The politicians led the way in a cynical scramble for personal gain; the officials, and the public followed. Probably the most demoralising factor was that of the refugees. Among the hordes of poor people fleeing for their lives, there were, inevitably, the cowards, the blackguards, the unscrupulous. As the refugees milled into squalid rest camps, and harassed officials attempted to allocate lands and houses to the throng, it was the unscrupulous who made the loudest clamour; who lobbied politicians, and who secured the largest share of the assets (often substantial) of the departed Hindu merchants and Sikh yeomen. Having made their haul, they used every device to retain their loot. Officials were offered bribes to provide legal titles, or to look the other way when the commissions of inquiry into evacuee property were investigating; politicians were bribed to promote protective legislation, and to exert influence. After the great wave of refugees, came a steady trickle of what might be described as 'professional' refugees—many from Hyderabad and Uttar Pradesh—not driven out by necessity, but deliberately making the move in a spirit of opportunism. Some found fortune in public office, others in business or land. The refugees spread a poison throughout the land. Within five years of partition, almost all the idealism had evaporated; replaced by an aggressive assertiveness, 'the world owes me a living', or a casuistical eye to the main chance.

The Governor-General gauged the temper of the country, and he approached the Commander-in-Chief, General Mohammad Ayub Khan, asking him to take over the government.[1] According to the General, he declined; and Ghulam Mohammad fell back on Muhammad Ali (Bogra). During his remaining months in office, Muhammad Ali was little more than the 'front man'. The three strong men in the Cabinet

[1] Ayub Khan was born in 1907, a Pathan of Peshawar District. He went to the Muslim University, Aligarh, and then to Sandhurst. Commissioned in 1928, he first served with the Royal Fusiliers, and then in the 14th Punjab Regiment, which he commanded during the Burma campaign. After the war he commanded a brigade on the North-West Frontier. His selection as Commander-in-Chief of the Pakistan Army followed the death in a plane accident of the designated C.-in-C. Ayub succeeded Sir Douglas Gracey in January 1951 as the first Pakistani C.-in-C. at the age of 44.

were none of them politicians. The Minister of the Interior was Major-General Iskander Mirza; the Minister of National Defence was General Ayub Khan, the Commander-in-Chief; and the Finance Minister was Chaudri Mohammad Ali, formerly Secretary-General, head of the civil service. A second constituent assembly was brought into being by indirect election. The provincial legislatures chose seventy-two candidates, while eight were filled from the principalities and tribal areas. East, and West each had forty seats. No single party commanded a majority in this new assembly, which convened on July 5, 1955 at Murree; the pine-scented hill station, within a few miles of the Kashmir Cease Fire line. The Muslim League was still the largest group, with thirty-five members (all but two from the West); followed by the United Front, led by Fazl-ul Haq, with sixteen, and Suhrawardy's Awami League with twelve. Suhrawardy was pledged to end the system of separate seats, and to base the franchise on joint constituencies for all communities. Because the caste Hindus supported this policy, others feared that this was a dark plot to re-establish Hindu supremacy, and Fazl-ul Haq joined with the Muslim League to continue the separate electorate system At their first meeting at Murree, the Muslim League Parliamentary Party elected their Leader: they ignored the Bengali, Muhammad Ali, and chose the former Finance Minister, Chaudri Mohammad Ali, who was a Punjabi. Bereft of party support, Muhammad Ali (Bogra) tendered his resignation. Ghulam Mohammad, ailing unto death, handed over the Governor-Generalship to Major-General Iskander Mirza in August. Mirza was a Pathan; he went from Sandhurst into the army, but most of his career had been set in the Indian Political Service on the North-West Frontier. Mirza had kept the peace among the unruly tribesmen by a *mélange* of inducement and coercion; he had applied this technique most successfully to Pakistan national politics. As Governor of East Bengal, he had restored order after the United Front had wrought chaos by their politicking after their 1954 triumph. Now, as Governor-General, it was not surprising that he chose as his first Prime Minister a fellow professional administrator, Chaudri Mohammad Ali. The Chaudri's premiership lasted only one year: but this short period included a considerable measure of achievement.[1] The new Prime Minister took

---

[1] The tenure of office of Prime Ministers was as follows: Liaqat Ali, August 1947—October 1951 (4¼ years); Nazimuddin, October 1951—April 1953 (1½ years); Muhammad Ali (Bogra), April 1953—August 1955 (2¼ years); Chaudri Mohammad Ali, August 1955—September 1956 (13 months); Suhrawardy, September 1956—October 1957 (13 months); I. I. Chundrigar, October-December 1957 (2 months); Firoz Khan Noon, December 1957—October 1958 (10 months).

over the four key portfolios (Defence, Foreign Affairs, Finance, Economic Affairs) himself. His ministers included Fazl-ul Haq, and other United Front men; Dr. Khan Sahib, the former Frontier Congress 'Red Shirt', and B. K. Dutta, former East Bengal Congress leader.

The first important measure was the Establishment of West Pakistan Act; passed in September, and largely a legacy from Ghulam Mohammad. The four provinces and ten small principalities of the West were now amalgamated into one 'unit'. Then, in February 1956, the constituent assembly passed into law the Constitution of the Islamic Republic of Pakistan.

The 1956 Constitution has now only an historical interest; but if only as a gesture to its prolonged gestation (eight-and-a-half years) it deserves a brief consideration. The Pakistan Constitution contained 234 Articles and six Schedules, compared to the 395 Articles and eight Schedules of the Indian Constitution (the longest in the world, to date). It began in the approved style, with a declaration of Human Rights, and Directive Principles of State Policy. These included the 'promotion of Muslim unity and international peace' and 'promotion of Islamic principles'; towards this end it was stated that 'steps shall be taken to enable the Muslims of Pakistan individually and collectively to order their lives in accordance with the Holy Quran and sunnat'. The Constitution itself did little to intensify the Islamic character of Pakistan. The President had to be a muslim; while Sections 197 and 198 instructed the President to set up an Islamic cultural institution and to appoint a Commission to make recommendations for bringing existing law into conformity with the injunctions of Islam. These provisions were never implemented.

The Constitution adopted the parliamentary system; defining parliament as the President, and the National Assembly, of one house of 300 members, half from each wing. Ten seats, in addition, were to be reserved for a period of ten years for women. The Constitution made no other decision on the vexed question of joint or separate electorates. The politicians supposed that, at last, the supremacy of Parliament had been established and the rôle of the Executive scrupulously defined. Article 37 read, 'The President shall act in accordance with the advice of the Cabinet...' What could be more explicit? Yet, within three months the new constitution had been suspended throughout East Pakistan, following yet another ministerial crisis at Dacca.

The eternal triangle of East-West-Centre was again causing tension. As chief minister of the newly amalgamated West Pakistan, Dr. Khan Sahib quickly assumed an independent rôle. The President and Prime

Minister had played the ancient political game of disarming a rebel by giving him office. Thereby, they also hoped to disarm the formidable Khan Abdul Ghafur Khan, Khan Sahib's brother and the lustiest champion of a separate Pathan state, Pakhtoonistan. However, the new premier promptly formed his own party, the Republicans, and attracted considerable support from the Muslim League. By August 1956, the League numbered only ten members in the central Assembly, while twenty-six took the Republican ticket. Chaudri Mohammad Ali was placed in a dilemma; should he accept the changed situation, and change horses also? President Mirza was plainly lending his influence to the new party. Instead, the Chaudri took what he called the 'agonising decision' to resign from office and from leadership of the League.

The President invited Mohammad Ali to reconstitute his administration, but he declined, and on September 12, 1956, Suhrawardy was sworn in as Prime Minister. His majority in the Assembly was composed of thirteen Awami League members, seven members from the minorities, and thirty Republicans. This unnatural alliance came about largely because of Suhrawardy's personal and political eminence: on a less heroic scale, this was a repetition of Churchill's emergence in 1940. The strangeness of the alliance was illustrated by its first important move: the introduction of a bill to establish an electoral system providing for separate seats in the West, and joint seats in the East. The Republicans had resolved to fight for separate electorates throughout Pakistan. But Dr. Khan Sahib was compelled to accept this hair-splitting formula, or face a show-down with the President, who favoured the joint scheme. The compromise formula was accepted by the Assembly, and subsequently (April 1957) an amendment was passed extending joint electorates to the Western wing.

The next crisis came in March 1957, when the West Pakistan Legislature plunged back into the 'one unit' controversy. Khan Sahib found his majority dissolving, and he was compelled to advise the President to suspend the Constitution in West Pakistan. President Mirza made a memorable broadcast in which he analysed the 'malaise' into which the country had declined, and went on 'I recommend to your consideration a careful study of the American system of administration, with necessary modifications to suit our own conditions'. This was, of course, a plea for a strong presidential executive. The President's views met an immediate rebuff from East Pakistan, where in April the legislature voted unanimously for full autonomy in all subjects except defence, foreign affairs, and currency. This was interpreted by some as an indication of Suhrawardy's loss of standing in his home province.

Meanwhile, there was the pending problem of creating a balance in West Pakistan. There, public opinion had never been tested by a general election, and the assembly members had been returned by a curious mixture of methods. Khan Sahib had failed to hold his party together, but now he sought to re-establish a majority by doing a deal with his opponents. Elements of the Awami League had defected to set up a National Awami Party, with which Abdul Ghafur Khan was associated. Khan Sahib bid for their support by offering to introduce legislation to dismantle the 'one unit' and recreate four provinces: this met Abdul Ghafur Khan's Pakhtoonistan demand. The President continued to support the Republicans; partly because he did not wish Suhrawardy to become too powerful. While the Prime Minister was en route from America (a dangerous moment for Bengali premiers!) the President reinstated the West Pakistan ministry, in the face of protests from the Governor of West Pakistan, Mr. Gurmani. Gurmani was thereupon dismissed, on the pretext that he had 'interfered in politics'. On his return, Suhrawardy took the offensive. He toured Punjab, denouncing the Republicans, and calling for the preservation of the 'one unit'; and he called upon the President to recall the National Assembly so that he might demand a motion of confidence. The Prime Minister calculated that he could pick up enough support to see him through from the Punjabis (the only Westerners broadly in favour of 'one unit') together with other dissidents and his own supporters.

At this point, it is not entirely clear whether Suhrawardy resigned, or was dismissed: at any rate, his request for a fortnight's grace in which to attempt to reconstitute his government was refused. The President now personally took on the task of forming a government. For his Prime Minister, he called upon an old-guard Muslim Leaguer, I. I. Chundrigar; who at least was outside the East-West imbroglio, being a Bombay man by origin. The new coalition was formed around the rump of the League, and the Republicans. Bitterness between old colleagues who have decisively fallen out is not easily healed. The Republicans suspected that the League intended to exploit its return to power to injure its supplanter. Suhrawardy made overtures to the Republicans: if they would not interfere with the joint electorates, he would support a Republican ministry, without requiring office. With this offer in their pockets, the Republicans withdrew support from Chundrigar. The President, inevitably, called on them to form another ministry: the sixth in six years.

The next Prime Minister, and the last, was Firoz Khan Noon. Noon came from a great Punjabi landlord family which virtually controlled the Shahpur District. He had served as High Commissioner for India in London, as wartime Defence Member of the Viceroy's Executive Council, Governor of East Bengal after partition, and chief minister of West Punjab: he was one of Pakistan's outstanding public servants. Surely, such a man would re-establish the now somewhat tarnished reputation of the premiership?

Unhappily, within the existing system, such a renascence was impossible. Power rested, formally, upon the support of a majority of the National Assembly, of which half was not even nominally responsible to an electorate. Power actually rested on the ability to manipulate the machinery of administration so as to gratify or terrify the legislators. Because almost all the West Pakistan members were great landlords, no land reform measure could even be planned: but this was respectable, above-board politics compared to most of the dealing. Was a political demonstration desirable in this district? Very well: the Deputy Commissioner, and the Superintendent of police must be informed that arrangements should be made for transport to bring in the rural crowds, cheer leaders must be instructed, the local gentry must be politely but firmly told to put in an appearance. Had a minor, but persistent opposition politician become an intolerable nuisance? Surely there had been a dispute over the family lands: could not that be revived? His younger brother was said to be a gay chap: what about sticking a charge of rape on him, to make the politician sweat? Did the Deputy Commissioner hesitate? Was the Superintendent squeamish, after all his years of handling doctored evidence? Let us try the effect of ordering him off to distant posts, where schools are non-existent, and malaria rampant. Let us see the effect of three such transfers within twelve months: the wife has gone home to her parents, the family is dispersed ... and promotion is clearly gone for ever ... better not to try to oppose the system. After all, everyone else co-operates with the politicians. What was it his old English chief had taught him about duty, responsibility and moral courage? Well, the old man had cleared off to England as soon as things became really tough, where nobody would try to stop *his* pension. Better to be accommodating. ...

This was the moral climate in which Firoz Khan Noon took office, and he operated within this miasma. Support was given to his Republican ministry by the Awami League, the Hindu Congress members, and other Bengalis: the price they required was a free hand in the East Bengal legislature. Elections were coming in February 1959, and it was believed that control of the legislature would supply the power to rig the elections. Noon bolstered his mainly Western Government by including regional bosses in his Cabinet; Rashid from the Frontier; even the unspeakable Ayub Khuhro from Sind.

The year began with violence; Dr. Khan Sahib, the former chief minister was assassinated. Violence flared up in Bengal, as the parties tried their strength. The opposition succeeded in having the Speaker of the legislature certified as insane; his place was taken by the Deputy Speaker, an opposition sympathiser. Incensed, government supporters arrived to get rid of the Deputy. The proceedings degenerated into a riot. Balks of wood were heaved around; one hit the Deputy Speaker, and he was killed. This took place in September 1958.

These disgraceful events in Dacca soon had repercussions in Karachi, and Noon's government began to totter. Instead of once again searching for a paper majority among the cardboard political leaders, the President took over power. On October 7, 1958, Iskander Mirza declared martial law, dismissed the central and provincial governments, abolished all political parties, abrogated the Constitution, and appointed General Ayub Khan as chief martial law administrator.

President Mirza might disassociate himself from the politicians, and avow that his only motive was to 'clear up the mess'. But to the martial law administrators, not only the politicians but also many officials were implicated in 'the mess'. Only one month later, Mirza was visited at night by a military deputation which forcefully requested him to leave the country. Somewhat reluctantly, the ex-President boarded a plane for England and exile. General Ayub took over the office of President. When he became martial law administrator, Ayub declared 'My authority is revolution; I have no sanction in law or constitution'. The genial, tweedy ex-Sandhurst general did not, of course, mean to imply that he was setting out on a Leninist or Mao-ist transformation; the political and social ethos of the new régime was more in tune with the heyday of Lord Curzon. Yet it was genuinely revolutionary in renouncing the dogma nurtured by generations of Westernised nationalist leaders that the inevitable goal of Asia was a parliamentary, party system; and in rejecting the belief that these institutions could be brought about by the efforts of learned legal draftsmen, spinning their clauses, articles, and schedules.

The first phase of military rule was devoted to 'cleaning up the mess'. Military men were given desks in most of the civil departments, and they proceeded very briskly to instruct the officials in their jobs. Results were astonishing: prices came down, scarce goods appeared on the market, arrears of income tax to the tune of £25,000,000 were hastily paid. Perhaps best of all, the misery of the Karachi refugees, who had endured a bestial existence for over a decade in gunny and kerosene-tin hovels, was terminated. A new town, Korangi, was swiftly erected on the edge of the desert; a drab, bleak place; but not entirely inconsistent with human dignity.

Attention was also paid to the promoters of the former régime. Some, like the former Defence Minister, Ayub Khuhro, could be prosecuted for abusing their office by blatant black-marketeering. Others could be accused of nothing more definite than going along with the system. Most of the leading politicians were given the alternative of signing an undertaking to retire completely from public life for five years, or face proceedings under a new version of PRODA, the Electoral Bodies (Disqualification) Order, EBDO. Most politicians deemed it prudent to sign and retire. H. S. Suhrawardy preferred to face definite charges: the vague attempts to prove that he was in league with Indian interests were not very convincing. Eventually, in February 1962, he was placed under arrest.

One cannot avoid a certain sympathy for men like Suhrawardy, Firoz Khan Noon, or even Iskander Mirza. They were undoubtedly patriots, who wished to see their country great. Under their direction, Pakistan did not succumb to anarchy, or Fascist or Communist dictatorship— like some Asian lands whose leaders are still venerated in undiscerning circles. Their crime was to find themselves within a vicious system, and to imagine that they could manipulate this system for the higher good. It was the old error of self-deception, of justifying the means by the ends. They were more unlucky than most political leaders in the speed with which nemesis caught up with them; that was all.

Having dealt with the politicians, Ayub turned to the senior civil servants, the lawyers, and the intellectuals. A high-level committee was set up to review the records of service of all senior civil servants. The upper ranks of the civil service emerged from the review relatively untouched, but 1,600 middle and lower grade civil servants were dismissed or compulsorily retired for misconduct or inefficiency. Of the judicial system which Pakistan had inherited from its British mentors, Ayub observed it was 'at once the most expensive and the most dilatory'. The President sensed that his most persistent critics were the lawyers, who could not reconcile themselves to the régime's extra-legal origins and attributes. His relations with the legal fraternity remained cool. The universities in Pakistan had fallen into a low state of morale and indiscipline: as an influential report observed: 'The politician has ... continually attempted to embroil the academic community in partisan politics. To achieve his purpose he has pitted student against student, student against teacher, and ... both against the lawful authority of the university.'[1] University staff were ordered to turn their attention to the welfare of their students, and students were ordered to stick to their studies.

Having thus given the quietus to the only active element in the nation, the Westernised urban middle class—officials, lawyers, and intellectuals —the President had placed himself in a dilemma. Who was to provide leadership for Pakistan? The army, for the present time; but there was no wish to perpetuate this situation. The army wanted to return to its professional duties. What did the nation need? It urgently needed economic development; for ten years, the standard of living in Pakistan had remained stationary, and agricultural production in particular had disappointed expectations. The nation required character building; the fostering of a spirit of leadership and enterprise, based upon service and sacrifice. Then who should speak for the nation? Ayub turned to the same class as had British officials in the nineteenth century, to the 'natural leaders of society': not the great landlords who had dominated West Pakistan politics, but the local squirearchy and yeomen farmers. The institutional means whereby this rural leadership was to be mobilised also resembled that of the British nineteenth-century precedent—local self-government in the 'Basic Democracies', brought into being on October 27, 1959.

Many observers underestimated the new scheme, just as they underestimated General (later Field Marshal) Ayub, with his apparently simple, bluff, soldierly demeanour. Basic Democracy, they derisively hinted, bore the same relation to Democracy as Basic English to English. Yet the new system introduced two principles which, if they were implemented, were fundamentally vital. The basis of the system was to be the Union Council, a local unit of approximately eight to ten thousand souls. By contrast the British scheme of rural self-government initiated in the 1880s had taken the administrative District as its principal unit, while the Indian community development schemes of the 1950s in practice did the same. Basic Democracy was also planned to overcome the 'Dyarchy' in local government in which centrally-directed departments controlled key functions, such as secondary education and medical services. Indian community development in the 1950s also had to shake

---

[1] *Report of the Commission on National Education, January—August*, 1959, Karachi 1960, p. 39. The Commission declare: 'Our fundamental need is for a revolution in attitudes through which the cynicism, lethargy, opportunism, suspicion, dishonesty and indifference that have characterised the outlook of so many of our people and officials in the past will give way to a spirit of initiative, personal integrity, pride in accomplishment, trust in one's fellow-men, and a private sense of public duty.'

free from departmentalism. The Pakistan scheme visualised Basic Democracy as the means of building *national* development from a *local* base; development was to be integrated and comprehensive.

The vital question was whether Ayub and his advisers recognised all the political implications of their proposal: the transformation of a centralised, autocratic system into a decentralised, popular system. The first pronouncements appeared to indicate that Basic Democracy was influenced profoundly by military thinking and the military outlook of the old British-Indian Army (which is analysed in greater detail in Ch. VII, pp. 151-7). A presidential train, the *Pak Jamhuriyat Special*, or 'Democracy Express' made a whistle-stop tour of the countryside, to enable Ayub to explain his scheme to the countryfolk. The peasants were gathered together, and the President sat down in their midst and very simply discussed what had gone wrong, and revealed his plan for a new deal. He explained 'it was his desire to see the country as organised as her army'.[1] The Pakistan Army was, in many ways, the most progressive force in the country; it would have no truck with religious obscurantism, and over the question of purdah, the commanders had made a point of encouraging their officers' wives to appear in public and to take part in social activities. But its philosophy had a certain simplicity which (quite attractively) appears old-fashioned. The country, above all, needed self-discipline and character building. The country needed leadership; of the kind which an officer owes to his men, exacting obedience, but in return always placing the welfare of the men above his own. The social and political order would reflect the pattern of the army. Officers (or leaders) were appointed partly because they had received superior education and training, partly because they showed qualities of leadership. Under them were the special class of warrant officers (see p. 156) whose influence among the men entitled them to consideration from their officers, but who would not expect to have any say in wider issues beyond their ken. And in the ranks were the simple peasant mass; solid, honest, industrious, deserving of upright leadership, but not really qualified to understand or take decisions on grave and complicated issues. This was a not unworthy vision of a society 'where none were for the Party and all were for the State', but it obscured certain inescapable facts. First, one could not expect the new Union Councils to function within a wider polity as a section or platoon functions within

---

[1] Quoted in *Middle East Journal*, Summer, 1961, 'Pakistan's Basic Democracy', by Khalid Bin Sayeed. Sayeed is also author of *Pakistan; the Formative Phase*, Karachi, 1960, which has been considerably drawn upon in preparing the present chapter.

an infantry battalion: the integration of stagnant rural communities into a developing economy is a complex socio-economic process. Second, the dichotomy between a politically active urban middle class, and a politically inert rural mass might be deplored: but it could not be changed, merely by stifling the urban middle class, and telling the peasants that they were now to have their turn. Pakistan had its middle class—paper-thin though it might be—and for half a century they had enjoyed political aspirations. The lawyers, doctors, professors—and even the civil servants and army officers—would not just passively accept the proposition that parliamentary government was not for them. Equally the peasants, and even the yeomen and squirearchy (conservative, like small landowners in every country) could not be expected within a brief period to become a dynamic, creative force. Somehow, Ayub and his government had to stimulate a progressive spirit in a country where economic life, religion, the social structure were all obstacles to change. How to channel existing political consciousness into a constructive rôle? How to avoid a return to the sterile East-West rivalry? How to enlist rural support for a dynamic programme of economic and social development? These were the almost impossible, and mutually-contradictory dilemmas which faced the President as he sought to formulate a new constitution.

First, he obtained a mandate for his own assumption of office. Between the end of December 1959 and mid-February 1960, the new Basic Democracies were elected. The number of seats to be filled was 40,000 in East Pakistan and 38,457 in the West, with 1,389 for the Karachi central area. Of the 80,000 new members, 18,000 were returned unopposed. For contested seats, the average vote was 73.3 per cent of the electorate in West Pakistan, and 65 per cent in East. An educational analysis of the new members showed that in West Pakistan almost 70 per cent were literate; and of the literates, about one in twelve was a matriculate, or had a higher qualification. In East Pakistan, all but 2 per cent were literate, and almost one in nine were matriculates, or above. In East Pakistan there had previously existed Union Boards, not dissimilar to the new Councils, and the largely middle-class members of the old Boards secured election to the new bodies. The Union Councils in West Pakistan tapped a largely new source of members, and these were mainly of the yeoman, retired army officer, or small hereditary landlord class.

The new 'Basic Democrats' (as the members are inelegantly termed) were promptly required to give a vote of confidence to the President: 95.6 per cent signified their support (there were no alternative candidates). After this indirect election, the President formally took an oath of office, and thereafter announced the composition of a constitutional commission, headed by Mr. Justice Mohammad Shahabuddin of the Supreme Court. The ten members, all civilians, were equally representative of each wing.

Different organisations throughout the country were invited to submit proposals; and, as might be expected, legal associations came out forcibly for a return to the parliamentary system. Chaudri Mohammad Ali was bold enough to criticise the basic democracies, and to demand a return to party politics. Political education could not advance under a dictatorial system, he said: 'The school in which this experience is gained is free elections, and the instrument for imparting this education is open public debate between political parties. Both the school and the instrument may not be perfect, indeed, far from it; but the modern world has not seen a better means of educating the people.'

The constitutional commission submitted draft proposals to the President midway through 1961. They attempted to find a *via media* between the former parliamentary set-up and the President's known preference for a strong executive. The President would select his own Cabinet, and govern independently of the legislature. But the legislature would have power to override the President by a two-thirds majority vote; and they would have control over the budget. Members would be directly elected, but an interim legislature would be chosen by vote of the Basic Democrats. Against the President's wish for a unitary government, the commission recommended a federal system, with two provincial legislatures.

The President was somewhat taken aback by these recommendations; he was really surprised that sensible men should want to go back to anything like the discredited party and parliamentary system. He declined to give any indication of his intentions until the actual appearance of the constitution.

The constitution which was promulgated by the President on March 1, 1962 made some concessions to the commission's views (notably, in accepting federalism) but its general tenor reflected Ayub's determination to create a strong, stable system of government. The President expounded the underlying philosophy of the new constitution in a long broadcast to the nation which included some trenchant comments in his usual forthright manner. 'People shall have the right to hire and fire their rulers. This is basic,' he declared. He went on:

We have adopted the Presidential system as it is simpler

to work, more akin to our genius and history, and less liable
to lead to instability—a luxury that a developing country like
ours cannot afford. The other alternative was the Parliamentary system. This we tried, and it failed. Not that there is
anything inherently wrong with it. The trouble is that we have
not attained several sophistications that are necessary for its
successful operation. . . . Above all, you need really [a] cool
and phlegmatic temperament, which only people living in
cold climates seem to have. Also it requires [a] long period
of probation. For instance, the British took six hundred years
of trial and tribulation to reach this stage. . . . So don't let us
kid ourselves and cling to clichés and assume that we are ready
to work such a refined system knowing the failure of earlier
attempts.

The most obvious feature of the new constitution is the concentration of
power in the hands of the President. It specifically lays down that 'all
executive authority of the Republic is vested in the office of the President'. He appoints the commanders of the armed forces, the Governors
of the provinces, the Ministers of the national government, and their
Parliamentary Secretaries; and he appoints the Chief Justice 'in his own
discretion'. The office of Prime Minister is non-existent. The President
can issue ordinances, valid as law for six months' duration; he may refuse
his assent to bills passed by the National Assembly; he may refer any
dispute between the Assembly and himself to a referendum of the
members of the Basic Democracies; and he may dissolve the Assembly
at any time. The President is elected by the Basic Democrats, and is
eligible for two five-year terms in office. A provision that a candidate
for President must not have held the office previously for eight years,
appears to afford Ayub some latitude in calculating the ten year rule. He
may choose to stay in office until 1972, or thereabouts, when he may
feel due for retirement.

The President can be impeached by the National Assembly, but a
vote of three-quarters of the total membership is required to make this
effective. An impeachment motion first requires the signatures of one-
third of the members; and in the event of the motion failing to obtain
the support of half the total membership, the original signatories will
forfeit their membership. When the floating loyalties of the members of
the former legislatures are called to mind, it can be seen that it will
require a desperate situation, and bold, iron-nerved members before
any attempt to remove the President is ever initiated.

The legislative will consist of a National Assembly and two provincial legislatures. Dacca will form a 'national capital area', and will be 'the principal seat of the central legislature'. The National Assembly will consist of one chamber, composed of the President, 150 members (drawn equally from both wings) and six special women representatives. Similarly, the provincial legislatures will comprise the Governor, 150 members, and five women representatives. The Basic Democracies again provide the electoral college. They will be grouped according to constituencies. Each constituency for the National Assembly will be composed of about 550 Basic Democrats. Ayub attaches great importance to this method of election, which he believes will make it more difficult to 'fix' the electorate, as each Basic Democrat member of the college will be 'a person of substance in his community'. It is provided that representation in the West Pakistan Assembly will be distributed as between the former Punjab province and Bahawalpur, 40 per cent, and Sind, Baluchistan, and the former North-West Frontier Province, 60 per cent. This will load the dice heavily against Punjab, which contains more than half of the population of the western wing: presumably this is to ensure that no single language group can dominate the provincial Assembly, as the Punjabis certainly did domineer over the former West Pakistan Assembly.

The field of legislation will be allocated to national and provincial lists. The legislatures will find difficulty in extending the range of their influence. The Ministers, who will be the agents of the President or Governor, will not be members of a legislature; although Parliamentary Secretaries will be appointed to provide a link between executive and legislative. The annual Budget will be laid before the National Assembly.

It will have no power over prevailing taxation and expenditure, but may give or withhold assent to demands for new grants. Political parties will not, initially, be permitted, but they may be revived in future, with the assent of the National Assembly, if they have 'respectable and healthy national programmes'.

What possibilities are there that the legislatures may be able to shrug off the straitjacket? The assemblies are permitted to choose their own Speakers, and the Speaker of the National Assembly will act for the President if he is abroad, or incapacitated (there is no Vice-President in Pakistan). Previous to the election of a President, the national and provincial assemblies, meeting jointly, will screen the aspirants and select three suitable candidates for office (the incumbent President, if eligible, can automatically qualify as a candidate). Perhaps these and other functions will help to give the legislative a worthier rôle in the nation.

The constitution provides for a Supreme Court, and High Courts for both wings, but the power of the judiciary is strictly defined. There will be no such nonsense as there was in 1954 of the judges presuming to interpret constitutional authority. Ayub has laid down that 'No Court shall be at liberty to refuse to enforce a law because it is of the opinion that the law is not in accordance with the principles of law-making. The relevant opinion for this purpose is the opinion of the law-makers and nobody else.'

The disputes which brought ruin to the former régime mainly revolved around three issues: the relationship between the executive and the legislative arms, the relationship between East and West Pakistan, and the rôle of Islam in the state. The first issue has been firmly decided: the executive is in full control. Regarding the other two major issues, the President has made considerable effort to meet grievances fairly. Urdu and Bengali continue to enjoy parity as the national languages. The creation of two capitals, Dacca, as the seat of the legislature, and Islamabad as the seat of the central government, also promotes parity. It is provided that the Supreme Court will hold sittings at Dacca and, eventually, at Islamabad also. The President has indicated (though it is not formally included in the constitution) that a convention will be established that the Speaker of the National Assembly, the second citizen in the republic, shall be chosen from the wing to which the President does not belong. It is provided in the constitution that Governors and provincial Ministers must be natives of the province they administer, so that East Bengal will be governed by Bengalis. This should quiet the murmurs that are heard today at the predominance of Punjabis and Pathans in the administration of the eastern wing.

The Islamic provisions in the 1962 constitution go somewhat further than those of 1956 to propitiate orthodox opinion. As before, the President must be a Muslim. The Preamble states that 'the Muslims of Pakistan should be enabled, individually and collectively, to order their lives in accordance with the teachings and requirements of Islam'. Or, as the President preferred to put it, 'whilst making material progress, we naturally wish to do so under the umbrella of Islamic spiritual and moral values'. This will be implemented by an Advisory Council of Islamic Ideology, to be appointed by the President from 'experts' and research scholars. In law-making, the President and the legislatures will seek the advice of this Council as to whether any proposal is repugnant to Islam.

There will also be an Islamic Research Institute, set up by the President, 'to undertake Islamic research and instruction in Islam to assist in the reconstruction of Muslim society on a truly Islamic basis'. All this may mean a great deal—or nothing.

The 1962 constitution perpetuates the paradox that has prevailed since 1958. It establishes a framework out of which the people of Pakistan can, if they have the will, create a modern and not illiberal polity. It can also provide a legal cloak for the continuation of military dictatorship and bureaucracy. Few will doubt the sincerity of the President in concluding his explanation of the new constitution with the wish that it will promote 'a sound, vigorous, progressive and powerful state'. When Field Marshal Ayub Khan first assumed power he promised that 'Our ultimate aim is to restore democracy'. How can the present system, an enlightened despotism, gradually become more democratic? The Field Marshal asserts that the *clou* is to be found in the Basic Democracies. It remains to be shown, first whether his faith will be translated into endowing these bodies with genuine, independent powers; and second, whether the Basic Democracies will prove themselves 'sound, vigorous and progressive' in the discharge of their responsibilities.

The first elections for a National Assembly underlined the difficulty of finding any alternative to the old, supposedly discredited politicians of the lawyer, landlord class. The Basic Democrats proceeded to return many of the old guard leaders, including the former Speaker of the first constituent assembly, Maulvi Tamizuddin Khan, who became Speaker of the new Assembly, and Muhammad Ali (Bogra) who was appointed Foreign Minister. By contrast, in the elections to the provincial assemblies many of the old politicians suffered defeat; with the result that there was great difficulty in providing parliamentarians competent to take charge of the assemblies' affairs.

Soon after the National Assembly was inaugurated on June 8, 1962, a cleavage appeared between the government and the politicians. Sixty Bengali members of the National Assembly presented a series of demands for the restoration of political rights; this was followed by a joint statement from nine senior Bengali political leaders, calling for an entirely new constitution on parliamentary, federal lines.

Behind the parliament men, the Islamic zealots, and the forces of law and order stand the mute peasant masses. They are loyal to President Ayub: but how can their dumb, passive loyalty be made dynamic? All the obstacles to Pakistan's evolution into a democracy remain in the way.

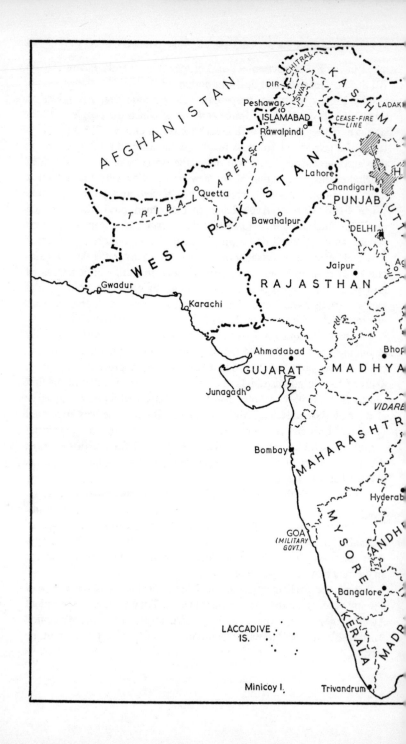

INDIA AND PAKISTAN
POLITICAL DIVISIONS 1962

Miles

0   100   200   300   400   500

Protected State   Union Territories

H.P. Himachal Pradesh   M. Manipur   T. Tripura

C H I N A

NEPAL

SIKKIM

N.E. FRONTIER AGENCY

BHUTAN

NAGA HILLS

Lucknow

RADESH

A S S A M

Patna

Shillong

BIHAR

EAST PAKISTAN

DACCA

WEST BENGAL

Calcutta

Chittagong

B U R M A

ORISSA

Bhubaneswar

RADESH

Madras

ANDAMAN IS.

NICOBAR IS.

V

THE PARTIES: ORGANISATION AND POLICIES

A DESCRIPTION of party politics in India and Pakistan must necessarily be somewhat speculative. At the time of writing (Spring 1962) there are no recognised parties in Pakistan, and it is doubtful whether the pattern which evolved between 1947-58 will recur again; while in India the accepted system is under attack and will almost certainly be modified. Moreover, though it is possible to produce a satisfactory analysis of party, in terms of leadership, personalities, and organisational structure, it is much less simple to analyse the ideological content of the various policies. Some parties have a clear enough 'brand image'; but one discovers on closer examination that the image exists in the eye of the beholder rather than in party manifestoes. We can trace easily enough the gradual erosion of the 'Freedom Movement', the growth of splinter parties, and the emergence within the main parties of divisions between the 'ins' and the 'outs', i.e. between the ministerial group and the party organisation: but we cannot state with much confidence what are the fundamental differences in ideas which separate parties and groups. As the Socialist leader Asok Mehta observes: 'It is a common characteristic of the new states that [their] political parties, by and large, share common objectives.'[1] These objectives include opposition to continuing colonial rule, an urgent sense of the need to raise living standards by modernising the economy, an acceptance (which may be only theoretical)

---

[1] Mehta tells how he commented to a New York group of diplomats, 'It seems in Ceylon everyone is a Socialist except Sir John Kotelawala' (one-time Right-wing Prime Minister), to which the Ceylonese Ambassador replied, 'Now he too claims to be a Socialist'. To Edward VII, as Prince of Wales, is attributed the saying 'We are all Socialists now'. In Victorian England this was merely a flourish; but in southern Asia today it is almost literally true.

of the need for national planning and a measure of national economic development for power, industry, irrigation, etc.; and, in most cases, the desirability of finding a foreign policy which emphasises the sovereignty of the new country. These, at any rate, are the common objectives of the small minority of the politically sophisticated. For the mass, politics may be simply equated again with 'the revolution of rising expectations'; they intend to gain for themselves, as individuals or social groups, a larger share of the national and international cake (not, by any means, a political objective confined to the masses of south Asia).

Before trying to analyse the growth of party, let us briefly subsume a climatic chart of political states of mind. Before independence, the population could be broadly divided into three categories; the loyalists, the moderate reformers, and the extremists, 'physical force' men—sometimes revolutionaries. By far the greatest part of the population belonged, either actively or passively, to the first category. They were carrying on the political tradition of centuries; ordinary men did not make governments; the most they could hope to do was to propitiate, and possibly manipulate the existing system. The active loyalists included the orthodox and conservative (who relied upon British rule to preserve existing social, religious, and economic interests), as well as some modernist, politically conscious elements who feared the effect of change of government upon themselves (such as the Eurasians, Dr. Ambedkar's untouchables, the tribal peoples' leaders, and even some Right-wing Muslims). The mute mass of the population exhibited what Gandhi called a 'pathetic contentment' in their lot. Congress politicians dismissed the loyalists as stooges of the British, sneeringly calling them *Han-Ji* or *Jo-Hukm* ('Yes Sir,' 'Whatever is your order [I obey]'). But they were by no means stooges; they merely accepted the same approach to authority as their fathers and grandfathers. It was Gandhi's achievement to persuade some of these ordinary folk to shake off this acquiescence, at any rate during the period of the satyagraha campaigns: but the proportion was never as high as Congress liked to proclaim.

When the Congress inherited the Government of India from the British they automatically inherited a major share of this automatic loyalty. The dispossessed, whether of the privileged, or the minorities, did not subscribe to Congress Raj; and neither did the Hindu bigots; but the mute masses of the countryside became the sold basis of Congress electoral support. In Pakistan, the Muslim masses gave their loyalty to Jinnah as the champion of their religion; they did not transfer this loyalty to the Muslim League. Only after the army dismissed the politicians did the ordinary Pakistan peasant discern a recognisable symbol of authority to which he could give his loyalty.

The moderate reformers provided the main element in both Congress and the League. They demanded independence, not because they wished to transform the whole ethos of national life, but because they wished to remove the government of their country from the grasp of middle-class Scots, Englishmen, and Ulstermen, and take it into the hands of middle-class Hindus and Muslims: their own hands. (Of course there were and are noble ideals in Indian politics; but in terms of power, this was what the struggle was all about). When put to the test in 1947, rather than face a fight, the Congress leaders accepted terms which had been theirs to take all along: terms laid down by the British Government, and by the Muslim League. For, although the leaders of the League were moderate, accommodating men, they had unleashed the forces of Islamic fanaticism, and against the cry of 'Islam in Danger' they could not hold their followers back.

The physical force or revolutionary element has always been small, numerically, but has often forced the pace for politicians in general. From the time of Tilak and the Bengal terrorists, Congress has been drawn into violence. Nehru (who has in his time assumed almost every colour in the Indian political spectrum) once wrote to Gandhi: 'For myself, I delight in warfare.' The attempt of Subhas Chandra Bose in the 1930s to launch Congress on the road to revolution was circumvented by Gandhi and the followers of non-violence; but in August 1942, the men of violence prevailed. The Socialist group, led by Jayaprakash Narayan, waged what an official report described as 'an underground revolutionary movement, with all the trappings of terrorism'. After independence, the Communist Party adopted a programme of guerrilla warfare in imitation of Mao Tse-tung's People's War. Only when this collapsed, did the Party switch to 'constitutional Communism'. Similarly, the Hindu bigots, the R.S.S.S. made a cult of violence, but after Gandhi's murder they were effectively suppressed, and compelled to act carefully in the following years. In the 1960s it seems probable that the Hindu bigots will again turn to violence and mob hysteria, to gain the power which they cannot win by appeals to faith and reason.

Similarly, in Pakistan, the Islamic fanatics and reactionaries exploited mob violence; and, paradoxically, it was the ability of the army to guarantee peace and order which reconciled the country to a period of military rule.

One political factor has been omitted from this triple political classification: that of Gandhi, and his heirs. Gandhi was a religious leader, but not a religious bigot; he was a revolutionary, but not in any Marxist or Nihilist sense.[1] Western revolutionaries to whom he shows some affinity are Thoreau, William Morris, Tolstoy, and Kropotkin. Almost every corner of modern Indian political, cultural and spiritual life bears the mark of Gandhi; yet how far has Gandhian precept been abandoned by being elevated into a higher ethic, an ideal which no-one applies in practice? This is the verdict of one of India's most acute political analysts, Frank Moraes; the 'new class', the Establishment of today, he says, 'has turned its back on most of Gandhi's cherished ideals'. 'Posterity will probably rate Gandhi as one of history's magnificent failures' he decides.[2] The political ideas and techniques of Gandhi are perhaps the most original and protean since Lenin; are we to say of him—and of his spiritual successor, Jayaprakash (who has emerged as the one Indian political leader today possessed of bold and basic political concepts)—that this is 'the voice of one crying in the wilderness'? Have fundamental ideas no place in independent India? Is politics just machine politics and a scramble for shares of the cake? And are the alternatives only Communism or the rule of the satraps, as in Pakistan today? This is the vital question: to which this chapter can provide only a tentative answer.

We have seen that in its claim to represent the 'Freedom Movement' the Congress professed to be greater than any party: and because after independence the Congress was the Government—still managing to hold most of the Right- and Left-wings within its fold—the claim was widely accepted. As the party of freedom, Congress continued for many years to spend much time in fighting the battles of yesterday. The leaders of the 1930s continued to dominate the stage, right through the 1950s. No politician stood any chance of recognition unless he was a 'jail graduate'; which meant an active worker during the civil disobedience campaigns against the British. Because they had led the struggle, these old Congressmen believed that they were now entitled to the fruits of office. Gone were the days of handloom weaving and third-class travel and other Gandhian simplicities. The old Congress-men moved into the palaces of the former British Governors, and took over the cavalcade of mounted

---

[1] Gandhi has worried and annoyed orthodox Marxists. The Programme of the Communist International, promulgated in 1928, had this to say: 'Tendencies like Gandhism in India, thoroughly imbued with religious conceptions, idealise the most backward and economically most reactionary forms of social life . . . preach passivity and repudiate the class struggle, and . . . become transformed into an openly reactionary force. Gandhism is more and more becoming an ideology directed against mass revolution. It must be strongly combated . . .'

[2] Frank Moraes, *India Today*, New York, 1960, pp. 89-92.

escorts and A.D.Cs and gold and scarlet peons. The rise of this Congress Establishment soon alienated the ordinary people. Yet they made an exception for one man, Nehru: Panditji could do no wrong, he could move in magnificence or lowliness, as he wished. For he is Panditji: their prince, priest, father, brother. As the years passed, Congress increasingly sheltered behind the popular image of Nehru.

To a corresponding degree, Congress national policy is the policy of Nehru. More than anything, it resembles Fabian Socialism; and its latter-day prophets are Harold Laski and Kingsley Martin. At the 1955 annual session, Congress adopted the 'socialistic pattern of society' as its programme. Although not a party document, the *Second Five Year Plan* offers as clear a definition as any of accepted doctrine; and a few key passages from Chapter II, headed 'The Socialist Pattern of Society', will illustrate its philosophy.

> A rising standard of life, or material welfare as it is sometimes called, is of course not an end in itself. Essentially it is a means to a better intellectual and cultural life. . . . The task before an underdeveloped country is not merely to get better results within the existing framework of economic and social institutions but to mould and refashion these so that they contribute effectively to the realisation of wider and deeper social values.
>
> These values or basic objectives have been recently summed up in the phrase 'socialist pattern of society'. Essentially, this means that the basic criterion for determining the lines of advance must not be private profit but social gain. . . . The benefits of economic development must accrue more and more to the relatively less privileged classes of society. . . . For creating the appropriate conditions, the State has to take on heavy responsibilities as the principal agency speaking for and acting on behalf of the community as a whole. The public sector [of industry] has to expand rapidly . . . it has to play the dominant rôle in shaping the entire pattern of investments in the economy, whether it makes the investments directly or whether these are made by the private sector.
>
> The use of modern technology requires large scale production and a unified control and allocation of resources in certain major lines of activity. The socialist pattern of society is not to be regarded as some fixed or rigid pattern. It is not rooted in any doctrine or dogma.

The whole of this statement is directly opposed to almost everything that Gandhi stood for; it also treads heavily upon the interests of big industrialists and entrepreneurs who have formed the most substantial contributors to party funds (the subscription of ordinary members is four annas, or 3d.). Free enterprise certainly has a sizeable part to play in present economic expansion, but (as the *Plan* emphasises above) only under rigid government control. Because of the regulations which circumscribe any transaction involving foreign exchange, import of plant, or even heavy use of national resources (such as a substantial demand upon power or transport), the Congress régime has been nicknamed 'Permit Raj'.

It is doubtful whether, except under Nehru's lead, Congress would have accepted so completely the necessity for overall national planning, development through public corporations, and continuous and minute regulation of economic life for over fifteen years. It is also very doubtful whether (without Nehru) Congress would have accepted the very full part India has assumed in international affairs, supplying observers, technical and administrative personnel, and large bodies of troops for U.N. operations, from Korea to the Congo.

During the whole period since independence, small shifts in the Congress position at the national political level have occurred. After 1951, there was a perceptible shift to the Left; about 1960 there was a moderate swing to the Right. These variations have come about partly in accordance with feeling in the party, and partly in response to the mood of the nation. They have been influenced hardly at all by pressures from rival parties.

The forum in which major decisions of policy are usually enunciated is the annual session of Congress, held each year at a different local centre. These sessions are much more like American conventions than any institution in British politics; the nearest equivalent is provided by the Labour Party's annual conference. The setting is that of a grand *tamasha* or circus, in which the leadership renews its ties of brotherhood with the rank and file. This is not the remote, seignorial visitation of a British party leader, but an apostolic communion with the discipleship, curiously combined with fraternal glad-handing, American style. Policy, as such, is decided in the back rooms. The All-India Congress Committee is supposed to be the policy-making body, but with a present membership of 500 it is far too unwieldy. A small minority, the Working Committee, the 'high Command' make all the important decisions.

The office of President of the Congress, wrested by Nehru from

Tandon in 1951, was held by him until 1954, when he handed over to his own nominee, U. N. Dhebar; a man held in respect by the party, but not a dominant leader. Nehru's daughter, Mrs. Indira Gandhi, stepped into the presidency in 1959, but she held office only one year, being succeeded by Sanjiva Reddy, the party boss of Andhra. These later changes have seen the prestige and influence of the party president steadily devalued. Another situation in which formal office has declined in importance is revealed within the Congress Parliamentary Party, the association of party representatives in the central legislature. The Prime Minister's title to the post of Leader has been automatic, but the Deputy Leadership has been valued as a symbolic indication of who is considered the heir apparent to the premiership. Maulana Abu Kalam Azad was Deputy Leader of the Parliamentary Party, followed by Pandit Pant, the Home Minister. Both were venerable figures within the party, and by right of seniority and standing might have had a good title to succeed Nehru. After Pant's death in 1961, two politicians competed for the post. Morarji Desai, the austere Finance Minister, often predicted as Nehru's successor, was the choice of the Right-wing. Jagjivan Ram, Minister for Railways, a Harijan, was sponsored by those who wanted to keep Desai out: he was selected mainly because he was considered harmless. The prospect of a contest induced both factions to appeal to Nehru to make the decision himself. The Prime Minister first made it clear that the Deputy Leader enjoyed no automatic right to the succession, and then resolved the contest by appointing two Deputy Leaders—one for each House of Parliament. This Delphic solution had the effect of draining this important party post of all significance, and also deprived Morarji Desai of any prior claim to the succession. Nehru has succeeded in papering over yet another cleft within the party by the exercise of his personality. Yet because high office in the party is only significant in relation to Nehru; because offices and institutions have not been built up to be important in themselves, the higher direction of Congress lacks viability. The annual session before the third general election, held at Patna in January 1962, found the party divided by faction, and confused as to long-term objectives. The Patna Congress demonstrated again the hold of Panditji over the affections of the rank and file. It also brought into the open the discord within the upper levels of the party, and its dependence upon the prospect of office, or other patronage, to hold together the middle-ranks of the membership. The most serious recent attempt to create a dynamism within the party, outside the orbit of Nehru's personality, and outside of machine politics, was the formation of the 'Ginger Group', 1957-8. This group tried to promote a more constructive programme on modernist-socialist lines. Even this effort drew reflected light from Nehru: Mrs. Indira Gandhi was a leading member. However, it is difficult to see any tangible results from the Ginger Group's activities. The only other notable development, in Congress ruling circles, is the emergence of 'the managers'. In place of the old-style 'Freedom Fighters', the modern Ministers have little popular appeal, but direct their departments efficiently and progressively; they are the 'Butskells' (or possibly the Dean Rusks) of the Congress Government. Lal Bahadur Shastri, Minister for Commerce, S. K. Dey, Minister for Community Development, and Humayun Kabir, Minister of State for Education are typical enlightened 'managers'. It is a reflection of Nehru's colossal stature that this 'management' is the only type of leadership to evolve.

However, those (among whom the present writer is possibly one) who are ready to equate the Congress with Nehru must remember that Congress still possesses an asset unique in India (and Asia)—a comprehensive party organisation covering every district in the country. First there is the Pradesh organisation: India is divided into twenty-six Pradesh. These are subdivided into District Committees, and Mandal (or Tehsil) Committees. Throughout all the former British provinces, this organisation is in working order, with paid officials and organisers in all the higher echelons. This organisation can 'deliver' the vote for Congress: and so long as the political scene is speckled with multiple parties, and so long as only about half the voters can be expected to enter the polling booths, if Congress can muster some 20 per cent of the electorate on polling day, it need fear no loss of control.

The very ability of the Pradesh Congress Committees to 'deliver' the vote is, however, a cause of division. The party organisers feel that they are the source of power, and that the Chief Minister and the State government are merely the façade. Recent political history has witnessed a tussle between the Ministerial group and the Pradesh Congress Committee in almost every State. In some instances, the conflict is also between the Old Guard, the Ministers, and the New Men, who have reached the higher levels of politics only recently, after working their way up the Pradesh organisation. Usually the two groups maintain an uneasy equilibrium, but from time to time there is a head-on collision: both sides attempt to win over supporters, and there is a danger of a collapse of Congress power. The first serious breaches were in the south, in Hyderabad and Mysore. The Hyderabad situation was restored to a semblance of concord by the personal intervention of the Prime Minister, but other splits have defied even his hypnotic powers of persuasion.

Uttar Pradesh, the supreme Congress stronghold, saw the vendetta fought out until the Chief Minister, Sampurnanand, was compelled to go; his duel with C. P. Gupta was partly on Ministry-Party lines of division, but was also a test between orthodoxy and modernism.

This situation favours the rise of the political chief who is also an organisation man. Bijoyanand Patnaik, Chief Minister of Orissa is the model of this new brand of politician. Patnaik first attracted fame when, as a pilot of Indian Airlines, he made a daring rescue of Sukarno in Indonesia. His first encounter with Nehru was a similar feat of *panache* (a breathtaking drive and flight to enable the Prime Minister to keep an important appointment). Subsequently, he went into pioneer branches of business, and made, and lost, and made again fortunes. He became Chairman of the Orissa Congress Committee at a time when its prestige had sunk to an all-Indian low. He severed the coalition, which the Congress had been forced to conclude with the Right-wing Ganatantra Parishad, and in consequence let his party in for a mid-term election: an election which all the political commentators predicted the Congress would certainly lose. Instead, they recaptured absolute control over the State legislature. Taking over the premiership at forty-five, Patnaik instituted a vigorous administrative programme. He displays the touch of a Kennedy, rather than of a Nehru: the comparison may, after a few years, prove not inappropriate.

A continuous fifteen years of almost unchallenged authority have made the Congress fat, complacent, and indecently preoccupied with getting and keeping power. But they have not disclosed any fundamental vulnerability within its ranks. The rival 'Freedom Movement', the Muslim League, revealed its fatal vulnerability within five years of its initial entry into office.

Before 1937, the League was mainly a coterie of landlords and retired senior officials. The disastrous consequences of the 1937 provincial elections to the League led to Jinnah undertaking the complete transformation of the party into a mass organisation. The annual subscription was reduced to two annas, and hundreds of thousands of new members were enrolled from among the Muslim peasantry. Provincial, District, and local committees were created (the latter known as 'Primary Muslim Leagues') to such an effect that in the 1945-6 elections the League captured the great majority of Muslim seats. This transformation of the League into a popular political force did not affect its central direction which, even more than in the Congress, was a dictatorship. The supreme political decisions of the Congress upon partition and independence were taken by three persons—Gandhi, Nehru, and Sardar Patel. There is no evidence that Jinnah deferred to anyone in making his decisions. There is clear evidence that any lieutenant who presumed to challenge his commands was jettisoned. Firoz Khan Noon, despite the considerable sacrifices he had made for the cause, was discarded by Jinnah (and received no appointment in Pakistan while Jinnah lived) because he questioned one of the Quaid-i-Azam's commands.

The All-India Muslim League held its last meeting in December 1947, when it was replaced by the Pakistan Muslim League. A party constitution was drafted which (like other Pakistan constitutions) was never fully applied in practice. Jinnah continued as the unquestioned President of the League. There was a Council, as the policy-making body, with provincial, district, and city Leagues as the national organisation.

This organisational structure was never kept in running order because the mandate of the people (which dominated the Congress-League tug of war, 1945-7) was not invoked. As the constitutional debate settled down into timelessness, so the prospect of an appeal to the electorate faded from political calculations. The uneasy triangle of power which subsisted between the Governor-General, the central legislature, and the provincial Assemblies depended on the successful manipulation of a few dozen professional politicians. In this situation, the League reverted to its earlier character as a coterie of landlords and lawyers, in conjunction with the senior officials.

The Presidency of the League, after the death of Jinnah, passed to Chaudri Khaliquzzaman, a politician from the United Provinces. He was no longer an active participant in the power struggle, being interested mainly in pan-Islamic movements. As Prime Minister, Nazimuddin also became President. When he was dismissed he clung to the party leadership for a while. Thereafter, the presidency became associated with the premiership, but Chaudri Mohammad Ali was uneasy about this identification. One of the elements in his rise to power was the transfer of Muslim League support from Muhammad Ali (Bogra) to himself, while the former was still Prime Minister. But the Chaudri was careful not to allow his administration to be identified with the party. In January 1956, Mohammad Ali moved the nomination of Sardar Abdur Rab Nishtar as President, and the constitution of the League was altered so as to separate the party leadership from the government of the country.

The League provided the cloak under which provincial elections in West Pakistan were sorted and settled by the landlord politicians. The tenants of the semi-feudal landlords, and the tribal followers of the

Frontier chiefs were compelled to follow their masters' bidding. Punjab and the North-West Frontier Province held elections in 1951, and Sind followed in 1953. Ayub Khuhro fought the Sind election with a party of his own making; but he took office as Chief Minister of a League provincial ministry. But, as we have seen, this 'boss politics', crudely stamped with the League brand, failed to maintain a hold in East Bengal. There, a motley assortment of candidates, with no semblance of party organisation sufficed to put the League to rout. The following year, largely over the 'one unit' issue in West Pakistan, the League blocs in the central and provincial legislatures suddenly dissolved, and a majority defected to the new Republican Party.

After 1956, the Muslim League was little more than a corpse. A League Prime Minister was propped precariously in office for two months in 1957: he departed as ignominiously as he had arrived. The League was dead: and few lingered to mourn its passing.

If the fate of the 'Freedom Movement' presents such a striking contrast in Pakistan and India, the rôle of Communism has been equally dissimilar. In Pakistan, Communism has remained a cult of a few intellectuals; in India, it has become the major challenge to the established government. During its early days, the Communist Party was a slender, scattered circle of intellectuals, drawing its nourishment from abroad, and without 'grass roots'. M. N. Roy, its leader, was an *émigré*, and almost all its directives came from the International, or from the British Communist Party. About 1936, a number of Communist intellectuals infiltrated the Congress, and attempted to influence it toward the Popular Front line. Nehru's private secretary at this period was a Communist, Nawabzada Mahmud-u-Zafar, and Nehru himself favoured a Popular Front. During the first years of the war, the Communists were in the forefront of militant activity against the Government; like all other Communist parties, they executed a rapid *volte-face* after the German invasion of the Soviet Union, and the Communist members of the All-India Congress Committee vehemently opposed the Quit India resolution in 1942. While the Congress leaders languished in confinement, the Communist Party enjoyed official toleration, and its membership increased from 5,000 in 1942 to 53,000 in 1945.

Communist leaders included quite a number of Muslims, some of aristocratic lineage, like the Nawabzada, and Mian Iftikharuddin. Others in the front rank were Dr. Z. A. Ahmed, and Sujjad Zaheer (both members of the A.I.C.C.). The Communist Party supported the Pakistan demand, from 1944 onward. However, it was not able to establish any solid Muslim proletarian backing, except in isolated areas of Bengal. Consequently, when Pakistan came into being, Communism played only a minor part in politics. Iftikharuddin became the Minister for Refugees in the West Pakistan Government: he called for revolutionary land reforms, and was compelled to resign by the dominant landlord interest (he was, himself, a wealthy but exceptional landlord). Subsequently he owned and ran the *Pakistan Times* newspaper, and founded a Left-wing party, Azad Pakistan. Sujjad Zaheer became Secretary of the Communist Party of Pakistan; on allegation of implication in the Rawalpindi Conspiracy he was arrested; Iftikharuddin secured his release on bail, and he disappeared to India. In East Bengal, Communism was mainly promoted by 'front' organisations, notably the Ganatantra Dal ('Democratic Party') founded in 1952. It was strongly neutralist and violently anti-Western, also stressing the evils of communalism. The Ganatantra Dal had an agreement to work in unison with Azad Pakistan in the western wing. The Communist Party was banned throughout Pakistan in 1954, at the time that an agreement was signed with the United States for military and technical assistance. There is little reason to suppose that, under the military government, Communist influence survives, except in attenuated form.

By contrast, in India the C.P.I., despite (in its own words) 'sharp twists and turns' of policy, with subsequent repercussions upon the Party's growth and popularity, has built itself up into the second largest party in Parliament and the only serious rival to Congress. This march forward has been punctuated by the familiar purges and self-criticism. An extraordinary dialectical debate has been pursued in the high counsels of the Party, which no sooner crystallizes over one major issue than it breaks out again over another.

The first post-independence phase was the period of extreme militancy, a would-be 'People's War'. Arson and sabotage were everywhere directed against landlords and other 'feudalists', while in Telingana the campaigns assumed the proportions of a minor rebellion. This phase came to an abrupt end; partly under pressure of tough internal security measures, and partly because of changes in the Party line as dictated from Moscow. A. K. Ghosh was appointed General Secretary of the Party in 1951 as the exponent of 'Constitutionalism'. The All-India Conference, held in October 1951, resolved to commit all the Party's resources to fighting the impending general election. The results were gratifying, particularly in Andhra, where forty-eight seats out of a total of 140 were taken by the Communists. The explanation of this success lies partly in the caste structure of the region[1] but it was also assisted

[1] See Chapter VI below, pp. 145-8

by careful organisation. As we have seen, Congress took great pains to ensure that mid-term elections, in 1955, told another story. The Communist vote was actually increased: but Congress did even better, and the number of Communist seats in the new legislature of 196 was only fifteen. This *débâcle* led to furious recrimination at the subsequent Communist meeting at Palghat, in April 1956. The Report submitted to the conference dwelt on the immensity of the struggle ahead: 'Advance will have to be made against resistance through the overcoming of big obstacles.' This admission led to the Party 'fully supporting all the progressive policies and measures of the Government', and also 'a correct attitude towards the political parties': that is, a democratic front with other Leftist parties as well as 'appealing to the Congress and its masses to hold hands with us'. This resolved (temporarily, at any rate) a long internal dispute as to whether Congress and the 'national bourgeoisie' should be regarded as enemies or allies. This policy of accommodating political rivals was adopted in part because of the complete change of attitude by the Soviet Union. During the early years after independence, Communist propaganda abused Gandhi as a traitor and called Nehru a 'running dog' of Imperialism. But the view of India as a semi-colonial régime was to be reversed (about 1954). Nehru was adulated as the architect of peace, and the visit of Bulganin and Kruschev to India in February 1956 set the seal on the new Soviet policy: and underpinnned the Palghat policy of co-operation. The success of the Communists in capturing the government of Kerala seemed to offer clear evidence of the success of the 'correct' policy. Next year, in 1958, at the Amritsar conference, A. K. Ghosh led the Party in adopting a specific commitment to parliamentary democracy and to achieving power within its framework.

The Communist honeymoon with democracy was shortlived. The following year (1959) the Communist Kerala Government was superseded, and the border dispute between India and China came to a head, inflicting odium upon the Indian Communists. Party difficulties were increased by the twenty-second congress of the Soviet Communist Party in Moscow, and the growth of a split between Kruschev and Mao Tsetung over the rôle of Stalin in international Communism. During 1961, these questions produced a division in the C.P.I. One group, which accepted the Moscow ideological line (also coinciding with those who advocated co-operation with Congress) joined in condemning Chinese aggression on the Indian border. The other group, which had leaned away from Moscow (and away from 'bourgeois' co-operation) and towards Peking, attempted to ameliorate the Indo-Chinese dispute.

A. K. Ghosh inclined towards the first, or so-called 'national' group. In November 1961 he issued a statement strongly criticising Chinese actions. 'Such actions,' he said, 'cannot but heighten tension, create deep resentment among the Indian people and further embitter the relations between the two countries.' He demanded that China 'must immediately put an end to such actions'.

The qualities that go to make up a leader in most of the parties in India and Pakistan are comparable to those required by different types of politicians in the West: the spell-binder, the parliamentary debater, the vote-gatherer are three important types. But in the C.P.I. leadership is associated with qualities of a different order. Discipline, indifference to personal and social relationships, intellectual austerity—indeed harshness, a clear acceptance of the right (or the 'correct') and repudiation of the wrong (or 'deviationist')—these are some of the very un-Indian attitudes required of Communist leaders. In addition, forms of leadership are dictated by the structure of the C.P.I.

Like all Communist parties, the C.P.I. is based upon 'democratic centralism'. There is a hierarchy of organisation, stretching up from the basic unit, the cell, through the town or local committee, district committee, and provincial committee to the Central Committee. There is also provision for the holding of periodical conferences, leading up to a national conference, called somewhat confusingly the All-India Party Congress. But this Party apparatus is not designed to promote the exercise of popular control over policy or administration. Thus: the all-India conferences are required by the Party constitution to meet biennially: but since the C.P.I. came into being in 1924-5 they have been summoned only in 1943, 1948, 1953, 1956, 1958, and 1960. Only during the period in which Ghosh was attempting to pursue a constitutionalist, parliamentary line was the two-year rule observed. Actual power has resided with the general secretary and the Politbureau—or rather, those few members of the Politbureau who happen to be at Party headquarters. To the general secretary and these few are entrusted plenary powers: provincial committees may be dissolved, members may be expelled (irrespective of seniority or office) and policy remodelled. Every major crisis in the Party has hinged upon a struggle for the post of general secretary. From 1935-48, the post was held by P. C. Joshi, a gifted organiser, from the United Provinces. When the C.P.I. adopted its militant line in 1948 he was removed from office, then expelled from the Party; being readmitted in 1951. His place was taken by B. T. Ranadive, a Maharashtrian, who had led the anti-Joshi movement. Under his leadership, the C.P.I. plunged into violence: he was removed from office in 1950, after his tactics had been censured by the Cominform (the International). His successor was C. R. Rao, a veteran worker from Andhra; he came of prosperous peasant stock, in contrast to the urban, intellectual origins of other holders of this office. Rao led the opposition to Ranadive, following the Mao-ist line (which envisaged purely temporary co-operation with the bourgeoisie 'from below'). As general secretary, his tactics were to encourage rural revolution behind a 'united front' façade; he was removed from office with a shift in Party policy. His successor, A. K. Ghosh, another United Provinces man, had formerly been a militant (indeed, he entered politics as a terrorist), but played a primary part in ousting Rao and revising the Party line. He was careful to keep closely in touch with Moscow at all moments of crisis, and his tenure of the general secretary's office was firm. His death, in January 1962, when the gulf between the 'national' and the 'Peking' groups was giving rise to another tussle, left the vacant secretaryship as an even more strategic position, more a focus of contention, than ever.

Membership of the Party has never been thrown open to the millions, as in Congress. The C.P.I. is based upon cadres, active workers, and as such its numbers have remained small: 125,000 in 1957. Whereas Congress strength is concentrated in U.P. and Bihar—the Hindi-speaking stronghold—Communism has made its greatest appeal in the 'anti-Hindi' areas, the south, and West Bengal. In addition, the great cities have largely abandoned Congress for the C.P.I. Calcutta is called the 'fortress of the Left', and Bombay City with its Communist mayor (1958-9) has not been far behind. Membership of the C.P.I. is largely replenished from the middle classes. A sizeable proportion come from professional families, many being the sons of administrators, judges, or doctors; while many are intellectuals, using the term fairly strictly, and including students, writers, artists, teachers, and scholars. Membership carries the obligation to submit, unquestioningly, to Party discipline, and to carry out whatever duties are laid down by the Party. A much higher degree of dedication is expected than from active workers in other parties. Communist M.Ps and M.L.As are required to surrender a fixed portion of their official salaries to the Party. E.M.S. Namboodiripad transferred the whole of his family fortune of Rs. 70,000 to Party funds. Within recent years this rigid austerity has been somewhat mitigated. Members are given *solatia* ranging from holidays in the Soviet Union for the upper ranks, down to free cinema tickets for the groundlings. But still, the members of the C.P.I. are driven much harder than their equivalents in other parties. The rigid scale of Party leadership and regulation does not fit well with Indian ideas of social amenity, and there is a steady falling away of disillusioned members. A notable leader who has drifted out of the Party because of harsh, unyielding treatment is Mrs. Aruna Asaf Ali, the former heroine of militant anti-British activity, who became Mayor of Delhi in 1958.

The Communist struggle for power has never been wholly concentrated upon parliamentary activities. Two other important agencies are the 'front' organisations, and the mass movements. The 'fronts' include a number of supposedly cultural societies, such as the All-India Progressive Writers' Association, in which a leading spirit is the well-known novelist Mulk Raj Anand (author of *Cooly*, *Across the Black Waters*, and many other vivid portraits of Indian life). Another is the India-China Friendship Association, which has numbered among its officers such influential public men as K. M. Panikkar. Dr. Gyan Chand, Dr. V. K. R. Rao, and Syed Mahmud: all respected figures in the Indian Establishment. The cloud which has gathered over Sino-Indian relations has not entirely dimmed the importance of this society. However, the mass labour movements form a more direct weapon of Communist strategy; and at this point we digress for a brief account of this quasi-political force.

The first Indian trade union of any consequence was the Bombay Millhands Association, founded in 1890, which had neither a regular constitution nor paying members. Unionism only became a force in industry in the 1920s. The All-India Trade Union Congress was set up in 1920, and in 1926 the movement was regularised and legalised by a Trade Unions Act. The first president of the A.I.T.U.C. was Lala Lajpat Rai, a veteran Congress leader from Punjab, belonging to the 'Extremist' wing. The Communists began to organise their own labour unions, aided by several British Communist union officials: the two most important were those of the textile workers and the railwaymen, with a combined membership of 95,000. When the A.I.T.U.C. held its annual session at Nagpur in 1929, with Jawarhalal Nehru presiding, the Communists emerged as the strongest force and were able to take over control. A Communist, S. A. Dange, became general secretary, and other important offices went to their nominees. A number of union leaders whose prime interest was the improvement of rates of pay and working conditions, rather than politics, seceded to create a rival Indian Trade Union Federation. Two years later, the Communists walked out of the A.I.T.U.C. to set up their own Red Trade Union Congress, in line with the current Comintern policy. In 1935, the Comintern line again abruptly altered, and the Red Congress unions returned to the A.I.T.U.C. Three years later, the Indian Trade Union Federation leaders (they had meanwhile changed their name to National Trade Union Federation) affiliated to the A.I.T.U.C. and in 1940 all the rivals were again completely reunited. During the 1930s, the Congress Socialists, like Jayaprakash Narayan, took the initiative and built up the Union organisation as the industrial wing of the nationalist movement. A peasant counterpart was created in 1936, the All-India Kisan Sabha (or 'peasant conference'), led initially by Swami Sahajananda Saraswathi, a quasi-religious peasant leader from Bihar. Almost at once, three factions emerged within the Kisan movement: the agrarian reformers, the Congress Socialists, and the Communists. The nationalist-Socialist-Communist tangle continued in both these labour movements until 1942, when the Quit India campaign and the subsequent internment of all Congress and Socialist leaders left the field clear for the Communists. By 1945, Communist leadership had greatly enlarged the mass membership of both movements: the Kisan Sabha claimed 800,000 members, and the A.I.T.U.C. had enrolled 451,915 members. After the war, the Socialists and other Congress workers attempted to recapture some of their former influence in the labour movements, but the Communists were too firmly entrenched to be shaken by these late-comers. The Congress reverted to the old technique of setting up a rival body, and in 1947 the Indian National Trade Union Congress came into being. The Socialists, on the point of withdrawing from the Congress fold, decided to hold aloof and in December 1948 sponsored a third body, the Hind Mazdoor Sabha, with Asok Mehta as general secretary.

When the C.P.I. launched its militant campaign in 1948, the Communist unions were plunged into a vortex of strikes, with mass demonstrations and violence. Industrial terrorism was most bloody in the factories and mills that form the Hooghley industrial complex. British managers were a special target, and after murder had been committed the West Bengal government banned the C.P.I. and closed the Communist unions. After this, such non-Communist leaders as remained in the A.I.T.U.C. withdrew, and founded a fourth 'all-India' organisation, the United Trades Union Congress. This splintering off inevitably weakened the labour movement. Of the four rivals, the Congress I.N.T.U.C. was the most powerful: the government (whether at the centre or in the States) is by far the largest employer of industrial and clerical workers, and was therefore able to offer facilities, or exert pressure, which was most efficacious in ensuring that the Congress unions attracted membership. The Communist A.I.T.U.C. still held its own, and where militant industrial action was possible (as in some sections of the textile industry, or among plantation labour) it showed much more vigour than its rivals. The Socialist Hind Mazdoor Sabha, and the largely Trotskyite U.T.U.C. were of lesser importance. During the early 1950s, attempts were made to bring together the three Leftist organisations, but unity could not be achieved: the non-Communists were not prepared to accept any merger in which the Communists would be left in control. During the period in office of the Kerala Communist Government the Communist unions were employed as a weapon of violence against the foreign-owned tea plantations. The Congress I.N.T.U.C. on behalf of its own members negotiated a settlement with the plantations, but the A.I.T.U.C. union men repudiated the agreement and intimidated members of rival unions. Pressure was brought to bear on the police and the courts to favour the militant unions. This incitement to violence in labour disputes was one of the factors leading to the supercession of the Kerala Government by the President.

The Kisan movement has undergone the same process of fragmentation as trade unionism. After unsuccessfully attempting to force their way back into the Communist-dominated All-India Kisan Sabha, the Socialists organised Kisan Panchayata with some success, especially in the Hindi areas. The C.P.I. exploited the Kisan wing during the period of militancy, yet even then there was an element of compromise in their policy. Communist strength in Telingana depended on the support of the Kamma caste, mainly wealthy landowners. It was laid down that landlords who remained aloof from the struggle should be classified as 'neutralised', and left alone. An Andhra Communist statement of policy laid down that 'Assurance should be given that we should not touch the land of rich *ryots*'. (*Ryot* means 'cultivator' or 'peasant', not 'landlord'; but here as often the Communists juggled with semantics). As the C.P.I. changed over to constitutional methods, so their dependence on the rural middle class, the wealthier peasants, for political leadership led them to soft-pedal the Kisan movement. Also, Vinoba Bhave's land-gift campaign, and the government Community Development programme both had the effect of polarising rural support around different objectives. The Communists may revitalise the Kisan movement later on, but in the early 1960s it was in eclipse.

After the general election of February 1962, the C.P.I. was required to carry out a re-evaluation of policy and strategy. The most weighty study of Indian Communism concludes with the following observation:

The C.P.I. is neither monolithic nor unchanging, and it is sure to be shaped by future events in India and elsewhere. Up to now, its nature has been more Communist than Indian. But it has shown some flexibility and adaptability—especially in the realm of tactics. Should it ever become even a little more Indian, it will be truly a force to be reckoned with.[1]

The Communist Party may become the party of the future: the Socialist Party already looks like the party of the past. Britain, in the decade 1945-55 adopted a Liberal policy, yet showed no interest in the Liberal Party. The same may be said of Socialism, and the Socialist Party in India: and in the 1960s Indian Socialism fails to show any of the promise of rejuvenation and renewal that distinguishes English Liberalism. The decline of the Socialists is all the more unfortunate because their leaders have shown by far the greatest originality and vision in drafting programmes and policies designed to meet India's unique needs. In part, their lack of success has been due to their finding themselves midway between the Communists and the Congress ('in the unenviable position of the proverbial earthen pot between two brass vessels', to quote again the words applied by an Indian Liberal to his own dilemma at an earlier period). Their potential vote tended to be drawn away towards rivals who outbid them in both directions. But the Socialists have also been plagued by an internal weakness; the continual defection of front-rank supporters, due to differences on points of policy and strategy. Their very strength—ideological inventiveness—has been their Achilles Heel, for every major party decision entails a debate over method and doctrine, in which, very often, at least one leader, or faction is unable to accept the majority ruling. And whereas the Socialists in their earlier phase understood the necessity of tackling power politics from the base, by mobilising the masses, in its latter day, Indian Socialism has allowed itself to be displaced in popular support by rivals, whose appeal is crude or emotional.

The Congress Socialist Party was founded in 1934 out of Marxist-Socialist groups which had been formed in Bombay, Bihar, and elsewhere. Its aim was to exert pressure to force the Congress leaders upon a revolutionary path; and the C.S.P. was received with considerable reserve both by the hard-headed, orthodox wing led by Sardar Patel and associated with big business, and also by the liberals, such as Rajagopalachari. Gandhi, however, despite a complete divergence of aim and purpose was kindly disposed to the Socialists. Their greatest moment came in August 1942, when they stampeded Congress into discarding

[1] G. D. Overstreet and M. Windmiller, *Communism in India*, University of California Press, 1959, pp. 538-9.

Gandhian non-violence for a revolutionary campaign of terrorism and sabotage. Their failure cast something of a cloud over their prestige, and they played virtually no part in the negotiations for independence. This forms a striking contrast to the situation in Burma, where the Thakins, the Marxist-Socialist group, thrust aside the moderates and constitutionalists and dictated their own terms to the British Government under the threat of a national strike and possible rebellion.[1]

Far from capturing the 'Freedom Movement', the Socialists were elbowed out of the Congress early in 1948. Resolving to function as a separate party, the Socialist leaders adopted a resolution stating: 'For the maintenance of [the] democratic climate, an opposition becomes necessary. The Socialist Party alone can provide this opposition.' From acting as a revolutionary spearhead, the Socialist Party now accepted the rôle of a constitutional opposition—the negative rôle which had soured an earlier generation of Indian political leaders. The psychological effect of this deliberate decision to play a waiting game must have been profound. The following year, at the Patna Convention, the implication of the change of front was given doctrinal form. The Socialists have always adhered to the Marxist practice of issuing elaborate dogmatic rationales of what are sometimes the shifts of expediency. 'Democratic centralism' was thrown overboard in favour of mass organisation; instead of the cult of revolutionary leadership, emphasis was placed on the solidarity of the party members. Full membership was now thrown open to all prepared to pay an annual subscription of one rupee. However, a distinction was retained between ordinary members, and active members, prepared to give fourteen hours a week to party work. A comprehensive programme was issued in July 1951 as a prelude to the election called *We Build for Socialism*. Great emphasis was placed on land reform, and new agricultural techniques, including co-operatives and collective farms. The state is to be reorganised upon Four Pillars: the village, the *mandal* or district, the province, and the central government. All are to be integrated in a system of functional federalism; with the community taking over responsibility from the executive. A Fifth Pillar is also envisaged: world government. The progenitor of this plan was said to be Dr. Ram Manohar Lohia: born in 1910, he is the youngest of the front rank Socialists. The plan is also very close to the thinking of Jayaprakash Narayan.

Immediately before the 1951 election, another Socialist party appeared, as a result of differences within Congress, the Kisan Mazdur

[1] See the author's *The Union of Burma; a Study of the First Years of Independence*, Oxford University Press, 3rd edn., 1961, Chs. I and II.

Praja Party. The new party was led by Acharya Kripalani, a former Congress President. Kripalani belonged to the previous generation of leadership, being a year older than Nehru. He joined Gandhi in his first campaign in Bihar in 1917, and thereafter was at the heart of the movement. He was general secretary of Congress from 1934 to 1946, when he was elected president. At the apex of power, his position crumbled. As a Sindhi, his province now formed part of Pakistan, and he therefore disposed of no political strength. In the general share-out of patronage, his suggestions were ignored. His control over the High Command wavered. In November 1947 he resigned from the presidency. His next bid for power—the contest in 1950 against Tandon for the presidency —ended in disappointment. Two weeks later, in association with an equivocal Congress Muslim, Rafi Ahmed Kidwai, Kripalani headed a bloc of fifty Congress-men in a 'Democratic Front' in order to 'energise the organisation [Congress] and rid it of the corrupting influence of power politics'. Nehru and others exerted steady pressure to dissolve the Democratic Front, and in May 1951 it was disbanded. Kripalani resigned from Congress, along with other dissidents, and the K.M.P. was launched at Patna in June.

Both Socialist parties went into the first election with high hopes: their pretensions to provide an effective opposition were almost everywhere deflated. The two parties agreed to merge in September 1952, on a programme of socialisation, emancipation of the workers, and decentralisation of political and economic power. The Socialists still insisted on the purity of their Marxism; Jayaprakash Narayan declared at this time: 'The Socialist Party is the only Marxist party in India.' But the whole Socialist ethos was being transformed; the concept of the class war was giving way to the idea of sarvodaya, or harmony, with consequent effects upon relations with other parties. During 1953, Jayaprakash conducted negotiations with Nehru to bring Congress and the P.S.P. into closer accord and co-operation on the task of national development. Asok Mehta supported Jayaprakash, but Lohia opposed any rapprochement, insisting that the Socialists were 'equidistant' from both Congress and the C.P.I. His stand earned the approval of rank-and-file Socialists. The 'Allahabad thesis' adopted in 1953 approved electoral pacts to avoid three- (or four-) cornered contests against the Congress, but ruled out coalition deals. Lohia's disagreements with his colleagues reached breaking-point in 1954. The occasion was the responsibility of the curious minority P.S.P. Government of Travancore-Cochin (later Kerala) for dispersing a crowd of Tamils, agitating for their language rights, by police firing. Lohia called on the party to demand the resignation of the P.S.P. ministry. Failing to carry the party with him, he resigned from his post of general secretary. The question of the position of Congress, having adopted the goal of a 'socialistic' society, injected further heat into the dispute. In July 1955, Lohia was suspended by the Executive of the P.S.P. and his supporters began to establish local associations. As a result, a separate Socialist Party of India came into being in December 1955.

The two Socialist parties approached the second general election from diametrically opposed points; the 'Lohia Socialists' were ready to take on all comers; the rump P.S.P. negotiated electoral deals with every party from extreme Right to extreme Left. Neither policy paid off. Between the second and third elections, the Socialists floated in limbo. Meeting at Bombay in October 1959, the P.S.P. adopted a coherent radical programme, with firm emphasis on the needs of the land. Its appeal was weakened by the withdrawal of Jayaprakash into the rôle of a latter-day John the Baptist, adapting some of the Socialist policies towards his own *Plea for Reconstruction of Indian Polity*.

The eclipse of the Socialists is the more unfortunate because they have directed their thinking towards some of India's vital problems. Indian Socialism went beyond Marx, who dismissed the peasantry as a reactionary element, and focused upon the urban proletariat. Indian Socialists looked for solutions to the problems of the villagers, pointing to the primal necessity for an end to caste conflict. Indian Socialists have tackled the subject of planning from below, instead of from above like almost everyone else. Yet, lacking internal unity and a popular appeal, the Socialist bid to offer an alternative to Congress has petered out.

Membership of the Socialist Party, like that of most parties, is predominantly middle class. Originally, the Socialists showed the same regional limitations as Congress and other parties. Bombay was their first stronghold. The P.S.P. has duplicated Congress in finding its principal support in the Hindi-speaking north; but it enjoys a respectable following in many other areas; West Bengal and Madras especially. It follows Congress in deserving to be reckoned as an all-India party. In view of these factors, the current failure of the Socialists to create a popular following need not necessarily be taken as the final verdict on the party.

The Socialist Party of Pakistan was even less successful in putting across its appeal. After partition, only a fragment of the former Socialist movement survived in the region which now became West Pakistan. Two men, Mobarak Sagher and Mohammad Yusuf Khan represented virtually the only element of continuity upon which Socialism could depend. Despite associating with certain popular demands, such as a free plebiscite in Kashmir, the Socialists were called 'disloyal'; and the continual drift of party workers into India appeared to confirm such accusations. The party secured its only parliamentary representation in the 1954 landslide in East Bengal, when four representatives entered the provincial legislature. They were elected under 'united front' labels and, significantly, three were Hindus. Some attempt was made to develop trade union activity as a means towards political power. The Socialists succeeded in gaining control of the Pakistan Trade Union Federation from the Communists in 1951; Sagher became president, and Mohammad Yusuf vice-president. The Communists held on to a minority in the P.T.U.F. and they reformed an organisation, retaining the old name. The new Socialist body became known as the Pakistan Mazdur Federation. However, the main stream of the labour movement (if one can use such dignified terms of something so unimportant) was outside both of these bodies, being controlled by the All-Pakistan Confederation of Labour, which enjoyed a regular standing with the government. Even before the military *coup d'état*, the Pakistan Socialist Party had ceased to be an active force: its failure (in the words of the principal writer on Asian Socialism) 'seemed to provide illustration of the inability of a Socialist Party to flourish in a Muslim environment'.[1]

What did flourish in the Muslim environment of Pakistan were the various groups which professed to interpret the political implications of the teaching of the Holy Prophet. The impact of religion was made through two opposed approaches—political parties, claiming to speak with the authority of religion; and the religious groups, exercising an external pressure upon political activity.

There were two main avowedly religious parties, the Jamaat-i-Islami ('the Islamic party') and the Nizam-i-Islam ('party of the Islamic order'). The Jamaat-i-Islami was founded in 1941 by Maulana Abu Ala Maudoodi, a conservative divine, and a powerful writer and publicist. Its objective is the establishment of the Islamic state: yet this is not to be equated with the frontiers of Pakistan; the goal is the *Millat-al-Islamian*, or the Islamic polity, comprehending all the lands inhabited by the faithful. Consequently, Maudoodi was opposed to carving up undivided India, and renouncing the 40,000,000 Muslims who were necessarily excluded from Pakistan. Within the new state, the Jamaat-i-Islami worked for the acceptance of an Islamic order—as interpreted by Maudoodi. The party made no attempt to become a power on the parlia-

[1] Saul Rose, *Socialism in Southern Asia*, Oxford University Press, 1959, p. 67.

mentary stage; but it carried on a powerful propaganda campaign, through publications and lectures. Its organisation and membership afforded remarkable parallels with that of the Communist Party. Nizam-i-Islam was founded in East Bengal by Maulana Athar Ali, and was a similar alliance of divines, scholars, and conservatives. Two other religious parties are, perhaps, worth a passing mention: the Anjuman-i-Shabal-Muslimeen (Muslim People's Organisation) was founded by Chaudri Khaliquzzaman to work for the establishment of a pan-Muslim bloc; the Millat Party was founded by the former Major-General Akbar Khan (convicted for the Rawalpindi conspiracy) with the objective of the liberation of Kashmir.

Finally, there were religious movements which claimed the right to influence politics; of these, the Ahrar movement was the most powerful and the most peculiar. The Ahrars came together in 1930 as a nationalist Muslim adjunct to Gandhi's civil disobedience campaign. Their philosophy at this time was that of Hindu-Muslim unity, and they attempted to oppose the rise of the Muslim League. However, their popular following was almost entirely absorbed by the League, and the Ahrars were left to confront the Pakistan demand by a somewhat apocalyptic vision of 'the Kingdom of God'. The principal Ahrar appeal lay in their leader, Attamullah Shah Bokhari, a spell-binding orator who urged his followers to fight the British by copious appeals to the Holy Quran. Partition left the Ahrars without a cause and without a country. For a time, the movement 'went underground'. It emerged in 1953 as the apotheosis of Islamic bigotry; its target was the heterodox Ahmadiyya community, and its weapon was a crude appeal to mob emotionalism. Possibly, its ultimate aim was the disruption of Pakistan; resting, as it did, on an uneasy compromise, compounded of the Islamic heritage and Western democratic theory. The swift facility with which the army suppressed the anti-Ahmadiyya rioting served to demonstrate the incoherence of the aims and methods of the Islamic theocrats.

The impact of militant Hinduism on politics in India is also dualistic; directly applied by avowedly Hindu political parties, and indirectly asserted by quasi-political movements. The Mahasabha, the oldest association, cannot be assessed according to its party or parliamentary strength. It has devoted most attention to propaganda; to creating an awareness of the legacy of Hinduism, and to awakening the Hindus to their rightful place in *Bharat-varsa*. The Mahasabha encouraged volunteer movements, in which young men learnt drill and rifle shooting. Such were the Maharashtrian Militarisation Board at Poona, and the Rashtryia Swayam Sevak Sangh which originated at Nagpur. The

Mahasabha called for fuller participation by Hindus in the regular and territorial forces, and in private armies as storm troopers. Although the Mahasabha had a free hand during the incarceration of the Congress leaders, 1942-5, it was completely over-shadowed before and after independence; while the supposed implication of the R.S.S.S. in Gandhi's murder led to its being banned, February 1948-November 1949. A new and ultra-orthodox Hindu party, Ram Rajya Parishad, was started by a Swami Karapatri in 1948, but Hindu politics received its main fillip when the Jan Sangh came into being in May-June 1951. Its leading spirit was Dr. Syama Prasad Mookerjee, member of a leading intellectual Calcutta family, himself Vice-Chancellor of Calcutta University, and a Minister in Nehru's first Cabinet. Dr. Mookerjee was no wild-eyed fanatic; he was a constitutionalist and parliamentarian; a conservative, in the best sense. He was to resign from the Cabinet in 1950 over the conclusion by Nehru of an agreement with Pakistan. After a year in the political wilderness, he founded the Jan Sangh, with much support from discontented R.S.S.S. members. The Jan Sangh claims that it is not a communal party: its goal is not *Hindu Rashtra* but *Bharatiya Rashtra,* not Hindu India, but a Hinduised India. It even includes a few Muslim Uncle Toms to prove its non-communal character. The re-union of Pakistan with India in *Akhand Hindustan* is given high priority. Dr. Mookerjee organised a small coalition of opposition members of the Union parliament, and he might have given Right-wing politics some purpose, had he not died in 1953, after leading an agitation in Kashmir against the Muslim control of the State ministry. Leadership of the Rightist coalition was taken over by N. C. Chatterjee, a leading lawyer and president of the Mahasabha; but he lacked Mookerjee's exceptional personality. The Jan Sangh has received sufficient electoral support to be classified by the Electoral Commission as an All-India party: but in practice its main strength lies in *Arya-varta,* the classical Hindu (and Hindi) homeland. Its main electoral gains have come in backward Rajasthan and Madhya Pradesh, with some militant support in Uttar Pradesh. Despite the Bengali background of its founder, it has made little headway in West Bengal, even among refugees from East Pakistan.

Pandit Nehru, Krishna Menon, and other spokesmen of the 'secular' school of politics have so frequently argued that the Hindu communal parties have failed to gain a footing, that the argument has been widely accepted. Yet, over the central feature of Nehru's secular programme, the Hindu Code Bill, the communalists have to a large extent had their own way. The Hindu Code Bill was first introduced by Nehru in 1950 as a comprehensive measure to reform the whole structure of Hindu marriage, divorce, inheritance rights, and adoption custom. The Bill met with widespread opposition, in and out of Parliament. In October 1951, President Prasad threatened to use his power of veto, unless the measure was withdrawn. The Bill was delayed, and its provisions whittled away. At last in 1955, a major part of the code was placed on the statute books as the Hindu Marriages Law. The ranks of the Congress parliamentary party contained few prepared to support the measure, and many who spoke against it: but when the vote was taken, the party whip was obeyed. As a demonstration of the secular spirit, all this was not very impressive.

M. R. Masani, as an independent M.P., drew attention to the 'lop-sided' ideological balance in the Indian Parliament. Three major parties, Congress, P.S.P., and C.P.I. all claim to be Socialist: 'We do not have a single party which takes what I would broadly call a Liberal stand—a stand based on enlightened individualism. . . . The fact that no liberal or conservative or centre party exists which is non-socialist is, in my view, a great weakness of our democracy.' In order to combat what he calls the 'slave state', Masani, together with the aged and vastly respected Rajagopalachari, founded in 1959 the Swatantra or 'Freedom' party. Masani and Rajagopalachari have every right to call themselves Liberals and they succeeded in attracting a certain amount of moderate support from business men, retired judges and officials, and other men of good-will. But in order to obtain mass support, they were compelled to accept obscure and reactionary recruits into the party. Nehru once observed, in conversation with Asok Mehta, 'Who says that opposition forces are weak in India? The opposition we have to fight is obscurantism and inertia of the people.' The Prime Minister had in mind mass lethargy and ignorance: but the record of both the religious and the secular Rightist parties is a sad commentary on this maxim.

Certain of the parties in Pakistan which emerged as successors to the Muslim League may properly be classified as secular, conservative parties: such was Dr. Khan Sahib's shortlived Republican Party. The most consistent of these was Suhrawardy's Awami League. Suhrawardy's philosophy was nothing more sensational than party politics; he was a journeyman Edmund Burke. He was prepared to take the unpopular line; to categorise Nasser at the height of his powers as an adventurer; to dismiss the pan-Islamic cult as a string of zeroes which, added together (the 'Islamic brotherhood'), remained a zero. But in order to play a dominant rôle in the politics of the 1950s he was compelled to play the politics of accommodation, and he took as his principal West Pakistan ally a *flâneur*, Iftikhar Hussein, Khan of Mamdot. As in India, the attempt to create a conservative position in politics merely ended in the politics of compromise and retrogression.

As the 1950s drew to a close, the whole concept of party politics was under question. In Pakistan, Field Marshal Ayub was declaring: 'We are not yet ready for democracy.' In India, the Speaker of the Lok Sabha was concluding: 'We have to follow a policy which is evolved according to our own pattern and which is consistent with our own historic tradition and the feelings of our own people.' Even such a confirmed believer in the parliamentary party system as Asok Mehta was driven to state that 'the main function of the opposition is to exercise vigilance ...', and that 'opposition, if confined to the political plane, remains anaemic'. Significantly, he added: 'Opposition, to become strong, often utilises the deeply felt loyalties of religion, language, tribe or caste: and so does a government, driven to a corner.'

Politics in the 1960s looks for a theoretical rationale to the concept of sarvodaya or the general will or (in Ayub's phrase) to democracy 'of the type that people can understand and work'. Yet, as the locus of government shifted away from the control of an enlightened few, into the hands of the many, so local party politics acquired a new intensity, based upon a new consciousness that power might be acquired by organisation and agitation.

VI

THE POLITICS OF LANGUAGE AND CASTE

THE nation-state, as it has been created in the West, is normally rooted in cultural assimilation and absorption. Religion and language are the two main factors in creating the sense of nationhood; and although there are exceptions—such as Canada, Switzerland, or Czechoslovakia —a common language has proved the outstanding means of knitting together separate groups into a nation. The Asian pattern (outside of the Middle East) is different. Only two states, Japan and Thailand, enjoy linguistic homogeneity. Several Asian countries do possess a recognised major language (as in China, Vietnam, and Burma) while most other countries are able, artificially, to create a national language, whether by compromise (Tagalog in the Philippines), coercion (Sinhalese in Ceylon), or synthesis (as in Indonesia with its syncretic *Bahasa Indonesia*). However, in two countries the complexity of the problem defies any simple solution: in the Soviet Union, with sixty-four distinct main languages, and India with sixty-three major tongues.[1] The Soviet Union has, to some extent overcome the problem of linguistic diversity by evolving a kind of Russified-Communist type, the product of conquest, ideological uniformity, and the ascendancy of technology. Indian acceptance of the legacies of British conquest—among which, the English language was supreme—has been selective and critical. India has no unifying ideology, no common religion or creed. Apart from the millions of Muslims, Sikhs, Christians and animists, Hinduism itself is

[1] Some 46 of the languages of the U.S.S.R. belong to the Asian group, and out of the grand total of 64, only 18 are spoken by over half a million people. Of the Indian languages, about 25 can claim over half a million speakers. The reader should recognise a distinction from 'languages of literary record': the latter are far fewer in number.

divided into manifold cults and beliefs; and the sacred system it has produced, caste, is a unique system of classification and subdivision. The influence of caste has penetrated almost all other religions in the sub-continent; including Islam, and even, perhaps, Christianity. Language and caste permeate politics in India, and to a lesser extent in Pakistan. To understand their power, a brief historical retrospect is necessary.

The speech of the earlier inhabitants of the sub-continent survives among the aboriginal tribal folk: the most important of this 'Munda' group of tongues is Santali, spoken by over 2½ millions. Waves of immigration overwhelmed the aborigines. The first folk-immigration was that of a palæo-mediterranean people bringing the proto-Dravidian speech. The later Aryan invaders brought their Indo-European tongue, which achieved Homeric stature in the *Rig Veda,* composed between 1500 and 800 B.C. Religion and law were preserved in a ritual language, Sanskrit. As Brahmanical Hinduism penetrated southern India, so Sanskrit percolated into the Dravidian vocabulary, just as Latin permeated the vulgar tongues of north-west Europe. The widespread use of Sanskrit was preserved by the Brahmins, as the vehicle of the sacred texts and of ritual usage.

Among the languages of the present day, the first to attain something like its present form was Tamil, which has a continuous literary tradition going back over two thousand years. Kannada and Telugu emerged a few centuries later, with Malayalam as the last to achieve an independent literary form. The vernacular forms of Sanskrit, or Prakrits, developed into Apabhramsha ('falling away') from which descend the modern languages of India north of the Narbadda. The mid-western branch, Sauraseni Apabhramsha, was the main source of Hindi; Rajasthani and Gujarati are linked with Najan Apabhramsha; a southern branch produced Marathi; a north-western branch contributed Punjabi and Sindhi; while the eastern branch, Magadha Apabhramsha (the supposed native language of Lord Buddha) was the seed of Bihari, Bengali, Assamese, and Oriya.

The Muslim conquest, from the twelfth century onward introduced Persian, Arabic and Turki into India. The trans-Indus languages, Pashtu (in all its forms) and Baluchi, are Iranian off-shoots. Because of the political dominance of the Muslim invaders, many loan-words from their native languages were absorbed into the general vocabulary, in north India especially.

A new language emerged from the encounter of Muslims and Hindus, in the market place, the darbar, and the parade ground: Zaban-i-Urdu (from Turki, 'language of the camp'). One form of this hybrid tongue became known as Hindustani. The relationship of Urdu, Hindustani, and Hindi is complex, and it has been further obscured by the smoke-screen of propaganda put out by the growing school of language fanatics which has flourished in recent years.

Two dominant forms of Hindi arose in the districts between Saharan-pur and Agra, 'Hindustan' in the most narrow meaning of the term. Brajbhasha, from the vicinity of Mathura, developed a flourishing literary style as the language *par excellence* of the Krishna cult, and continued as a poetic vehicle until late in the nineteenth century. Khari-boli ('straight talk') had its centre around Meerut, and provided the basis for both Urdu and modern literary Hindi. 'Hindi' as understood today includes not only the literary Khariboli and the poetic Brajbhasha (both of the western Hindu group) but also the literature of an eastern group; Awadhi in particular, the language of the northern Rama cult; and, less justifiably, that of some languages of Rajasthan and Bihar; in both these areas (literary) Hindi is the prestige speech. Urdu was taken south to the Deccan, flourished especially at Hyderabad, and from there re-fertilised the Mughal capital. It is grammatically identical with Hindi, but draws its learned vocabulary from Persian and Arabic and is written in the Persian script. Hindi depends for learned vocabulary and script on Sanskrit. Both Muslim and Hindu poets composed in Urdu. Raja Shiva Prasad popularised a literary form called Khichri (kedgeree) Hindi, a deliberate amalgam, which was the basis of Hindustani. This word is often loosely applied. It may refer to 'the lowest common de-nominator' of Urdu and Hindi, the *lingua franca* of north India; or to the language of the 'Hindustani movement' (virtually, Urdu written in the Hindi script); it may also refer to the mother-tongue of the country to the north-west of Delhi.

Hindi, then, took on a dual rôle. It was the colloquial speech of the peoples of the Ganges plains and around Delhi; and it was the matrix of urbane literary styles. While this development was going forward, there were other notable literary movements among other regional lan-guages. The period from the twelfth to the fifteenth century has been called the seed-time of the vernacular literatures; the early nineteenth century saw the harvest. Bengali and Gujarati were the most important northern regional schools. Court patronage was important, but the regional literatures more often grew out of popular demand; such was the widespread *bhakti* movement for religious reform. It encouraged a popular religious literature, in place of classical Sanskrit, the preserve of the Brahman priesthood. There was also a secular literature, of which

Mukundaram, the documentary poet of rural Bengal, is an outstanding example. The priestly preservation of Sanskrit militated against the rise of the vernaculars in polite literary esteem until the Christian missionaries began systematically to develop the regional languages as a means of evangelism. The Baptist missionaries with their great printing press at Serampore were the pioneers of this renascence. Bengal was their first concern, and Bengali flowered most brilliantly; from Ram Mohan Ray down to Rabindranath Tagore, Bengal took the lead in developing new techniques and new modes in drama, the novel, and poetry. Bengali literature was nourished by the new Westernised middle class. Its themes were mainly secular, and soon included a political content. One landmark was the publication in 1883 of the novel *Ananda-math* by Bankim Chandra Chatterji, with its hymn *Bande Mataram*, 'Hail to the Mother', which was later adopted by the Congress as the national song. The first great issue upon which the Moderates and the Extremists united to oppose British policy was over Lord Curzon's partition of Bengal in 1905 as a measure of administrative reform. Because of the volume of protest against the 'bisection' of the Bengali people it was necessary to rescind the partition in 1911.

However, the primacy of Bengali in the vanguard of the national movement was outpaced by the Hindi revival. Dayanand Saraswati, founder of the religio-political Arya Samaj, was a Gujarati Brahmin; but to emphasise his Vedic inspiration he chose to write in a Sanskritic Hindi modelled on Kharibol. His influential *Satyarthaprakasa* appeared in 1875, and thereafter 'standard' Hindi in the Deva-Nagari script began to establish a hold, especially in Punjab and western U.P., the Arya Samaj stronghold. Gradually, the Hindi newspapers of Delhi and U.P. began to change over from publication in the Urdu or Arabic-Persian script to the Deva-Nagari script. The promotion of Hindi as the national language was taken up by another Gujarati-speaker: Gandhi. From 1917 onward, he urged the acceptance of Hindi as *Antar Bhasha* or the national language. But to him, Hindi meant Hindustani, the *lingua franca*: neither Hindi as a neo-Sanskritic literary style, nor as the language of the Ganges plains. Here is Gandhi's interpretation of his definition of Hindi.

> The distinction between Hindus and Muslims is unreal. The same unreality is found in the distinction between Hindi and Urdu. It is unnecessary for Hindus to reject Persian words and for Muslims to reject Sanskrit words from their speech. A harmonious blend of the two will be as beautiful as the

confluence of Ganga and Yamuna [Ganges and Jumna rivers] and last for ever.... There is, no doubt, difficulty in regard to script. As things are, Muslims will patronise the Arabic script while Hindus will mostly use the Nagari script. Both scripts will therefore be accorded their due place.... In the end the script which is the easier of the two will prevail.[1]

Gandhi made this statement in 1918, and he went on saying much the same thing until the end of his life. Under Congress auspices, the teaching of Hindi was introduced in the schools of Bombay and Madras, where Rajagopalachari sponsored the experiment; it met with strong local opposition. Right up to independence, Congress, as a mass party, drew its strength from U.P. and Bihar, which accounted for over two-fifths of the total membership. To be a force in Congress, one had to make allies of the Hindi-speakers; yet the Hindi-speakers never constituted a majority, and they were sometimes compelled to make concessions to the others. After five years of passive and active opposition, the Congress accepted in 1920 a motion declaring that the Congress provincial committees should be organised not according to the arbitrary boundaries of the British provinces but upon a linguistic *pradesh* basis. In deference to this decision, three new *pradesh* were recognised: Andhra, Utkal (Orissa), and Sind. Among the changes wrought by the 1935 Act were the hiving-off of Orissa and Sind as separate Governors' provinces; Telugu-speaking Andhra remained a part of the Madras Presidency.

Thus Congress had committed itself to supporting two conflicting policies: the promotion of *Antar Bhasha,* the national language, and also of *Swabhasha,* the mother tongue, or regional languages. The Congress provincial governments, 1937-9, being led, for the most part, by upper middle-class barrister-politicians with a genuinely all-India viewpoint, worked to promote Hindi. In U.P. and Bihar this entailed strong pressure in the schools, local government, and the provincial administration to change over from Urdu (the language of public affairs next to English) to Hindi in the Nagari script. Not all the Congress leaders were committed to Nagari: Nehru advocated the adoption of the Roman script as a compromise (after the model of Turkey under Kemal Ataturk). But Nagari was pushed assiduously; to the growing alarm of the important U.P. Muslim leaders, who valued the reputation of Lucknow as the foremost Urdu cultural centre. The threat to Urdu was one of the

[1] Quoted in *Report of the Official Language Commission,* New Delhi, 1956, p. 380.

fundamental causes of the growth of the Pakistan demand; outsiders found it puzzling that this demand was loudest in U.P., an area that could never by any political conjuring form part of Pakistan; the explanation lay in the special Urdu heritage of the U.P. Muslims, and the need to discover a means to repel the attack of the Hindi fanatics.

Language had demonstrated its potency as a political issue before independence; caste had also assumed new forms and a new harshness in a climate of economic and social change, and growing political experience.

Caste has to be considered from two contrasting aspects: as a means of social classification and division, and as a system of inter-group relations. Caste is usually treated as a system whereby society is immutably graded and divided.[1] These divisions are enforced by customary laws, or taboos, which operate in three main spheres of activity: domestic life, kinship and marriage, and occupation. The 'domestic' taboos which surround eating, drinking, etc., are highly important, but are not highly relevant to problems of political analysis. Hindu marriage custom is based upon endogamy; a man can only marry within his own caste; but also he must not marry within the circle of his own relations, or his particular sub-caste, and normally the practice of hypergamy is followed. This situation has two political consequences. First, brides are customarily taken from certain associated villages, so that there is a local network of kinship associations between villages; and, more important, because of caste endogamy it is almost impossible (without breaking caste) for anyone, however wealthy or talented he may be, to throw off his own caste folk. If men aspire to rise in the world, they must carry the whole caste upward with them.

This leads to the third attribute of caste—that which is normally associated with the term, but which is least precise as an indicator— caste as a sign of economic, social, or ritual standing. Caste is of two main varieties: tribal, and functional. Caste may be determined by agnatic relationship; this is general among two contrasted sections of the population, the aboriginal peoples of south and central India, who form 'tribes' as the term is usually understood; and the agriculturalists of north-western India, such as Ahirs, Awans, Gujars, who (whether

---

[1] A 'working definition' of caste is offered in *Social Service in India*, ed. Sir E. Blunt, HMSO, 1939, Ch. 11 'The Structure of the Indian People', p. 50: 'A caste is an endogamous group, or collection of endogamous groups, bearing a common name, membership of which is hereditary; imposing on its members certain restrictions in the matter of social intercourse; either following a common traditional occupation or claiming a common origin; and generally regarded as forming a single homogeneous community'.

Muslim or Hindu) are descendents of nomadic tribal groups. Caste is also derived from traditional functional duties; these castes are often sub-divided minutely, according to original tribal origins. There are castes corresponding to every possible form of economic activity, ritual function, and hereditary right. It is usual to assign a place for all these castes and sub-castes to some section of the four main 'orders' or 'limbs' of Hinduism. These are ascribed to the Institutes of Manu, a legal authority which has the same ancient sanctity for the Hindu that the Mosaic decalogue has for the Christian. Manu defines four *varnas* (the term is derived from 'colour'), the *Brahmans*, the priests; the *Kshattriyas*, or warriors; the *Vaishyas*, traders and cultivators; and *Sudras*, servants and menials. Outside of caste altogether are the despised *Mlecchas*, foreigners or untouchables. The pre-eminence of the Brahmins has been perpetuated through all time, but the inheritance of the other three varnas is open to debate. The Rajputs claim to be the sole heirs of the Kshattriyas, but others also claim the title, while acceptance of the status of Vaishya or Sudra is also disputed. The Indian term for 'caste' (which itself is of Portugese origin) is *zat* or *jat*, literally 'breed', and has no occupational connotation. At the top, and the base of the caste edifice, the functions are clearly defined. The priestly office, whether in temple, home, or serving the needs of a caste-group, can only be performed by a Brahmin. Similarly, the unclean tasks of scavenger, tanner, and leather-worker (unclean because contaminating Mother Cow) will only be discharged by the lowest of all the untouchables. In between, despite claims to ancient precedent, high and low castes will be found in contra-position. For example, the Khatri, claiming descent from the Kshattriya, provides the main element in commerce and trade in Punjab. The Kayasthas of Vaishya origin, by their literary skill, have attained a position as high as that of the more literary Brahmins. Although no one individual can escape from his caste-origin, castes may rise and fall in the hierarchy. Change in social and economic practices will contribute to elevation or depression. Upward movement may be attained by abandonment of degrading occupations; by giving up the consumption of meat, by giving over liquour, and by ceasing to practise widow re-marriage. One branch of the despised Chamars (tanners) abandoned eating flesh and leather-working and took up weaving as their occupation. The new caste, Julaha, was grudgingly admitted within the pale of Hinduism. The status of a caste may vary from region to region. In South India, the Brahmin is supreme; but in Punjab he is little more than a dependent of more prosperous and powerful castes. The Rajput has retained his feudal princely superiority in Rajasthan; but in Punjab and U.P. he is often no more than a yeoman. One who has made a study of caste and politics, Dr. F. G. Bailey, finds 'a high degree of coincidence between politico-economic rank and the ritual ranking of caste'.[1] Where a caste has attained wealth, or administrative importance, it has been able to improve its status, *vis-à-vis* other castes.

The last census to enumerate in full detail the castes and tribes of India was that of 1901: a total of 2,378 castes was listed (castes, not sub-castes); some microscopic, but others running into millions. At the census of 1931, it was calculated that there were approximately 15,000,000 Brahmins and 10,000,000 Rajputs. In most cases the zat as a whole is too large and too scattered to constitute a unit, and caste membership is effectively organised in the *biradari* or *bhaiband*: the brotherhood. The *biradari* may be limited to a village or town, or it may have jurisdiction over a hundred miles of territory. Its executive organ is a panchayat of prominent members, and the *biradari* fulfils functions of social security and welfare for its members, as well as insisting upon conformity to its code of morals and action.

So far we have considered the 'exclusive' aspect of caste: but as Dr. Bailey emphasises, caste is also 'a system of relationships *between* certain groups'. Traditional village India (it was observed earlier) was a nexus of complementary activities. Every village artisan or servant had a circle of clients, usually fixed on a hereditary basis, in a relationship called *jajmani*. The family priest or *purohit* was in a similar *jajmani* relation with his 'parishioners'. The wife of a Chamar would be the midwife for a circle of high caste families. Sometimes *jajmani* would extend far beyond the village—many castes had their family recorders, living far away at Hardwar on the Ganges, or Pryag, where ancestral registers were maintained. Some castes had their hereditary bards, who perpetuated the family saga in song: they too were in *jajmani* relations. The patron-client pattern tied together many relations within and without the village.

The web of caste entwined around the communities formally outside of Hinduism. Many movements which began as revolts against caste ended by merely creating yet another caste; such was the fate of the Lingayats, and the Kabirpanthis; such, even that of the Sikhs, who broke away from Brahmanical Hinduism, but created a miniature caste system within Sikhism. Islam, the brotherhood of equal believers, never accepted restrictions on eating and drinking, but otherwise adopted Hindu customs, if never so straitly. Muslims of high degree known as

[1] F. G. Bailey, *Caste and the Ecomomic Frontier*, Manchester, 1957, Ch. XII, 'The Changing Village'.

ashraf, 'noble' (such as Sayyids, Quraishis, and Shaikhs) would never intermarry with their inferiors, *ajlat*. Even the minute Jewish community of Cochin permitted no intermarriage between its two groups of 'White' and 'Black' Jews!

Economic change and the spread of education brought substantial changes upon caste from about 1860 onwards. Two opposing trends emerged. With improvement in communications, caste became more systematically organised. Caste associations were founded, beginning mainly with mercantile castes (for example, the Chettiars, the Madrassi banking caste) and frequently becoming the instrument whereby humbler *Vaishya* castes sought to enhance their status. At the same time, Western influence was beginning to spread the concept of civil equality, and both Christian missions and the Arya Samaj worked to dissolve the grosser inequalities of caste.

With the beginning of popular representation under Dyarchy, these trends assumed a political form: for the first time, the lower castes perceived they had a weapon to enable them to challenge the supremacy of the higher castes, especially that of the Brahmins. Unrest was particularly strong in the south, where the Brahmins constituted about 3 per cent of the total population yet enjoyed a near-monopoly of posts in government service. A Justice Party was formed to fight Brahmin dominance, and succeeded in becoming the strongest force in Madras, with some success in Bombay also. An even more significant phenomenon was the beginning of political organisation among the untouchables. Even as late as 1910, upper caste politicians were demanding that they should be excluded from the Hindu fold in the census of that year. Dr. Ambedkar, a member of the sweeper community, organised an Independent Labour Party in the 1920s, largely composed of the Bombay untouchables. Later, when they became known under the 1935 Act as 'scheduled castes', the party became the Scheduled Castes Federation. Dr. Ambedkar succeeded in obtaining separate electorates for his people, but thereby ran up against the policy of Gandhi. Should the 50,000,000 or 60,000,000 untouchables become a separate political force, along with 90,000,000 Muslims, also moving towards separatism, the Congress claim to speak for India would be shattered. Gandhi undertook a political fast to bring pressure to bear upon Ambedkar to withdraw his demand. Instead, Gandhi offered to allow the scheduled castes to choose their own candidates at a primary election, prior to putting up for seats specially reserved for them, in which the electorate was composed of Hindus of all castes. As an allurement, Gandhi offered to give the untouchables 148 'reserved' seats, instead of the seventy-eight separate seats to which they were entitled. Ambedkar capitulated: and signed his own political death warrant. There were now vastly more untouchable representatives in the legislatures: but as the Uncle Toms of the Congress. Gandhi also set himself the task of raising the status of the untouchables: he called them *Harijans,* 'children of God', and agitated to gain them entry into the temples from which they had always been rigorously excluded. This campaign is generally regarded as having been a failure.

The Sikhs also became acutely active in a politico-religious rôle in the 1920s. Many Sikh shrines had fallen into the control of Hindu managers or *mahants* who exploited them for profit. A committee, Shiromani Gurdwara Prabandak, took up the task of regaining control of these shrines; organising a militia, the Akalis, to achieve their purpose. The Akalis formed the spearhead of Sikh resistance in the grim days of partition, under the leadership of Master Tara Singh.

With the attainment of independence it became necessary to attempt to reconcile the social conflicts which had been created by Western influences, and the aspirations and tensions within the 'Freedom Movement'. The Western concepts of civil equality, of individual liberty, and individual political choice had to be reconciled with ancient attachments to religion, caste, and family. The unresolved dichotomy between national and regional or local loyalties had to be assimilated.

The Indian Constitution represents a superb effort to comprehend these dilemmas. As Law Minister, Ambedkar was in a strong position to uphold the rights of his own people. He was to claim, after his retirement, that he had been used by Congress as a figurehead: nevertheless, to the extent that any legal document can excise the prejudice and ingrained tradition of centuries, the Indian Constitution does set out to clear away caste repression. Among the Fundamental Rights is included the Right to Equality. This (among much else) prohibits any kind of discrimination against any citizen as, for example, restriction upon access to shops, hotels, or restaurants, or to the use of wells, tanks, or bathing ghats. A further clause (added in 1951) provides that the state may discriminate *in favour* of 'socially and educationally backward classes or for the Scheduled Castes and the Scheduled Tribes'. Another article allows the state to reserve categories of appointments for the 'backward classes', while the Directive Principles provide for the promotion of the educational and economic interests of the 'weaker sections of the people'. Above all, Article 17 states: ' "Untouchability" is abolished and its practice in any form is forbidden. The enforcement of any disability arising out of "Untouchability" shall be an offence punishable in accordance with law.' The precise nature of such offences, and punishment therefor, were spelled out in the Untouchables (Offences) Act of 1955.

There was a certain amount of oblique opposition to these revolutionary measures in the Constituent Assembly; but in general the legislators were in agreement on their desirability. Far different was their reception of the official proposals on language. The non-Hindi speakers mounted a prolonged filibuster to postpone the dreaded decision. According to Dr. Ambedkar, the meeting of the Congress Party which considered the constitutional draft was at first deadlocked over the question, and finally only resolved in favour of Hindi by one vote. At length, into the Constitution went a provision (Article 343) making Hindi the official language: but not the national language. English was to continue as the joint official language, initially for a fifteen years' period. Article 345 provided for the use of Hindi, or of a State language as the official language for State use: the Eighth Schedule enumerated fourteen languages.[1] Article 351 declared: 'It shall be the duty of the Union to promote the spread of the Hindi language, to develop it so that it may serve as a medium of expression for all the elements of the composite culture of India and to secure its enrichment by assimilating ... the forms, style and expressions used in Hindustani and in the other languages of India specified in the Eighth Schedule.' Here was yet another linguistic form to which the Hindi label would be applied: a kind of Indian Esperanto, a syncretic national language.

Congress had been identified again with the Hindi campaign, and both Nehru and Patel stood out as opponents of devolution and decentralisation. The Communists came forward as protagonists of linguistic nationalism. As early as 1942, they had postulated sixteen 'nations' within the sub-continent, and at the time of the constitutional debate, the C.P.I. came out strongly against Hindi as the national language. However, Communist policy now took one of its periodical 'twists and turns' and in 1953 cautiously accepted the use of Hindi as a common language. This did not prevent the C.P.I. exploiting the linguistic issue for all it was worth, notably in the battles within Bombay City between the Maharashtrian and Gujarati interests; the former, mainly allied to the C.P.I., the latter mainly Congress-led.

The struggle for linguistic States was actually decided, as noted earlier, by the fast unto death of Potti Sriramalu in December 1955. Nehru abandoned his attempt to maintain Indian unity by denying lin-

---

[1] Assamese, Bengali, Gujarati, Hindi, Kannada, Kashmiri, Malayalam, Marathi, Oriya, Punjabi, Sanskrit, Tamil, Telugu, Urdu.

guistic claims. The last effort in this direction was a proposal to unite Bihar and West Bengal into one State. Like Curzon's measure it had a basis in administrative rationalisation: but it was bitterly assailed as another aspect of Hindi imperialism. A Commission was appointed to review the entire Indian scene. Its members were Mr. Justice Fazl Ali, Dr. H. N. Kunzru (a veteran northern Congress-man) and Sardar K. M. Panikkar (from the extreme south, a former princely official). Their stated aims were the preservation of national unity, the formation of units based on linguistic and cultural homogeneity, and consideration for the national development plan. The reorganisation was most drastic and complete south of the Vindhya hills. Hyderabad, the premier princely state, disappeared from the map: indeed, the one Indian prince whose state survived in name, though not with its old boundaries, was Mysore. North of the Vindhyas, changes were marginal. Bihar was required to surrender a part of Purnea District to Bengal, thus reversing the previous attempt at a Hindi take-over bid. A minority suggestion (propounded by Panikkar) was to hive off the western districts of U.P., and to combine these with the Hindi-speaking parts of Punjab to form a new State. This suggestion reflects the suspicion with which the mighty Uttar Pradesh is regarded by other States. With a population of some 73,000,000, and a parliamentary bloc of eighty-six out of 449 in the Lok Sabha, U.P. has a determining voice in every decision. The creation of a new major Hindi-speaking State, Madhya Pradesh appeared to extend the Hindi Empire south of the Vindhyas.

The Reorganisation Commission recommended abolition of the distinction between Part A and Part B States (former British, and princely India, respectively). The new States were to enjoy equal powers. The Part C States (small, isolated units), were either absorbed by their neighbours or, as strategically-important areas, were designated Union Territories. The Commission was not able to satisfy all linguistic requirements. In the south, almost all the new States still included linguistic minorities, though on a much smaller scale. Hindi Madhya Pradesh included Dravidian and Marathi minorities. Most of the Commission's recommendations were accepted by the central government and a new pattern of States came into being in 1956. In total number, the States were reduced from twenty-six to fourteen.

The effect of the reorganisation was to give State politics a more intensely regional character: and to make the States a much more important level of power. As we shall see, State politics has become largely caste politics: but before that theme is explored, the linguistic consequences may be examined. The change is well exemplified in Madras where, in 1954, Rajagopalachari handed over the post of Chief Minister to Kamraj Nadar. Rajagopalachari—almost the archetype of the pre-independence political leader; a man of vision, of breadth of experience; a Gladstonian Liberal, whose mind moves in national and international terms. And Nadar—shrewd, competent, a hard bargainer; member of a once-lowly caste which because of its numbers and rising prosperity has become a political force; a veteran member of the Congress Party—and almost unknown outside Madras. Raja-ji, when he approached Nehru, came as an accepted insider. Nadar comes to Delhi as to a foreign city; he is not only outside of Nehru's political circle—he is an entirely different breed of politician. He even speaks to the Prime Minister through an interpreter, his secretary, as he professes to know no Hindi and little English (though this may be a shrewd move to assist him to keep up with the Prime Minister's quick-silver thought-processes). In the Madras Legislature, debates take place in Tamil and in English. There are still Westernised politicians (such as C. Subramaniam) who speak more fluently in English than in their 'native' tongue; at any rate, for political purposes (they like to introduce long quotations from Tamil poetry, to demonstrate their facility in their own language). But there are many more who follow English only with difficulty and who always speak in Tamil. In former days, such men were virtually tied to the back benches, and spent most of their time in silence. Now, they intervene with increasing effect.

The changeover from English to the regional language is going on at differing intensity in different legislatures. Already, in 1956, in Andhra 90 per cent of speeches were in Telugu, and only 10 per cent in English; Uttar Pradesh reported 100 per cent use of Hindi; West Bengal admitted to an equal use of English and Bengali; the Assam legislature heard 90 per cent of speeches in English, and 9.9 per cent in Assamese, with a plaintive .1 per cent in Bengali. Those States which have a bicameral legislature report a much wider use of English in the upper than in the lower house: in Madras for example the proportions were 82 per cent (upper) and 52 per cent (lower) house.[1] The extent to which the State politics are 'local' or 'national' is also quite unequal. West Bengal is highly conscious of its own cultural autonomy, but its politics are largely an extension of the national, party debate. More backward States, such as Rajasthan or Orissa, are almost entirely immersed in local questions revolving around local personalities. Even the

[1] A complete analysis of the use of different languages in all the legislatures is given in *Report of the Official Language Commission, op. cit.* pp. 451-5. However, it relates to States before reorganisation.

State represents a unit too large to have any sway over local loyalties in these backward tracts. For example, a major hydro-electric project, initiated by the central government, the Hirakud Dam, involved inundation of part of Sambalpur District in Orissa. The Sambalpur people were unmoved by any argument that Hirakud would give them cheap electricity, advance the industrialisation of Orissa, and contribute to India's prosperity. They could only see that their lands had been submerged in order that other districts might be spared seasonal flooding: and they signified their resentment by turning against their Congress representatives.

Because of the downward pull of politics today, genuine political issues increasingly give way to the politics of local demands and grievances. India is following the United States rather than modern Britain in a form of politics which revolves around the 'pork barrel', i.e. the ability of local politicians to get their hands upon State funds or services to distribute among their constituents. Because only Congress politicians have access to the 'pork barrel', Congress is assured of automatic adherents, whatever policies it may pursue, for many years to come. The only reply which opposition politicians can contrive is that of 'agitations'. Grievances are exploited, and where none exist (of a promising kind) they are artificially created. The techniques of agitation were thoroughly developed in pre-independence days. The simplest agitation is the public meeting, where inflammatory speeches are made, a petition is promoted, and a long protest procession, with banners and loud-speakers, wends its way through town. Politicians are assisted by the existence of large numbers of unemployed or semi-employed, including many of the educated lower middle class. Small fees will buy the cheer-leaders, and the remainder will follow in the hope of excitement. A more extended operation is picketing: perhaps of some rapacious shopkeeper, or some municipal institution which gives annoyance. Or a landlord's estate may be invaded, and his crops tampered with. In these forms of agitation, the purpose is to court arrest (the old satyagraha technique). The police will be tipped off in advance, but often they are too wily to play the politician's game. Then a little violence becomes necessary (and there are always hooligans, *goondas,* ready to make trouble). When brought to trial, the politician will refuse to plead; if fined, he will elect to go to jail. The whole purpose is to direct attention to himself, and create the image of a martyr, a latter-day John Hampden. The agitation is not, of course, confined to local politics. The archetypal Gandhian civil disobedience campaigns were cleverly designed to combine local and national grievances. Recent successful agitations have included protests against Nehru's supposed conciliatory policy towards China: but the agitations which have stirred up the most turbulence have been those in areas where there is still linguistic and communal dissatisfaction: Bombay, Punjab, and Assam.

The 1956 Reorganisation Commission was baffled by the Bombay problem. They had to find a solution to satisfy two communities, both of which had played leading (and militant) parts in the 'Freedom Movement', the Maharashtrians, and the Gujaratis. The nub of the dilemma was Bombay City. This is a cosmopolitan metropolis, with the proud civic motto *Primus in Indis*. Its population includes all the peoples of India, with the Parsis as by far its most public-spirited citizens. But a majority (including many of the labouring mass) are Marathi-speakers: yet the largest investment in the textile mills and other Bombay industries has been made by Gujaratis. The Commission favoured two alternatives. One was to create two new States for Gujaratis and Maharashtrians, but to exclude Bombay City from either. The city (which has by far the proudest record of civil and municipal activity in India) would then be administered from the centre as a Union Territory. The second alternative (which eventually became the Commission's recommendation) was to maintain Bombay, including the city, as a bi-lingual State. In order that the Marathi-speakers should not command a permanent majority; and also, perhaps, as a sop to the demand for a separate State, those Marathi-speaking districts which were to be hived off the previous hybrid Madhya Pradesh, would become a small Marathi State called Vidarbha. The central government turned down the latter proposal, and from 1956 Bombay became a swollen bi-lingual State. Immediately, a militant agitation began. Neither Gujaratis nor Marathas were at all pleased with the compromise, and there were violent disorders in Bombay City, in Ahmadabad, and even at Delhi. The Congressite Gujaratis backed the central government; but at the price of bitter unpopularity. The Maratha Congress leaders demanded separation: they had no choice, the opposition was capturing municipal and local power under their noses by noisily banging the linguistic drum. At length, in 1960, the central government acquiesced in the inevitable. Bombay was bifurcated, with Bombay City included in the new Maharashtra. Even this solution left open the question of Vidarbha. The city of Nagpur, especially, resented subordination to distant Bombay. Nagpur had been the capital of the old Central Provinces in British days, and local feeling was strong against its decline from eminence. However, for the moment, this question could wait.

Not so, the demand for the bisection of Punjab into separate Punjabi-speaking and Hindi-speaking States. Before 1956, the former Sikh princely states had been combined in a Part B State (PEPSU) now these were merged into one Punjab State of 20,000,000 people. The demand for a Punjabi-speaking State was voiced by the militant Sikh Akali Dal, and was virtually a demand for a Sikh State. Master Tara Singh stated plainly: 'We have adopted the linguistic principle because it suits. We know that a genuinely Punjabi-speaking state will be such that the Sikh religion will be safe in it.' The agitation entered the militant phase in May 1960, with Akali volunteers courting mass arrest. Although the *kirpan,* the Sikh ceremonial sabre, was ritually unsheathed, the Akalis did not give way to the violence of 1947. Some 20,000 went to jail in 1960, but Nehru showed no sign of acceding to their demand. In December, Sant Fateh Singh, a 'religious-political', began a fast unto death in the Golden Temple at Amritsar. Tension mounted, and attempts were made to persuade Nehru to adopt some face-saving formula, and so avoid the perilous situation which had attended the death of Potti Sriramalu. After twenty-two days, the Sant broke his fast. Master Tara Singh had been released from jail, and had met Nehru, but no other very obvious concession had been made. The Sikhs clearly believed they had made some headway, but in the following months, Nehru confined himself to appeals to Hindus and Sikhs within the existing Punjab State to work together in unison. Finally, in August 1961, Master Tara Singh embarked on a fast unto death in the Golden Temple amidst the most dramatic publicity. For forty-seven days bulletins were issued recording the failing condition of the Master. At length, the fast was broken. Some words by the Prime Minister were cited as evidence that discussions would take place. Nehru's Delphic utterances are often capable of alternative interpretations: but on this occasion there really was no confusion. Nehru had not given way, and the Sikhs knew it. The panchayat of Master Tara Singh's biradari met and ordered him to perform certain menial duties, as punishment for having failed in his word. With this defeat, the political fast was exhausted as an effective means of exerting pressure. It had always had undertones of blackmail, and of duplicity; even when sanctified by Gandhi. Except in the case of Sriramalu, it was never clear how far a fast included or excluded fruit juice, or even glucose, taken as 'refreshment' (but, of course, not as 'nourishment'). Despite this grave loss of face, Master Tara Singh continued to be accepted as leader. A three-man Commission was appointed by the Prime Minister in October 1961 to inquire into Sikh grievances, but with no power to recommend constitutional change. With a representation of nineteen for the Akali Dal in the Punjab Assembly elected in 1962 (which totals 154), the Akalis cannot by parliamentary means be more than a nuisance. For the time being, they have reached deadlock.

The year 1960, which saw the linguistic struggle reach a climax in Bombay and Punjab, also saw tension reach breaking-point in Assam. The attention of the outside world has been focused on the long-drawn out guerrilla war of the Nagas to attain some form of 'independence'. But this is mainly a dispute between the Nagas and the central government; as Naga country is classified as a Tribal Area, administered by the Governor of Assam as Agent of the President. But another unhappy minority is the Bengali population of Assam, who live mainly in the Surma Valley. Assam was formerly the hinterland of Bengal, yet now these Bengalis are completely cut off from their 'home' in West Bengal by a solid belt of Pakistan territory. In their isolation, they have attempted to secure recognition from the Assam Government of their separate cultural status. But if the Bengalis despise the Assamese as semi-savages, the Assamese hate and fear the Bengalis as traditional oppressors. Widespread attacks were made on Bengali settlements in the first half of 1960, and 7,000 huts or houses were destroyed. The Government of West Bengal ardently espoused their cause, and the heated inter-State dispute was transferred to the corridors of supreme power, in New Delhi. Despite attempts by the Assam Government to ameliorate the dispute, rioting broke out again, only twelve months after it had been checked; largely because the Bengalis rashly renewed their demand for the recognition of their language by the Government of Assam. The only compromise that offered any hope of peace was the acceptance of English as an interim official language until it was replaced by Hindi. This might be acceptable to the hill peoples who form about one-third of the population of Assam. But this raises again the vexed question of a national language policy.

The promotion of a national language has stirred up two strongly opposed currents of feeling. At the practical level of usage in public life, the central government still employs English for almost all written and printed communication. About 83 per cent of the speeches in the Lok Sabha are delivered in English, with 16 per cent in Hindi, and under 1 per cent in all other languages. In the Rajya Sabha, English is even more widely used. The Hindi-speaking States have actively promoted Hindi throughout public life: thus, in U.P. almost all university teaching is now in Hindi. Outside its homeland, Hindi made some headway in Bombay as an obvious compromise in that bi-lingual State; but since

1960, the trend has been reversed. In other States, the regional languages have been encouraged, but English still has an important rôle in education, administration, and the law courts: indeed, in the former princely areas, English has been gaining ground.

The encouragement of Hindi as a national language, which before independence enjoyed support from leaders like Raja-ji of Madras, and B. G. Kher of Bombay, has now become almost wholly a cult within the Hindi homeland. To these 'Hindi chauvinists', as their enemies term them, the national language will inevitably be Khariboli with the addition of a synthetic, Sanskritic learned vocabulary. The argument involves double-think on the part of the Hindi promoters, and undue suspicion on the part of their opponents. The opponents usually begin by pointing out that other Indian languages, notably the Dravidian group and Bengali, have ancient origins, are much more highly developed, and possess a much richer literature. The Hindi publicists attempt to disarm their opponents by disavowing any claim to cultural superiority: the case rests, they say, simply on the Hindi-speakers forming by far the largest group with a common mother-tongue. By lumping together Hindi, Urdu, Punjabi, Rajasthani, and Bihari, the 1951 Census of India managed to produce a total of 149,000,000 'Hindi-speakers' constituting 46 per cent of total population. But this makes nonsense of the whole argument. As speech, these tongues are undeniably separate and different. The area possesses two common denominators, a debased Hindustani, *bazaar bat,* which is a genuine *lingua franca,* of little value outside the market place; and literary Hindi, Khariboli, understood and used by a small minority among the mass. The language fanatics reject the *lingua franca* form, and press for extension of so-called 'standard Hindi', i.e. Sanskritised Khariboli. The opponents counter by insisting that this Hindi is still inferior as a literary form to older tongues, and by pointing out that this is a thinly disguised attempt to pass off a regional language as the national language: Hindi has a Jekyll and Hyde quality, as one southerner termed it. The Official Language Commission, which reported in 1956, comprised four members from western India, three from the south, three from eastern India, and the remainder from the Hindi orbit, or *Hindi Sansar.* Three of the non-Hindi speakers insisted on appending notes of dissent, and the Commission did little more than traverse well-worn ground. The 'moderates' in this controversy have, more and more, taken their stand on an insistence that English must continue, for many years to come, to take its place alongside Hindi, as a nation-wide, if not national language. A Three Language policy (English, Hindi, and the regional language) has been laid down for secondary schools throughout the country. Meanwhile, the south has become morbidly averse to Hindi (Dr. P. Subbarayan told the Language Commission: 'There is a feeling among some of the Tamil people that English is easier to understand than Hindi') and three political parties have emerged which openly advocate the formation of a separate Tamil state, independent of the rest of India. The largest of these parties, Dravida Munnetra Kazhagam, succeeded in winning fifty seats in the Madras Assembly elected in 1962: one quarter of the total. Perhaps this portent will do something to make the north understand that a national language imposed by one region is a source not of unity but of disunity.

The course of events in Pakistan has been very similar. As we have seen, the demand for a separate Muslim national state was partly to protect Muslim, that is Urdu and Persian culture. Urdu is like Hindi in having a dual quality: as an elegant, literary language, and as a *lingua franca*. It differs, in not being a regional language. Whereas the speech of 56 per cent of the Pakistan population is Bengali, and that of 29 per cent, Punjabi; only 7 per cent are classed as Urdu-speakers—and these are mainly refugees from India. While Urdu is widely spoken in the Western wing as a second, polite language by townsfolk, and the middle and upper class—and is also the means of communication in the army (mainly recruited from the West)—in the East it has no real place. Educated Bengalis fall mainly into two categories; the English-speaking Western-educated, and the orthodox religious, whose second language is Arabic. Only a very small Bengali group possess any feeling for Urdu: the great landowners, among whom the second Prime Minister, Nazimuddin, is pre-eminent. Speaking at Dacca in February 1952, Nazimuddin announced that Urdu would be adopted as the state language of Pakistan. Thereby, he lost the confidence of the Bengali politicians (removing his only political backing) and he brought to a head the discontent which had been brewing in East Bengal at its neglect by the central government, and at the arbitrary treatment of its administrators, mainly Punjabis. Almost immediately, language riots flared up, and in October 1953 a mass meeting at Dacca passed resolutions demanding autonomy for East Bengal, and Bengali as the state language. Over in Karachi, a mob rioted in March 1954 against the admission of Bengali as an official language. In the same month, came the total defeat of the League in the Bengal elections, with language as a major cause of their *débâcle*. Two months later, in May, the Constituent Assembly recognised that a majority of the citizens of Pakistan could not be expected to see their language overruled: both Bengali and Urdu were recognised as the national languages.[1] This became a provision of the 1956 constitution, and it has been embodied in its successor of 1962. All probationers for the Civil Service of Pakistan are required to pass an examination in whichever of the two national languages is not their own tongue. However, the constitution also recognised the continued use of English as the language of government; this, also, is perpetuated by the 1962 Constitution, which ordains that the use of English in administration will be reviewed in 1972.

A secondary cause of linguistic unrest was the formation of the 'one unit' for West Pakistan in 1955. By this measure, Lahore became the centre of government and of the High Court for all the West; apart from the tribal area of the North-West Frontier and Baluchistan; and certain tiny Frontier princely states. This appeared to confirm the predominance of the Punjabis, which had already been a grievance with Sindhis, Baluchis, and, above all, the Pathans. The Pathans have, perhaps more than any other people in the world, a fierce spirit of independence. Their national poet, Khushal Khan Khattak (1613-87) writes equally ardently of love, and of resisting the Mughal Emperor. There are approximately 10,000,000 speakers of Pashtu and its 'brother tongue' Pakhtu. Of these, less than one-quarter live in the regularly administered districts along the Indus, within Pakistan proper. The remainder live in a tribal society under their chiefs or *maliks*. These tribes: Afridis, Mohmands, Khattaks, Mahsuds, and the rest, acknowledge the right of no man to intervene in their affairs: but in 1893, an imaginary frontier, the 'Durand Line', was traced across their barren hills, to determine the respective sovereignty of the British Raj and of the Amir of Afghanistan. When British rule ended, Afghanistan refused to recognise the validity of the Durand Line in the new situation, and claimed that all the lands to the west of the Indus were Pathan. This area was termed, by the Afghan Government, 'Pakhtoonistan'; and a propaganda campaign was launched to stir up the tribes to fight for Pakhtoonistan. To this claim (which still continues to be asserted) India gave covert recognition and assistance. Pakhtoonistan, as represented on propaganda maps, stretches from the Indus to the Durand Line: but approximately half the Pashtu and Pakhtu speakers live beyond the Line, within Afghanistan. Nothing whatever is said about autonomy for them. Altogether, this is a thinly-disguised attempt by Afghanistan to seize Pakistan territory, and certainly cannot be taken at its face value.

[1] According to the 1961 Census, the population of East Pakistan is 50,844,000; and of West Pakistan, 40,814,000, to which must be added the central district of Karachi with 2,153,000.

However, the Pakistan Government cannot ignore the threat: the Pathans have to be given solid evidence that their citizenship pays off. After 1955, their own province, the North-West Frontier Province, no longer existed; and there might be a violent reaction to any assertion of the authority of Lahore, rule by the despised Punjabis.[1] And so, compensation was offered. The Warsak Dam has been built, to bring new economic opportunity to the Frontier. The University of Peshawar has been elaborately expanded, and Pathans brought in to fill its higher posts, so as to create an athenæum of modernist Pathan culture. The Ministry for the Tribal Areas has its offices at Peshawar, and the Minister is on the spot. Other Pakistanis will say that the efforts to mollify the Pathans have been grossly overdone: today, they say, in Pakistan there is Pathan Raj. And it is true that the President, the Governor of East Bengal (General Azam Khan) and the Commander-in-Chief (General Muhammad Musa) are, all three, Pathans.

The politics of language and region, then, has formed a powerful, and mainly divisive influence in Pakistan. The main reason why President Ayub preferred a unitary to a federal constitution was to eliminate regional feeling. Pakistan has not yet experienced the politics of caste or localism. While caste is nothing like so pervasive as in India, it is not entirely absent. Even in the villages of western Punjab and Sind, there is an occupational or functional caste hierarchy. The village community is divided between the *zamindars* or cultivators, and the *kammis* or craftsmen and labourers; the jajmani system also operates, being known in Punjab as *seypi*. About one-quarter of the population of East Pakistan belong to the Hindu minority, of whom over 50 per cent are members of the Scheduled Castes. The upper Hindu castes are mainly Brahmins, Kayasthas, and Baidyas (physicians).[2] The Bengali Muslims are also divided into functional groups; cultivators, for the most part, with weavers, fishermen, boatmen, and artisans. There are other marks of difference; for example, the people of Chittagong have an Arab strain in their blood, and the people of Noakhali District are ultra-orthodox Muslims, and look with suspicion on outsiders. Pakistan went as far as

[1] The author travelled through the mountains beyond the Malakand Pass in February 1958 (the setting of Winston Churchill's first literary masterpiece) and for some distance he was accompanied by a Punjabi official. Returning, a week later, a Pathan tribesman asked: 'Where is that black man?' The complexion of the Punjabi was approximately as black as that of the present writer.

[2] 'The Brahmin priest has fallen on very evil days; formerly he lived in comfort in the odour of sanctity, now he struggles along in an atmosphere which is little removed from contempt'. This illustration of the wealth-caste-status equation comes from *The Economic Life of a Bengal District*, by J. C. Jack, Oxford University Press, 1916, p. 90.

India in its 1956 Constitution in incorporating provisions to end 'man's tyranny to man'. The Fundamental Rights included safeguards against 'discrimination'; untouchability was abolished, and also, slavery and forced labour were prohibited. Special provisions were made to promote the advancement of the Scheduled Castes. Unhappily, the imposition of separate electorates, in the face of Hindu protest, appeared to be creating a class of *dhimmis* or second-class citizens in Pakistan, while the Islamic provisions, ensuring that 'No law shall be enacted which is repugnant to the Injunctions of Islam', might impinge on the rights and customs of non-Muslims.

Caste-ism, or communalism did not have direct repercussions in party politics, except in East Bengal where the Hindus were divided in their allegiance: some to the surviving rump of Congress, some to a branch of Ambedkar's Scheduled Castes Federation. In general, politics remained an upper-class affair, within the circle of the landlord and lawyer politicians. Perhaps the institution of the Basic Democracies (discussed in detail in Chapter IX) will uncover some basic political influences.

Meanwhile, as the 1960s are unrolled, the politics of caste provides the substratum of State politics throughout the greater part of India.

Caste politics is of maximum intensity south of the Vindhya mountains. The first post-independence phase saw a struggle to dispossess the Brahmin of power and position; that phase is now almost ended, and a struggle between the newly-dominant 'middle' castes and the submerged mass of lower castes and untouchables is only just begun. The basis of politics, right up to 1952, was manipulation. Power was based on prestige, on familiarity with the working of the administrative machine and ability to reach the key officials. These qualities were the prerogative of the Westernised, upper caste politicians. After 1952, the basis of political power changed to numerical strength. It was still necessary to organise, to 'deliver' the vote; the element of manipulation was still vital; but only as a first step. The mass vote must be won over, and this can best be obtained by winning the block vote of a large caste (what Dr. Bailey calls a 'vote bank'). Occasionally, a caste turns itself into a political party; and sometimes a caste, following its leaders, climbs deliberately on to one particular bandwagon; but more often caste and politics enter into *ad hoc* relations, rather like old-fashioned Hollywood marriages.

For a caste to become a significant factor in politics, the first essential is the expansion of the caste association. The resources of organisation and welfare services deployed by a flourishing caste sabha may be compared, say, to those of the Freemasons. The Chitrapur Saraswat Brahmins of Bombay issue their own caste census and directory, which lists twenty-two caste educational institutions, thirteen fraternal and social agencies, and twelve housing co-operatives: all for a community of 19,000 persons. The present-day 'total' caste association has become very Westernised in form. Membership does not follow automatically from heredity; joining the association is like joining the Automobile Association, a deliberate action, involving the payment of regular dues. The offices of President, Secretary, and Committee are defined in Western terms, quite unlike the ancient, indigenous organisation of the biradari. If the caste belongs to the Haves, its political activities may be discreet and indirect; but a Have Not caste will usually rate the political impact as the first of its priorities.

A few exceptionally well-organised caste associations have launched their own parties. In Madras, the Vanniyars (agriculturalists) formed the Tamilnad Toilers' Party in 1951, while another branch of the caste rallied to the Commonwealth Party. Both managed to win seats in the Madras Assembly, and by skilfully exploiting their ability to secure a Congress majority, they obtained two posts in the Cabinet. Having demonstrated the power of the Vanniyar caste, they agreed to merge their parties into the Congress.[1] The Adibasis, or tribal people of the Bihar-Orissa border, have organised their own Jharkhand Party, which has been able to capture many of the seats 'reserved' for the tribes in the area. More often, a caste association will climb onto an existing bandwagon. The Lingayats put their caste resources behind the demand for a separate Kannada-speaking State, in which they would form the largest group, about 20 per cent of the Kannada people. Although they were content to adopt the Congress platform, they are in a position to demand full representation, including a permanent lien on the post of Chief Minister of Mysore State. It is unusual for one caste to dominate State politics; more often, the largest castes can only function as one factor among many. In Rajasthan, the Jats form about 9 per cent of total population, with the Rajputs numbering 6 per cent. Both castes have struggled to control the State Congress organisation, the Jats supporting Sukhadia, the Chief Minister, and the Rajputs forming a dissident group, rallying behind a former Rajput Chief Minister. One state where politics can be nearly equated with the rivalry of two great castes is Andhra. Before the days of universal suffrage, the Congress Party in Andhra was Brahmin-dominated. A caste of wealthy landowners, the Kammas, began to produce Western-educated leaders in the 1930s

[1] See L. I. and S. H. Rudolph, 'The Political Role of India's Caste Associations', *Pacific Affairs*, March 1960.

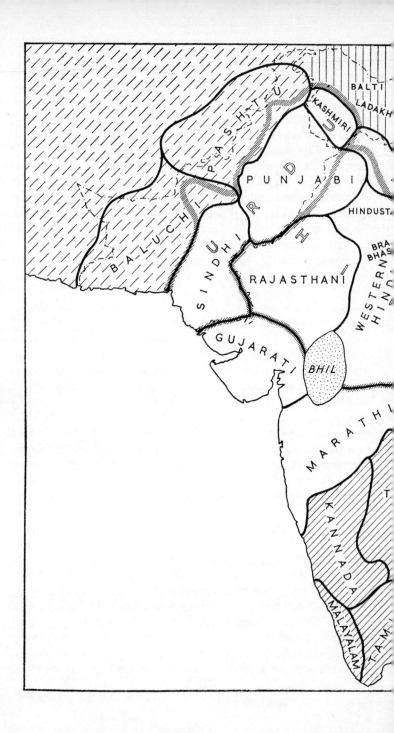

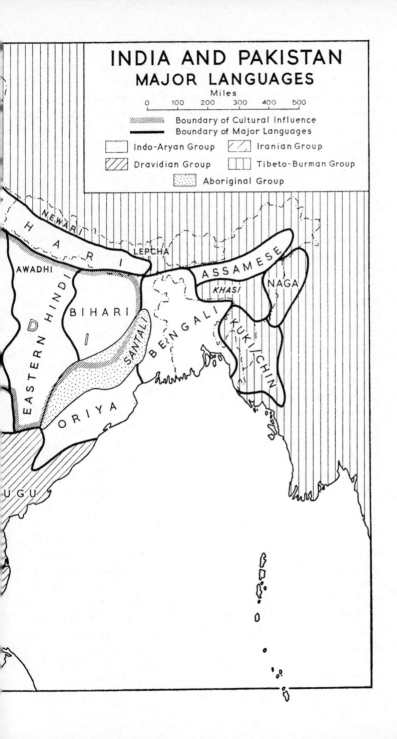

INDIA AND PAKISTAN
MAJOR LANGUAGES

Miles

0   100   200   300   400   500

////// Boundary of Cultural Influence
——— Boundary of Major Languages

☐ Indo-Aryan Group   /// Iranian Group
/// Dravidian Group   ☐ Tibeto-Burman Group
⋮⋮⋮ Aboriginal Group

NEWARI

LEPCHA

ASSAMESE

NAGA

AWADHI

HARI

KHASI

EASTERN HINDI

BIHARI

SANTALI

BENGALI

KUKI CHIN

ORIYA

D

UGU

who, in the face of the Brahmin control of Congress, joined anti-Brahmin parties, like the Justice Party, and in due course turned to Communism. As we have seen, in its militant phase, the C.P.I. was compelled to issue special directives to take care of its Kamma landlord supporters. The other great landowning 'middle' caste was that of the Reddis, whose emergence into political literacy came later. Their main political objective was to get even with the Kammas, and so they joined Congress; first as junior partners with the Brahmins, and then as their supplanters. However, in the 1955 election, when Congress was fighting back, after the Communists had scored on the language issue, it was decided that the caste game must be played with even greater finesse. The coastal, delta region was Kamma territory; the uplands were held largely by Reddis. Congress held off until the C.P.I. had filed its list, and then, candidate for candidate, it matched the C.P.I. slate with a Congress slate of opponents belonging to identical castes. That way, with superior organisation and funds, Congress could successfully trade upon caste loyalties everywhere. When Telengana was joined to Andhra in 1956, this brought such an accession of Reddi territory that they were ensured of an almost permanent majority, Sanjiva Reddy was elected president of the all-India Congress Party, not for his gifts of intellect or leadership but as undisputed boss of the Reddis.

Caste operates, not only on this total basis of the zat, but also on the local basis of the biradari. If the biradari is widely entrenched in a constituency, then a party may decide to run one of their caste for office. The opponents will probably try to reply by organising an alliance of the smaller castes against their more numerous neighbours. But often the bid made by a candidate for the block support of a biradari will be made on jajmani terms: he will attempt to enter into a contractual relationship based on mutual interests. In return for the vote, he will promise a school, or jobs in the public service, or some other reward.

Traditional, quasi-ritualistic ties may stretch even higher. One constituency in Madhya Pradesh is the pocket borough of a former raja: any candidate from any party that he chooses to nominate will be elected. The efforts of the Congress State Government to tarnish the prestige of the prince in the eyes of his people only appear to have cemented his hold over their loyalties still more securely. The Ganatantra Party in Orissa has built itself up as a challenge to the State Congress Party almost entirely by drawing upon the traditional sense of relationship between the former local rulers and their people.

The general effect of caste politics is to transfer power to the big battalions: and as the low castes are often the largest, political power has been shifting. Under the constitution, the Scheduled Castes and Tribes are given definite quotas: in educational institutions, and in public employment. This has led to a clamour from many other castes to be classified as 'backward', and so enjoy special consideration. A commission appointed to attempt to make an objective assessment of 'backwardness' ended up by listing 2,399 communities whose claim has been admitted. These represent over 120,000,000 people, to which the 70,000,000 Scheduled Castes and Tribes must be added. Clearly, it will not be possible to give special assistance to about one-quarter of the people of India.

In the south, the demand grows for posts in the public services to be awarded in proportion to population. This means that, in an open competition, the first sixty places may be taken by Brahmin candidates, of whom none can expect to be selected; forming only 3 per cent of total population, they are thrust aside to give places to members of the populous castes. Everywhere in the south, the Brahmins are abandoning the public services and the liberal professions and turning to commerce and industry.

The beneficiaries of the Brahmin eclipse have been the 'middle' castes who now control politics, and to an increasing extent, the public services. But the pressure of numbers will, in the end, compel them to share power with the lowly. An electoral reform, the abolition of double-member constituencies, has had the effect of increasing the representation of the Scheduled Castes. Andhra, which has already proved to be a bellweather in State politics (first seeing the rise of the Communists, then the victory of linguism, and then the capture of the parties by the 'middle' castes) may now be about to see the seizure of power by the Harijans. When Sanjiva Reddy went off as Congress President, he handed the State premiership over to a Harijan, Mr. Sanjiviya: firmly believing that this was the best means to prevent a rival taking over in his absence. Sanjiviya did not intend to be *roi fainéant*. He consolidated a following; organising the Scheduled Castes and other backward classes. When Mr. Reddy came back to take up the premiership, he refused to give way. In the struggle which followed, both sides fought to gain control of the State Congress and to nominate their own men for the party ticket. Despite attempts to unseat him, Sanjiviya was re-elected in 1962, and the struggle for power goes on. This internal struggle cost the Congress dearly; their strength in the Assembly before the election was 232; afterwards it was only 142. This setback will compel Congress in Andhra to give more attention to the claims of the underprivileged.

Timely recognition of the probable change in the balance of power in caste politics was given in the election of a new president of the Congress Party, early in June 1962. The All-India Congress Committee selected as successor to Sanjiva Reddy, the middle caste boss, D. Sanjiviya, the Harijan leader. It is by such strokes of political good sense that Congress demonstrates its continuing vitality and disarms rivals for its leadership.

Inevitably, State politics will be caste politics throughout most of India for many years to come. Even in West Bengal, where politics has more of an ideological tinge, and where caste has largely lost its hold, it was considered necessary in the 1962 elections to select candidates for caste or communal reasons. Under these conditions, is democracy, according to accepted definitions, possible? Even a brief acquaintance with— let us say—the politics of New York State will demonstrate that there is nothing unique about the present situation in India. For the foreseeable future, no Indian politician or party will be able to ignore caste; while the politics of language will inevitably create divisions between State and State, and State and centre. Indian politics will never be like British (or should one say, here, English) politics. But perhaps, in the future, it may produce many similarities to politics in Canada and the United States.

VII

THE PUBLIC SERVICES

JUST as Montesquieu's concept of the three branches of government (Executive, Legislative, and Judiciary) has largely shaped modern western European notions of government (especially in the United States) so, traditionally, government in south Asia was conceived as possessing three arms: criminal justice (law and order), the treasury (responsible for assessment and collection of revenue) and the army—upon which Imperial power finally depended. This triune system, brought to its height by the Mughals, outweighed English influence, with its emphasis upon the subordination of the military to the civil power. This was because the army was, and is, a living institution, within the experience of an important section of the community; whereas civil government has remained a power apart, something to be shunned; while Western innovations like parliament, or even the English-style legal system, are accepted and understood by few outside the middle classes.

The Royal Navy enjoys a unique place in the affections and the folk culture of the British people; yet one cannot compare its actual significance in the social and economic pattern, with that of the old Indian Army in the north-western provinces of the old India.

Enlistment in the army opened the way towards gaining two of the rewards most highly prized in life's lottery: honour, and land. All the attributes summed up in the oft-used word *izzat*—honour, esteem, status —are highly valued. Caste, and face are involved. Face means holding one's head high in personal and public relations—giving a grand entertainment for the marriage of one's daughter, being offered a seat by the magistrate, are two obvious aspects of face. Military service provided an escalator to honour. In the Hindu scale, the warrior, kshattriya, was second only to the Brahmin (and a very good second too). The British adaptation of caste recognised the same scale of value. If promotion had come, and the pensioner retired as Honorary Captain or Lieutenant, then he was reckoned one of the big men of the district. But even if he retired as a simple soldier, on high days he could put on the white cloth, *safed posh*, of respect, with his medals on his chest; and no British official would pass him by without a man-to-man salute. But honour was not just outward show. Honour was self-respect. The villages of the north-west all have their memorials, erected after the first World War; and the roll call of the dead, in many a village, is as long as that carved on the cenotaph of an English market town. These men had stood vigil on the Frontier, had shed their blood in Mesopotamia and Flanders. They had eaten the salt of the British Government, and they had kept faith. Those who came back did not hold their heads high just for a title or a medal. And their deeds were honoured by their village brothers.

The boy from the plough-tail enlisted, then, for honour; but he also hoped that service might lead to land. In south Asia, land has the same symbolic importance that formerly it had in France. Land means a firm hold on the real; stability, continuity, a future for one's family. The ancient reward for loyal military service was the *jagir*, the land-grant; and the British took this idea over with so much else. During the late nineteenth century, the arid wastes which spread, desolate, between the Five Rivers of Punjab were gradually opened up, by what became the biggest irrigation scheme in the world. After the first World War, many old soldiers were given grants in these canal colonies: some of the best land in India. Army service, dignity, and economic reward marched together. The military families had a major stake in the land, and were conscious of their duties and privileges, as leaders and shapers of public opinion. The British system of recruitment followed the caste concept and concentrated on the 'martial races'. This narrowed the field of military service to the north-west, roughly between Peshawar and Delhi.[1] Here, the army was the community. The writer recalls the villages of Jhelum District during the second World War: only the old men and the boys remained: all between sixteen and sixty were away in Egypt, in Italy, in Burma. This spirit breathes in the sentiments of the Punjab Premier, Sikander Hyat Khan (himself the first Indian to receive the

[1] Before 1939, the sources of recruitment for the Indian Army were as follows: Punjab, 54 per cent; Nepal (Gurkhas), 12 per cent; United Provinces (mainly western districts), 11 per cent. Other provinces making important contributions were, in descending order, Bombay (Marathas), Rajput states, Kashmir (Poonch Muslims), North-West Frontier, Madras (mainly Sappers). Bengal, with 50,000,000 population, contributed none.

King's Commission) speaking to the representatives of all communities in the provincial legislature:

> Punjab provides the bulk of the Indian Army—our proportion in the peace-time strength is about 52 per cent; our war-time contribution is even higher (*cheers*). Why? Because from time immemorial we have had to bear the brunt of attacks by invaders from the north-west and have a long and glorious tradition as clean and stout fighters (*hear, hear*). We are the natural custodians of India and have proved our worth on the battlefields at home and abroad and have thus acquired the proud distinction and title of being known as 'the sword arm of India' (*cheers*).

Let us look again at the three arms of Mughal Government, and what became of them under British rule. The first arm, criminal justice, had in Mughal times been a Muslim preserve; under the British, the legal system had very largely been taken over by Hindus; Brahmins and Kayasthas. The treasury had been largely Hindu under the Mughals, and Hindu it remained. The Mughal army had been mainly Muslim, with Hindu martial elements, such as Rajputs and Jats; and whereas the Muslims had nearly lost one arm of government to the Hindus, they had retained their strength in the army. Right into the twentieth century, the Muslims formed half the strength of the army. As the remainder included Sikhs, Gurkhas, and southern Christians, it will be seen that Muslims were a more important component than Hindus. After the belated bestowal of King's Commissions upon Indians (in 1918) Muslims secured a fair proportion of places, and held their own in advancement to senior rank.

The lawyers and landlords of the Muslim League seldom mentioned the army, but deep down, they recognised that here was the biggest guarantee of Muslim rights against Congress-Hindu domination. The Congress constantly attacked military expenditure, and demanded the reduction of the army. They also called for an end to enlistment of the 'martial races' only, and the formation of a genuinely national army, recruited on an overall basis. In the late 1930s, the Muslims saw Hindu plots everywhere, and they suspected that these were further examples of Congress determination to reduce the Muslims to hewers of wood and drawers of water.

During the enormous expansion of the Indian Army in the second World War, the Muslims retained their proportionate strength: large numbers of Bengali Muslims were enlisted for the first time in motor transport, as well as in the new Indian Navy. Jinnah was able to demand and obtain parity for the Muslim League with Congress largely because the Muslims actually enjoyed parity in the wartime army.

The partition entailed partition of the Indian Army. Almost all units had been formed on a 'class' basis: a typical infantry battalion would contain two companies of Punjabi Muslims, a Sikh company, and a Hindu company (Rajputs, Jats, or Dogras). These class units had now to be laboriously taken apart and rebuilt anew. The old regiments possessed a family character, son followed father, and also the different religious affiliations represented in the unit were tempered by long association and a common regimental loyalty. The new armies of India and Pakistan could not preserve this unique loyalty which transcended religion, but they did perpetuate the old regimental spirit as far as possible. There was a direct continuity between the regiments founded by British officers a 100 years ago or more, and the new formations of the new armies. The raising of Skinner's Horse, the 'Yellow Boys', took place in 1803; 160 years later, it not only flourishes, but is commanded by the great-great grandson of the eponymous founder. This is only the most extraordinary example of the continuity between past and present which persists in both these armies. It is worth underlining, because the regiments of India and Pakistan still preserve values and traditions which are unique: they form a distinct element in the national life.

It was not, perhaps, surprising that the first leaders of Pakistan, whose outlook was conventional and conservative, should have been glad to retain a great tradition at a time when so much was in ferment. But it is somewhat astonishing that the Congress politicians should have likewise acquiesced in conserving a tradition which was to them anti-pathetic. The new Indian Army is still organised upon a regimental system which enshrines the model of caste in the 'martial races'. Among the infantry we find the Mahratta Light Infantry, the Rajput Regiment, the Dogra Regiment, the Mahar Regiment, the Sikh Regiment, and the Sikh Light Infantry: all based upon caste. Be it noted, the Sikh Regiment recruits Jat Sikhs of the yeoman caste, and the Sikh Light Infantry enlists Mazbi Sikhs who are by origin untouchables. In British times, the Gurkha Rifle regiments were cited as the worst example of colonialism, being composed of mercenaries (like the Hessians whom the British employed in the American War of Independence). But Congress readily took over the task of paymaster to the Gurkhas, with everything else.

The continuing dominance of the 'martial races' produces political repercussions of a communal or sectional character. In Pakistan, by far the largest element in the army comes from Punjab; and Punjabi domineering is a standing grievance among their fellows. In order to mollify the unruly frontier Pathans, they have been given generous opportunities for service in the army, and in the quasi-military Scouts and Militia which guard the Frontier. The Pathans also are alleged to have acquired altogether too much power in national life. By contrast, the Bengalis only have a meagre opportunity for service in the East Pakistan Rifles, and they are sensitive about their underprivileged and exposed position.

Among the military castes in India today, the most obvious political problem is posed by the Sikhs. The Sikhs lost some of their richest agricultural land by partition, and have nourished a sense of grievance ever since. They would dearly like to take another crack at Pakistan, and their tough bellicosity has been channelled into army service. Their sense of grievance and isolation has led to the demand for a Punjabi-speaking Sikh state. So long as the Sikh forces are occupied on field service, they may be content to leave politics alone. But if they are ever left to brood in cantonments, they may serve as the spearhead of a Sikh rising.[1] None of the other martial groups has nourished separatist political grievances (except, perhaps, the Marathas) but, by default, the south is conscious of the effects of the present concentration of recruitment north of the Vindhya mountains. Like the Bengalis, in comparison to their numbers, their share in military service is distinctly inadequate. Some south Indian political parties have made this an issue.

However, it would be misleading to over-emphasise the rôle of the army in underlining fissiparous tendencies in either country. The main influence is towards a sense of nationhood. The old Indian Army was the only truly supra-communal institution in the old India, and the only institution of government established in the regard of the people. The new armies, even more forcibly, symbolise the nation. We have noted how the Muslims regarded the army as 'theirs'; and fear of the consequences of Congress reprisals against 'their' army was a contributory cause of the demand for separation. When Pakistan came into being, the army was its main guarantor. Only the army, it was believed, stood between the new nation and reabsorption by Hindu India. In the Kashmir struggle, the army salvaged something out of an operation that had been bungled by religious fanatics: and the only hope of winning back Kashmir one day from Hindu occupation lies in the army.

The army also serves as the instrument of the national purpose of the

---

[1] Sikh units had a deplorable record of discontent and mutiny in the old Indian Army: they never mutinied in the face of danger, but always in the boredom of inactivity.

new India; particularly in the field of national consolidation. India has only realised its 'rightful' limits by virtue of the army. Kashmir, Hyderabad, Junagadh, Goa: all these were reclaimed by the army. In each instance, India's claim was dubious at law and morally none too salubrious. In each instance it was the achievement of the army to mount such a rapid, cleanly-executed operation that adverse world opinion had no opportunity to challenge the action. (Speed is the essence of machiavellian politics in this age: Suez was a blunder from any point of view, but even at the machiavellian level it was maladroit to enter an operation in which, necessarily, execution had to be delayed for over a week after declaration of intention.) Indian policy may have had its odious aspects. It has also had its feats of high idealism, and it has been the army's privilege to make effective the Indian vision of international co-operation: in the exchange of prisoners in Korea, the supervision of a cease-fire in Indo-China, the policing of the Gaza strip, the Congo operation, the Indian Army has made it possible to implement noble intentions.

The character of both armies is still extraordinarily similar to that of the old Indian Army. In the Pakistan Army, Islam is a question of private conscience; it obtrudes into military matters hardly at all. In the new Indian Army, neither Gandhian precepts, nor modernist ideologies have had more than a faint influence. The ranks are still recruited from the sturdy peasantry: few come from the towns, and there is still a living connexion between regiment and countryside. Both armies still include in the chain of command those ranks formerly called Viceroy's Commissioned Officers, now Junior Commissioned Officers—veterans, selected from the ranks, to carry out duties discharged in the British Army by subalterns. Their long service and weight of experience entitles them to respect, even from senior officers. They serve as a cement, knitting together the regimental structure; and being conservative, rural in origin, isolated from the changing world, they play a large part in perpetuating the traditional flavour of the service. The officers still take their tone from the handful of Sandhurst-trained Generals who remain. The Indian Military Academy at Dehra Dun took over the whole circus of Sandhurst tradition, and so did its Pakistan counterpart at Kakul. Most of the young officers who have joined the service since independence still appear to accept the code: one which has much to offer them. In between these juniors, Captains and Lieutenants, and the seniors, the Colonels and Brigadiers, there is the strata which entered the army in wartime. Among them are some who are radical, dissatisfied with the conventional; but they are not, as yet, influential.

Both armies are conservative in outlook, yet both embody aspects of modernity. First, there is the increasingly technological milieu of the modern army; all, officers and men, have to handle technical equipment, and therefore, partly at any rate, can enter the world of the scientist and engineer. Both armies have carried on the methods of organisation, operational planning, and general efficiency upon which their British commanders set such store. Know-how, and the ability to deliver the goods: these proven military qualities, together with morale, and *élan* add up to something quite formidable. The image of the army in the public mind is of a reserve of discipline, efficiency, and resource; available to put things right, when politicians or officials have blundered. The cautious military outlook militates against the army assuming a revolutionary rôle: when the army intervened in Pakistan, it did so with genuine reluctance, and only in the interest of order. Intervention may be said to have been cumulative. The first important occasion was at Lahore, in 1953; when politicians, officials, and police had lost their heads, the army brought the city back from anarchy into order within a few hours. The next occasion, wider in its context, came in 1954, when General Iskander Mirza had to be appointed military governor of East Pakistan after the politicians had again, by irresponsibility and incompetence, produced misrule. The take-over of 1958, against this sequence, appears as only the largest of what in British-Indian military terminology were called 'operations in aid of the civil power'.

It is worth recalling that, through most of the area of West Pakistan, during the British period, it had been normal practice to appoint army officers to serve in the regular district administration alongside the civil servants, so that the admixture of a military element in government did not come as an innovation. These 'military civilians' were also employed during the nineteenth century in the Central Provinces (as in Burma) but the practice was unknown elsewhere.

Altogether, the military tradition is weak outside the north-west. From Delhi, north to Peshawar, and west to Quetta, almost every civil district headquarters is flanked by a military cantonment. Elsewhere there were dozens of districts containing millions of inhabitants with not one single soldier among them. This contrast should be remembered when the possibility of greater military participation in India's public life is canvassed. The British serving military officer's aloofness from politics and politicians is paralleled in India: but so it was in Pakistan, down to 1958. The possibility of military intervention could not be ruled out, if public order ever seriously degenerated, or if India was confronted by a grave external threat which was pusillanimously met by the politicians.

Military governments in Hyderabad and Goa were of short duration; but in Kashmir the army remains the real power behind the State administration. The cry of Indian publicists, 'It can't happen here,' has a shrill note: they know it could and might happen.

If the army has loomed large in the national life (absorbing 75 per cent of the budget of Pakistan, and 60 per cent of India's budget), to the ordinary citizen the civil service has continued to represent 'the government'. The humble man often still addresses a civil servant as *Sirkar* (ruler) or *Hakim* (lawgiver). The government, personified in the official, is the source of all things. It is the fount of blessings, so that British rule was often called *Mai-Bap,* or Mother-Father rule. It is also the origin of unaccountable pains and penalties, so that an old Punjabi proverb advises 'Never stand behind a horse or in front of an official'.

The ordinary public continues to regard the whole array of officialdom as alien, outside their control; but they are also very conscious that officialdom is a soaring pyramid. The administrative hierarchy, as it was perfected in the latter days of British rule, possessed a refinement of calculated gradation: it embodied both the Hindu caste system and the English class system. A comparison is often made with the Chinese mandarin order, and in general this is apt; but while the Imperial mandarinate was a *carrière ouverte aux talents* in which the brilliant village lad, just occasionally, might by infinite exertion make his way *via* an examination ladder to the administrative summit, the heights of British-Indian administration were open only to a very restricted type of talent.

The stratification of the administration was completed, in the form which persists to the present day, about the end of the nineteenth century. Its genii might be described as the Emperor Akbar, Lord Cornwallis, Macaulay, Arnold of Rugby, and Jowett of Balliol. Akbar developed the *mansabdari* system; a class of Imperial officials, set apart, commissioned to govern. Cornwallis as Governor-General (1786-93), laid down that high administration must be entrusted only to a special cadre of British officials, and framed regulations whereby senior posts in India could only be held by these 'Covenanted' officials. Macaulay helped to ensure that at the upper levels of public life in India, communication should all be in English; he further insisted that entry into the higher Indian services should be through competitive examination, based on the Arts studies of Oxford and Cambridge. Arnold, of course, contributed largely to the nineteenth-century middle-class preoccupation with life as a 'competition of character', to be won by the application of certain rigid moral and intellectual standards. Jowett completed this ethos by encouraging the notion that the keenest intellects of Oxford could find their richest reward in serving the state. Thus was the apex of the pyramid chiselled and polished, and it was to this apex that British thinking was chiefly directed. Indians, in general, were mainly concerned with the base.

At the bottom were the patwaris, the village accountants, and the clerks in the district offices; these might hope for modest promotion, but in general these jobs led nowhere. Standing on the lowest rung of the administrative ladder was the *naib tahsildar*, a junior revenue official, who assisted the *tahsildar*, the officer in charge of the basic revenue area. The tahsildar enjoyed second-class magisterial powers, and was a member of the Subordinate Civil Service, a 'gazetted officer' (i.e. his appointment appeared in the Government Gazette). This represented the lowest stratum of the hierarchy proper. The next, and much more highly regarded grade was the Provincial Civil Service. All members of this service were graduates, many with good degrees. The area of their recruitment was their own province. A certain number were appointed on the Governor's nomination, from among 'loyal' and 'respectable' families of the administrative class and the landed gentry. But the majority (and in some provinces all) were selected by competitive examination. The apex was provided by the Imperial services; chosen on an all-India basis, and from Britain, by means of a severe competitive examination. Between forty and fifty were selected every year for the Indian Civil Service (I.C.S.). Before 1922, Indian candidates had to sit for examination in London; a severe limitation. With the introduction of Dyarchy, a determined effort was made to accelerate the 'Indianisation' of the Imperial services. The quota of Indian entrants was increased, with the aim of creating parity between Indians and British as members of the I.C.S. by 1939. In fact, whereas there were sixty-three Indians in the I.C.S. in 1915, forming about 5 per cent of the service, by 1939 there were 625 Indians occupying I.C.S. posts, about 45 per cent of the total.

Every year, the cream of the Indian universities (scientists, mathematicians, lawyers, as well as Arts men) competed for the I.C.S. and the provincial services. It would often happen that, out of an aggregate of 1,200 marks over the whole examination, one single mark would separate the last man selected for the I.C.S. and his nearest rival who, perforce, would enter the provincial service. The distinction between success and failure in this lottery remained with the candidates all their days. The successful I.C.S. entrant would be appointed a Collector, or District Officer after six to ten years' service, and he might aspire eventually to become a Governor or a Member of the Viceroy's Executive Council. The provincial service man would only be chosen for promotion to a

'Superior' post (such as that of District Officer) if he stood out above the average, and then only after twenty-five years' service or more. These sharp distinctions existed right down the hierarchy. The first appointment of a provincial service man would be as Deputy Collector: a post which would be the height of ambition for a tahsildar. Thus, a man of outstanding ability in any grade might by great effort attain the middle of the next grade above him; but no exertion on earth would take him any higher. All the glittering prizes were reserved for the I.C.S.—no wonder they were known (in imitation of the Brahmins, the Twice Born) as the Heaven Born.

A further advantage for the I.C.S. was their complete security of tenure: having been appointed by the Secretary of State for India, they could only be dismissed by him, whereas the provincial civil service could be dismissed by the provincial government (which, after 1937, meant an elected ministry). No member of the I.C.S. ever was dismissed, except for gross misconduct. The consequence of this invulnerability was, inevitably, that the service had to carry a few supine passengers. On the other hand, the rebels, the nonconformists, the men of strange ideas could not easily be muzzled. And because Governors and Chief Secretaries change every three or five years, the man who had made himself unpopular knew his fortunes could suddenly improve. F. L. Brayne was packed off to the barren wastes of Gurgaon District to teach him the folly of his cranky ways. But he persisted in his folly of rural reconstruction, and he ended his career as the apostle of a new creed, honoured by Governors and Governors-General. All this tended to accentuate the contrast between the I.C.S. and the lower services. The I.C.S. officer could do his duty, shoulder unpleasant responsibility, secure in his position—and in most cases, sure of the warm support of his own service. The provincial officer, faced with the same dire decision, knew that if his action was not approved he might be thrown to the wolves.

These differences meant that the ethos of officialdom varied all the way down the hierarchy. At the summit, there was a unique spirit of duty, responsibility, and moral courage (on the obverse side there was perhaps a consciousness that, like Curzon, one was 'a most superior person'). Among the provincial services there was a sense of dignity and honourable behaviour, of conscientious discharge of one's duties, linked with a good deal of caution and compromise; an emphasis upon doing the correct thing, rather than doing the right thing. At the tahsildar level there was little inducement to a higher ideal of service. The tahsildar was the factotum of district administration, summoned by higher officials to do their errands. His usual recourse was to take any sense of grievance out on his own inferiors, or out of the public in bullying and bluster; and to utilise his opportunities to further his own advantage (naturally, there are plentiful exceptions to all these generalisations). At the bottom, the clerks and patwaris were the helots of the administration. Many were highly competent (the knowledge of village economics possessed by some patwaris would put to shame many a professor of rural sociology) but they could never expect to advance beyond the routine upkeep of official records in some stagnant backwater. Small wonder that many of them exploited their official position for private profit. Humble though they were, in the official hierarchy almost the whole process of government had to be transmitted through their hands. Every application from a member of the public, the collection of taxes, the issuing of licences, all had to pass through their hands. On these millions of petty transactions, the petty officials levied their petty tribute. There was one instance of a patwari earning Rs. 35 (£2/10/-) a month, sending his son to Cambridge, and thence into the I.C.S. (although this was somewhat exceptional). The higher officials knew of these practices; the present writer, as an administrator in an Indian city, knew himself to be immured in a miasma of corruption. But the very ubiquity of the system was its protection; so many were interested in its preservation; while the public, conditioned by the folk-memories of generations who had submitted to arbitrary tribute, great and small, expected nothing else.

The rôle of the police was somewhat different again: their forte was toughness. The Mughal inheritance, the *faujdari* police, may be likened to irregular cavalry. Their chief, the *daroga* or inspector, maintained public order by carefully contrived exhibitions of terror. Where a crime had been committed in a village, and witnesses were not forthcoming, he might decide to raze the village and drive away its inhabitants as a lesson to their neighbours. This *zabardasti*, strong arm justice, was replaced in the 1860s by provincial police forces modelled on the Royal Irish Constabulary, with British district Superintendents. The new police was thoroughly overhauled in its discipline and organisation, but it did not entirely shake off the techniques and attitudes of its predecessors. The reformed police was still quite unable to draw upon public confidence and support. Even when villagers had been victims of *dacoits,* armed gangs, they were reluctant to give the police adequate information, for fear that the dacoits would retaliate. The divorce between public and police was accentuated as the nationalist agitations of the 1920s gathered way. Deliberately, Gandhi's supporters courted arrest and police retaliation. The technique of satyagraha, non-violence, was designed to place the forces of law and order in a moral dilemma. Provocation was frequently offered (though Gandhi stated that this was not his intention) so as to provoke, and then expose police 'brutality' before Indian and world opinion.

In this sequence of situations, police officers, whether they wanted to or not, were compelled to condone doubtful practices. In order to keep the peace it was necessary to secure convictions against criminals, especially known habitual criminals: but these were often the most experienced in arranging that witnesses mysteriously altered their stories, or disappeared. Where witnesses were reluctant to testify, methods of persuasion might have to be utilised by the police. Prosecutions, once initiated must be made to 'stick'. When the police had to operate within a violent society (as in Punjab) they were compelled to employ forcible methods.[1] Always, the main concern of a senior British or Indian police officer was to be able to rely upon his men: when twenty constables armed with smooth-bore muskets stood in a city street with missiles hurtling down, and a seething crowd baying for their blood, the readiness with which they would obey an order to charge, or fire, was crucial. In turn, the constables must be certain that, whatever they were compelled to do, their superiors would support them against criticism, or possibly legal action. Lacking public support, the police had to be assured of internal support. Once again, the high officials were ostensibly in command, but the whole tone of the police—and its relations with the public—were determined by its most lowly members. Most of the senior police officers were more sharply aware of realities than most administrators; but there was an obligation to adopt a policy of 'my men—right or wrong', if law and order were to be maintained. Because (unlike the soldier) the policeman derives no sense of izzat, of honour and esteem, from his status, he is therefore more likely to try to exploit his position to gain the money which will give him status.

The period between 1937 and 1947 was a stretching, testing time for the public services. From 1937 to 1939 they first experienced the unfettered control of politicians, mainly Congress ministers. On taking office, Congress set up a district organisation which paralleled the regular district administration. Complaints from the public to the Congress district officials were taken up by ministers, and district officers were required to investigate and report. A deluge of complaints and

[1] An excellent picture of rural Indian crime and justice is contained in the novel *Call the Next Witness*, by Philip Woodruff: Philip Mason, a distinguished member of the I.C.S.

petitions rapidly brought the district administration to a standstill. Perceiving that the government machine (on which they must rely to carry out their programme) was being choked, the Congress ministers quite quickly abandoned these practices. But the memory of them remained with the officials.

The Congress-inspired revolt of 1942 came as the greatest test of the British Raj since 1857. Strengths, and weaknesses were revealed. For historical reasons, the district revenue administration in Bihar and Bengal was much weaker than in other provinces. The August revolt largely overwhelmed the Bihar administration (as the great 1943 famine was to overwhelm the Bengal administration). But in the United Provinces the civil service and police held firm, and a sabotage campaign, planned with care, was rapidly defeated. Despite much behind-the-scenes pressure by Congress, the officials did their duty; only one senior officer was suspended by the government for alleged shortcomings. A terrible strain had been placed on the loyalty of these Indian magistrates and police officers. When the Congress leaders were released from internment in 1944 and 1945, a Black List was compiled of those officials, British and Indian, supposed to have acted harshiy in 1942. There was talk of legal proceedings against these officials. Congress had served notice to the officials: in future if you thwart our actions you may expect short shrift.

The war was a period of acute shortages in India and of widespread controls, as elsewhere. There were also vast sums spent on hastily conceived projects, such as military airfields, and supply depots. The senior officials enjoyed unprecedented powers—and opportunities for private gain. A few cases were uncovered of officials (mostly of the middle grade) who succumbed.

The administration throughout India emerged from the war weary, uncertain of the future, disheartened, and short of personnel. Against the too-clever gyrations of the Congress leaders and the unreasonableness of Jinnah, Lord Wavell had to balance the low morale of the civil service and police. This lay behind Wavell's final *démarche*: he recommended either strong reinforcements for the higher public services or else the reduction of the area of British responsibility. His successor, Mountbatten, went further: he told the British Government that the services had become so demoralised, so perplexed and communal-minded, that the remaining period of British rule must be reduced to a few weeks.

With the transfer of power, British civil servants were given the option of retiring, with compensation; or negotiating contracts with the new governments. Because of weariness and frustration, most British officials chose to depart. Those who tried the experiment of taking service in the new India mostly found themselves relegated to a corner; few stayed very long. British officials were much more welcome in Pakistan, and during the early years, the senior administration was more British than Pakistani. Gradually the atmosphere changed, and they too went away.

Indian Imperial Service officers were also given the option to retire or continue in service: most went the way of their religion, though a considerable number of Muslim officials of all grades chose to stay in India, in their native provinces. India inherited about 400 members of the I.C.S. Pakistan's share was a little over 100 of whom most were Punjabis, a sizeable number came from U.P. and Bihar, and none were Bengalis.

Both India and Pakistan retained intact the administrative hierarchy the British had erected. The pay of the superior posts was reduced; but the dignity of office remained. The Collector, the District Officer, still occupied the old Collector's colonnaded mansion, with an armed sentry at his gate, and the national flag waving above. Within his district he was still the supreme embodiment of government, and the claims of M.Ps and M.L.As to co-equality were acknowledged only by the most party-minded. Despite the enormous strain imposed on the civil service by the reorganisation caused by partition and unification, and by expansion of the concept of government to include planning, welfare, and national economic development, the compact, élite character of the old I.C.S. was continued in the new Indian Administrative Service (I.A.S.) and the Civil Service of Pakistan (C.S.P.). Between 1947 and 1953, the annual intake into the I.A.S. averaged under thirty-five; thereafter the number rose to seventy (this in a population of 400,000,000). For the C.S.P. the annual entry varied between fifteen and twenty-five. Entry was still *via* a highly competitive examination. The standard of the candidates may have fallen somewhat: some of the best qualified Indian and Pakistani graduates now prefer to enter British commercial and industrial enterprises operating in the sub-continent. The examination is still entirely 'academic'; 'technical' subjects (e.g. public administration or statistics) are excluded, and the aim is still to secure entrants who are intellectually first class, and who in addition show evidence of character and integrity. The I.A.S. entrance requirements are modified somewhat to enable a few members of the scheduled castes and tribes to secure places, but otherwise the principle of merit is rigidly enforced. Very few Muslims have sufficient educational attainments to succeed. About one-third of the candidates come from the south: Madras has largely inherited the predominance in higher administration which Bengal formerly enjoyed. Almost all the entrants still come from a narrow segment of the Westernised urban middle class, many being sons of senior civil servants and judges. Of the C.S.P. intake, 20 per cent is selected on absolute merit, while a quota of 40 per cent goes to East Bengal and 40 per cent is distributed between the regions of West Pakistan. The social range is somewhat less restricted than in India; a minority of the Bengali entrants come from the homes of traders, clerks, and even small landowners. One Hindu probationer was accepted in 1947; thereafter the C.S.P. was exclusively recruited from the Muslim majority.

The training of the probationers follows the former British pattern, with emphasis on law and revenue matters. The probationers live apart, in dignified, collegiate surroundings. They still acquire a definite *esprit de corps*: the I.A.S. training school was formerly at the Delhi home of Charles Metcalfe, a pioneer pro-consul, and I.A.S. men like to call themselves 'Metcalfians'. But does the former spirit of responsibility and initiative continue? The Indian Constitution, and the abortive 1956 Pakistan Constitution gave the administrators of today the same absolute security of tenure as did the old I.C.S. 'covenant' with the Secretary of State. However, politicians, especially in India, manifested strong suspicion, and sometimes resentment of the I.C.S. men who occupied key posts. In a few instances, a political deal clashed with an I.C.S. officer's sense of fitness: if he protested, usually, the officer was isolated, and sometimes relegated to obscurity. Promotion to the most desirable posts, more particularly under provincial or State governments, went conspicuously to the man who played the same game as the ruling party. (In fairness, it must be added that in most programmes and projects, the senior official's patriotism and professional zeal would find fulfilment rather than frustration). What all this signifies to the fledgling administrator has been aptly summarised by A. D. Gorwala, a former member of the I.C.S. who compiled a report on administration for the Planning Commission in 1951:

One of the principal merits of the [British] Indian system was that it taught a man to take responsibility. That which was his job he did. Those above watched him doing it, but left him to do it, only volunteering advice occasionally and hardly ever issuing instructions unless he was going very wrong. The young probationer for the administrative, police, and other services still receives the same training, but worldly wisdom, alas, soon teaches all but the exceptional to tread the modern path of discretion.[1]

The infrastructure of administration is still provided by the provincial, or State civil services, the subordinate services, and the clerical staff. The divisions between them remain almost insuperable barriers. In the present context, where selective promotion can so often be ascribed to nepotism, or political jobbery, it is not easy to depart from the safeguards inherent in open competitive entry, followed by promotion by seniority (which Admiral Lord Fisher elegantly described as 'Buggins' turn'). But the gradation of merit, between the many who are called and the few who are chosen, in the lottery for selection into the national, provincial, or subordinate services grows even more blurred: one government report on the examination results of candidates for the public services in Punjab comments on their 'terrible uniformity of mediocrity'. In this situation, jealousy between the priviliged I.A.S. and C.S.P. and their provincial service brethren is even stronger.

Because government is still a pyramid, and because independent judgement is no longer encouraged, decisions are made only at the summit. The files ascend the administrative escalator, receiving an addition here, an amendment there, but passed for action to the top. Reporting on reorganisation in the central government of India on the eve of independence, Sir Richard Tottenham declared 'We have too few officers of the right kind and too many clerks of the wrong kind'. This situation has subsequently only been further aggravated. Administrative inflation has prevailed, and the employees of the central government of India have increased from 49,000 in 1939, to 670,000 in 1956. But the decision-makers still number only a few score.

The system in both countries is better organised to conserve existing institutions than to foster new development. Nevertheless, the public services have carried the burden of transforming a largely 'law and order' administration into one increasingly concerned with economic and social development; and, by their own lights, they are making an outstanding success of the task. Between India—and also Pakistan—and the majority of newly independent countries (including those in the Middle East) there is a fundamental difference. In India, if legislation, or administrative decision lays down a course of action, then that course will in fact be followed. In most new countries, the government can de-

[1] A. D. Gorwala, 'The Public Services and Democracy' in *Leadership and Political Institutions in India*, ed. R. L. Park and I. Tinker, Princeton, 1959, pp. 333-4.

cide on policy and issue instructions to their officials and to the public: but there the matter rests. 'Between the decision and the action lies the shadow'—of inactivity, irresolution, and incompetence. But in India and Pakistan the machinery of government actually works. This machinery may not be adapted to the ideal functioning of democracy and the welfare state: but it does provide mechanism to execute the public will, such as many other countries envy and desire to emulate.

VIII

THE CHECKS ON GOVERNMENT

ONE major problem in planting democracy in Asia is to devise methods of making governments accountable for their actions. Even in Western countries which consider they are politically mature, no effective means has been devised for bringing a government which is failing the people to account, in the interval between general elections. This may occasionally be achieved by an internal party revolt, as happened in Britain in 1940; but the tendency of the British party system to become ever more rigid makes this possibility increasingly unlikely. Indeed, it is difficult to call to mind any political party in the West that has not, once it has achieved power, gone on its way, regardless, in between elections. Yet how much more difficult it is to establish government accountability in India and Pakistan. India appears to have become settled into a pattern in which nothing can shake the central government; and general elections take place not because the government has any sense of being called to account by the public, but merely because the Constitution requires that this process be followed every five years. Pakistan, of course, has not held a national election; and the 1962 Constitution makes it almost impossible for the President and the Executive ever to be challenged to account for their stewardship. 'Government of the people, by the people' has never been a description of actuality, even in the United States. In south Asia it remains an improbable dream. Under these circumstances, the forces of public opinion cannot exercise much influence on the government, and almost everything depends upon two institutions which, in the Anglo-Saxon political tradition have played an historic rôle as checks upon abuses by governments: the judiciary, and the press.

During the British period, both these institutions adopted an attitude of independence from the executive and its influence. When alien rule came to an end there was a natural tendency for these institutions to seek a closer identification with the national spirit as embodied in the national government. A critical attitude became almost tantamount to disloyalty. In this situation, only the higher judiciary felt sufficiently sure of its ground to maintain a spirit of independence. In one of its judgements, the Supreme Court of the Indian Republic has laid down that 'this Court . . . is the ultimate interpreter and guardian of the Constitution. It has a duty to see that its provisions are faithfully observed and, where necessary, to expound them.'

This watchful independence stems back to the earliest days of British rule when, by Royal charter, the King's Courts were set up in Calcutta, Bombay, and Madras, thereby providing a check upon the activities of the East India Company as the ruling power. Subsequently, as British power spread across the sub-continent, High Courts were established in all the major provinces. These were instituted by Royal Letters Patent, and their judges were not subject in any way to the executive authority of the provincial or the central government of India. One-third of the judges were required to be members of the English Bar, or members of the Faculty of Advocates in Scotland, of five years' standing. One-third were required to be members of the Indian Civil Service: but this implied no identification with the executive. After his first five or six years in the service, the young I.C.S. man was permitted to choose whether he would remain in the executive or the judicial line. Having made his choice, it was almost unknown for a transfer to occur. The 'judgee' attracted many I.C.S. men of an independent or disputatious disposition. Also, before the first world war, Indians in the I.C.S. found themselves somewhat isolated in the executive line, and a majority preferred the judiciary. Underneath the High Courts, and corresponding roughly to the Assizes in England, were the District and Sessions Judges. These judges were partly drawn from the I.C.S., partly from the Bar, and partly from the provincial judicial service. By the 1930s, over half of their number were Indians. Civil suits were heard by the District Judge; while his *alter ego* the Sessions Judge was responsible for criminal justice.

Below the level of District and Sessions Judge, the system was bifurcated. The civil courts were presided over by *Munsifs*, a body of professional judges recruited on a provincial basis from members of the legal profession. Criminal justice was almost entirely in the hands of the district revenue administration. All Tahsildars exercised Second Class magisterial powers. The District Officer was also District Magistrate; he supervised all magistrates within his district, though he himself did not try many cases. The concentration of magisterial powers in the hands of the executive was a standing cause of complaint to nationalist politicians nurtured in English political doctrine, with its insistence on the separation of judiciary from executive. But this concentration of powers represented another example of the perpetuation of Mughal methods, with administration of justice, and enforcement of public order delegated to one all-powerful official.

The law, which the early Courts set up by the British had to interpret, was a confused medley of tradition, custom, and Islamic jurisprudence. Gradually this was replaced. On the criminal side, there came the Indian Penal Code, largely drafted by Macaulay, which introduced a rational code of law to cover all offences. Civil law was modified less completely; Hindu and Muslim personal law was largely retained, though in other matters (for example, the law of contract) there was an almost complete break. These legal changes had important incidental political consequences. The introduction of a legal system based on the English Common Law did much to inculcate the idea of equality. Under the old Hindu law, a Brahmin murderer might not be put to death, while a Sudra who cohabited with a high caste woman would automatically suffer execution. Under the new law, Brahmin and Sudra were liable to the same punishment for the same offence. Secondly, a uniform code of law dispensed by judges who were not the servants of the administration revealed an aspect of government which out-reached the arbitrary sway of the Mughals or the authoritarian rule of British officials. The idea of the rule of law, omnicompetent, greater than the greatest of the governors, took a hold over the mind of the Westernised middle class. Even when, led by Gandhi, Congress rejected British rule in its entirety, there was no rejection of the rule of law. Indeed, it may be argued that it provided the essential basis for the success of civil disobedience. In the face of a Hitler or a Stalin, satyagraha would, at best, have been a brief, ineffectual gesture; snuffed out in the darkness of the inquisition and the gas chamber. Even in the face of the not illiberal British-Indian administration, when juridical safeguards were in abeyance (as in the war-time, emergency conditions of the 1942 Congress revolt) political protest—even when militant, as in 1942—was impotent before the security forces. But in the 1920s and '30s, the successive Gandhian acts of defiance of authority were reviewed by the Courts. The judicial process, although (necessarily) applied to punish breaches of the peace, by its very nature tended to afford a means of justification for the Indian demand for rights to which English political belief entitled them. Gandhi and his followers were well aware of this paradox: that those who sentenced them, also indirectly provided them with a moral sanction. The satyagrahis were instructed to offer no plea in Court, and to refuse to accept the option of a fine, in token that they did not recognise the authority of British justice. However, Gandhi more than once acknowledged that his judges had, by their unbiased application of the law, shown that a system based upon equity and liberty, and a system based upon repression could not be combined. Any suspicion that a Court was in any way inclining towards the executive always aroused a furore among the Congress leaders. Indeed, the stature of Indian nationalism was not enhanced by the readiness with which they claimed that a wide range of acts of violence, even hooliganism, should be treated by the Courts as aspects of political protest. The moral confusion into which Gandhi sometimes plunged political India is illustrated by the case of Bhagat Singh, the terrorist. Having served a long sentence for exploding a bomb in the legislature, Bhagat Singh was sentenced to death for the murder of a police officer whom he accused (quite wrongly, as it turned out) of having struck the nationalist leader, Lala Lajpat Rai. Gandhi insisted that the murderer's sentence should be commuted, on the grounds that this was a political action. Thereafter, almost every goonda or ruffian was able to persuade some Congress-man to plead that his crime should be excused, as his motive was political.

Despite the strains to which they were subjected, from 1920 onward, the judges preserved the concept of law as an absolute, unimpaired. The reputation for impartiality of the Courts was not confined to the High Courts or those of the District and Sessions Judges. The lower Courts, presided over by munsifs, maintained a code of correct and conscientious dealing. However, partly because of the number of appeals to the higher Courts, which constantly increased, the munsifs paid excessive attention to detail, recording evidence with the utmost elaboration, disposing of legal arguments with perhaps over-much compunction and care. All this made the quest for justice a slow business. The list of cases pending was always long, and it was customary to grant adjournments, so that many cases dragged on for years. And so, to the common man, the operation of the law remained an enigma. Many folk looked upon the Courts as instruments for perverting justice only. In a society which still regarded land as the most precious commodity, and with land always scarce, litigation over land ownership was endemic. It was easy enough to start litigation: payment of eight annas stamp duty was the only fee required to bring a case before a Court. The volume of litigation in some provinces (such as Bengal) constituted a major social problem. Attempts were made in the 1920s and '30s to exclude the mass of petty suits from the Courts by reviving the panchayat as a judicial tribunal, and endowing panchayats with statutory powers to dispose of minor disputes and minor crimes. Despite Congress propaganda, urging the village people to boy-cott the panchayats, hundreds of thousands of petty cases were settled by them, out of Court, every year. These village tribunals worked towards arbitration or compromise, instead of the determining of guilt or inno-cence, right or wrong of the regular Courts. In this they reflected a signi-ficant difference between Western and Indian concepts of justice.

The attainment of independence made little difference to the judicial process in India. The value attached to the rule of law was aptly stated by Dr. P. Subbarayan, addressing the constituent assembly in 1949:

> There are two things that the British have left behind for us; one is the efficiency of the civil service and the other is the rule of law. . . . If there is anything I would like to cling to in the future of this country it is this rule of law. . . . I think we have provided in the constitution, in the powers vested in the Sup-reme Court and the High Courts, . . . for any citizen to have his right established as against the government of the day.

The Indian Constitution provides the most elaborate safeguards, both for the appointment of properly qualified judges, and for their further independence. The executive has no part in their appointment; even the district judges are appointed by Governors of States, in consultation with the High Court of the State. High Court Judges hold office, not for life, as in England, but until sixty years of age: possibly, a greater guar-antee of judicial integrity. The judicial processes which uphold the liberty of the citizen are the time-honoured pillars of British justice: Habeas Corpus, Mandamus, Prohibition, Certiorari, and Quo Warranto. Habeas Corpus has been invoked against the Preventative Detention Act of 1950, under which many hundreds of Communists, and others, have been held without trial. Mandamus has been utilised much more freely than in England, where it is a discretionary power, to be issued only when the Court is satisfied that there is no alternative remedy. In India, it is employed for the enforcement of the Fundamental Rights laid down in the constitution; to compel public officials or bodies to perform their duties; to direct officials not to enforce a law which is unconstitutional; to proceed against the Government of India or a State; to compel inferior Courts and tribunals to exercise their jurisdiction, when they have re-fused to exercise it; and to restore, admit, or elect a person to an office. These are formidable sanctions, and the constitution has served to endow the judiciary in present-day India with prestige and power even greater than before.

The influence of the English Common Law has continued, and the reception of English legal innovations has increased, contributing to the spread of the idea of equality. The much disputed Hindu Marriages Act of 1955, for example, strengthened the movement towards equality for women in India by abolishing polygamy. The Criminal Procedure (Amendment) Act of 1955, making women liable for jury service, and the Special Marriages Act of 1954, making provision for marriages between Hindus and Muslims, were steps in the same direction.

In an India in which the fissiparous forces of linguistic and caste politics are increasingly exercising their centrifugal pressure, the judiciary serves as a unifying influence. While the political structure is federal in character, the judicial organisation is purely unitary.[1] The whole judicial edifice culminates in the Supreme Court; the final court of appeal, and the arbiter of disputes between States, or between a State and the centre. The prestige of the judges has been recognised in their being appointed to inquire into allegations of misconduct by politicians or officials. The most discussed instance, the inquiry by Mr. Justice Chagla into the Life Insurance Scandal, has a significance comparable to that of the post-war Lynskey Tribunal in Great Britain. Judges have frequently participated in the Indian equivalents of Royal Commissions: Mr. Justice Fazl Ali was chairman of the all-important States Reorganisation Commission.

The judiciary has continued, then, according to its own lights to discharge the function of guardian of the public good; but there continues to be a divorce between the ideal, the rule of law, and the reality, compounded of delay, and the perversion of justice. The mounting pile of writ petitions is one reason why the higher Courts have been subject more and more to delay, despite the recall of retired judges, and other measures to accelerate the course of justice. As a partial remedy, the attempt to re-establish a network of village Courts or *panchayati adalat* has been redoubled. In Madras, 25 per cent of all civil actions are instituted in village Courts. Yet the *panchayati adalat* cannot be expected to meet all the needs of village life today, with its mounting emphasis upon

[1] In other federations (such as the United States and Australia) there are two distinct legal and judicial systems; the federal and the State. As a counterpoise to the growing sense of separatism in India which the linguistic States tend to foster, the States Reorganisation Commission proposed that in every High Court, one third of the Bench should be drawn from outside the State. This was accepted by a gathering of Chief Ministers in January 1958. The Chief Justices of the Mysore and Assam High Courts are outsiders, the former coming from West Bengal, the latter from Allahabad. This interchange is dependent, of course, on the continued use of English as the language of the higher Courts.

intercaste rivalry and individual economic gain. In the judicial, as in the political sphere, there is a dichotomy between the goal of harmony, or sarvodaya, or reconciliation, and the present reality of divided and conflicting interests.

Whereas Indian legal development has been predominantly in a Western, indeed Anglo-Saxon mould, Pakistan has experienced a sharp conflict between the supporters and the opponents of English legal methods and modes.

Muslims begin with a much more profound sense of the importance of law than the followers of other religions. The Quran and the Shari'a might, not improperly, be described as a corpus of statute and case law which regulates almost every action a Muslim may contemplate in life. The Islamic polity gave a prominent place to jurists and judges, and individual Muslims of the professional class were prominent in the judiciary during the British period, though in number the Hindus dominated the legal profession and the Bench. During the twentieth century, the growing Islamic consciousness was expressed in legislation to bring the personal law of indigenous Muslims into alignment with the Shari'a: examples were the Shariat Act of 1937, and the Cutchi Memons Act of 1938.

The concept of law was highly ambiguous in the new state of Pakistan. There was a strong element representing the spirit of the English Common Law: Jinnah had practised before the highest Court of Appeal in the Empire, the Judicial Committee of the Privy Council, and his every speech and act betokened the constitutional lawyer. There was no question of dismantling the High Courts or throwing out Macaulay's Penal Code; yet, from the beginning, the English legal heritage was under strong pressure, both from the executive, and from the Islamic extremists.

Pakistan retained all the emergency powers of detention which had existed during the British régime (including the venerable Bengal State Prisoners Regulation of 1818) and reinforced them with the Security of Pakistan Act. To some extent, the Courts were able to check arbitrary imprisonment: for example, in 1949, Suhrawardy (a leading proponent of the Common Law tradition) successfully moved for a writ of habeas corpus on behalf of a follower of Abdul Ghafur Khan, securing his release. Other extensions of executive authority were resisted; the High Court of West Punjab ruled, in 1948, that prohibition legislation was *ultra vires;* nevertheless, prohibition was imposed, despite the Court's ruling.

The climax of the tussle between judiciary and executive came in 1954 when the Governor-General, Ghulam Mohammad, dismissed the constituent assembly. The President of the assembly filed in the Chief Court of Sind, a petition for writ of mandamus, to restrain the Governor-General from giving effect to the proclamation of dismissal, and a writ of quo warranto to void the appointment of certain of the new Ministers. The Sind Court found against the Governor-General; but an appeal to the Federal Court reversed the decision. Four out of the five judges ruled that the prerogative power of the Governor-General 'must be held to have revived when it became apparent . . . that the constituent assembly was unable or had failed to provide a constitution for the country'. The new government proposed to frame a constitution by administrative fiat, but this was overruled by the Federal Court. The Governor-General decided to refer the whole constitutional question to the Court, and he propounded a series of questions to the judges. They stated plainly that a new constituent assembly must be convened. The 1956 constitution reproduced virtually the same safeguards for the judiciary as in India. It also guaranteed the writ petition process, among the fundamental rights, as in India. After 1956, the flow of writ petitions became a flood. They were invoked mainly to challenge decisions of the executive, great and small. For example, the Deputy Speaker challenged the changeover from communal electorates to joint electorates (although duly passed by Parliament) as an infringement of the constitution. In a society where politicians and officials were no longer trusted, the judiciary was the last repositary of public trust.

Beside the duel between executive and judiciary, a more indirect conflict was taking place with the Islamic zealots. Mr. Justice Munir put his finger on the dilemma when he pointed out that 'the legislature in its present sense is unknown to the Islamic system'; only acknowledged religious leaders, *ulama*, would be considered qualified to pronounce on legal questions. The school of Maulana Abu Maudoodi insisted that the state must be an Islamic theocracy, and that the pure Shari'a must be the paramount law. This would have gone beyond even the Ottoman Empire in accepting canon law as utterly voiding civil law. No other Muslim state today (except, possibly, obscurantist Saudi Arabia and Yemen) makes more than a perfunctory attempt to reconcile the requirements of the modern world with the Shari'a.[1] The Basic Principles Committee, which reported in December 1952, went as far as to propose that the Head of State should constitute a board of not more than five persons, well-versed in Islamic laws, to advise the Head of State about the repugnancy of

[1] Peter Partner, *A Short Political Guide to the Arab World*, 1960, pp. 11-12, 109.

new laws to the Quran and the sunna. This proposal met with steady opposition from the barrister-politicians, as introducing a power of veto, to be exercised by a body not clearly responsible to anything except their own scruples. Eventually, the constitution evaded the issue. A clause was inserted (Article 198) providing that 'no law shall be enacted which is repugnant to the injunctions of Islam', and requiring the President to appoint a Commission to make recommendations for consideration by parliament. Although the 1956 constitution was in force for two and a half years, no further action was taken on this issue. Any attempt to return to the Quran immediately raised practical difficulties: for example, if usury were to be abolished, as the Holy Prophet directed, how could Pakistan create an industrial class, or how mobilise foreign capital? And so the Common Law tradition continued to prevail in practice, however much the Quranic precept was honoured in theory.

All this was changed with the introduction of martial law. Ayub knew that, to the lawyers, his régime was a violation of all that they held dear: the rule of law, greater than rulers and ruled. Almost at once he indicated that the judicial system would be changed. He categorised the British system as 'at once the most expensive and the most dilatory'; the common people must have a legal system which they could understand and from which they could obtain prompt justice. As the martial law régime went on its way, with its draconian measures against those associated with the old order, there was a general acquiescence in the liquidation of political prerogatives, even among the more politically sophisticated groups of East Pakistan. But the lawyers did not acquiesce. The President of the Karachi Bar Association, Mr. Justice Z. H. Lari, spoke out in 1959 at the annual meeting of the Association in favour of restoring parliamentary democracy; and again in 1960 he criticised the military régime for what he called 'the complete withdrawal of freedom of speech and association'. For his pains, he was prevented from leaving the country. He was supported by Chief Justice Kayani, who also used the platform of the Karachi Bar Association to lament the lost independence of the judiciary and to criticise the Ayub régime for pandering to 'false notions of religion'. When H. S. Suhrawardy, perhaps the outstanding lawyer-politician, was arrested late in January 1962, the High Court Bar Association in Lahore issued a demand that he be brought to trial in Court. Similar resolutions were adopted by other Bar Associations in West Pakistan.

In view of this steady assertion of independence, it is not surprising that Ayub has clipped the lawyers' wings. He addressed the Karachi

Bar Association in October 1960, and took them to task for lack of appreciation of his objectives. In January 1961, trial by jury was abolished in Pakistan, and in the following November the High Court was forbidden to review any measure introduced by Martial Law regulation (this followed instances of the Court dismissing regulations as *ultra vires*). However, the Field Marshal has, it might be claimed, respected judicial integrity. He accepted, in May 1960, the appointment of Mr. Justice Cornelius as Chief Judge of the Supreme Court, though Cornelius had proved himself the most independent-minded member of the Supreme Court Bench (he is also, incidentally, a Roman Catholic and a Eurasian). Ayub also appointed an ex-Chief Justice, Shahabuddin, as Chairman of his Constitutional Commission. Yet the provisions of the 1962 Constitution gave small pleasure to the legal fraternity.

The powers of the higher Courts were straitly defined, while a Supreme Judicial Council was brought into being to regulate the activities of the judges. The Council, it is true, is composed of the Chief Justice of the Supreme Court and the other seniormost judges. But it is required to issue a code of conduct to be observed by the judges, while the President is empowered to direct the Council 'to inquire into the capacity or conduct of a judge of a Supreme Court or a High Court on ground of physical and mental incapacity or gross misconduct'. It remains to be seen how judicial independence will flourish under the ever-present shadow of Presidential intervention.

The creation of the Advisory Council of Islamic Ideology also takes the power of interpreting the law from out of the hands of the Common Law jurists and transfers it to the Islamic doctors and divines. The Courts are restricted to applying law which jurists thinking in a fundamentally different climate have determined.

The President has shown that he will not tolerate the claim of the Courts to function as 'interpreter and guardian of the constitution'; it seems unlikely that he will accept as binding the pronouncements of the Advisory Council should they clash with his avowed aim of establishing a 'sound, vigorous, progressive and powerful state'. Moreover, there can be no guarantee that the Advisory Council will speak clearly and together. Mr. Justice Munir, by his persistent questioning of *mullas* and *maulvis* in his inquiry into the anti-Ahmadiyya riots, demonstrated very clearly that there are as many interpretations of Islam as there are Islamic divines: he was compelled to conclude, from the conflict of evidence that was given to him, that the only acceptable definition of 'a Muslim' was 'one who calls himself a Muslim'. Faced with a comparable clash of learned Islamic advice, the President may be compelled to return to the more exact niceties of the Common Law judges.[1]

The record of the judiciary, both in Pakistan and India, as a restraining force upon abuse of power by the executive is impressive. The record of the press as a civic watchdog is less remarkable. With some notable exceptions, the press has done little more than echo the cadences of governments and parties. The verdict of future historians may be that the most important contribution of the press was made before, not after independence.

The first newspapers, in the English language, appeared in 1780, but they were mere scandal sheets. The true founders of a serious popular press, both in English and the vernaculars, were the Baptist missionaries of Serampore. In 1818 they began to issue a Bengali newspaper, *Samachar Darpan* (The Mirror of Truth). At the same time, the *Friend of India* began to appear, first as a quarterly, then as a monthly, and finally as a weekly. The circumstance that Serampore was then a Danish enclave gave the missionaries greater freedom of expression. Their journals were, of course, avowed vehicles of Christian propaganda, and a second Bengali paper came into being in 1821, *Sambad Kaumudi* (Moon of Reason), founded by Ram Mohan Ray, as the counter-voice of the modernist, Westernising Hindu viewpoint. Within a few years there were half a dozen Bengali papers, within the Calcutta area. Their circulations ranged from 400 to 800 copies, but their influence was out of proportion to their small-scale operation.

The pioneer administrator, James Munro, observed of these developments: 'A free press and the dominion of strangers are things which are quite incompatible . . . for what is the first duty of a free press? It is to deliver the country from a foreign yoke.' This clash of purposes soon led to the issue of a regulation introducing a censorship, in 1823. The first true political contest in India now began, between the Government, and Indian and British claimants of freedom of speech. The response of the Government was mainly influenced by the outlook of the Governor-General. Metcalfe, as acting Governor-General, abolished all restrictions in 1835. Restrictions were re-imposed during the Mutiny, and rescinded by the Liberal Viceroy, Ripon, in 1882. The terrorist campaign at the beginning of the twentieth century led to further Press Acts in 1908 and 1910. The owners of printing presses were required to furnish security as token of good behaviour; newspapers could be confiscated for offences.

---

[1] Ayub recognised the unique impartiality of the Common Law judges by appointing members of the judicial service to supervise the elections for the new legislatures in April 1962. When the President re-formed his cabinet in May 1962, the outspoken Mr. Justice Munir became Minister of Law.

These repressive measures were relaxed in the 1920s but were revived by Lord Irwin during the civil disobedience campaign of 1930.

The major newspapers came into being at a relatively early period. The *Friend of India* enjoyed its greatest influence during the twenty years before the Mutiny. At this time, the Governor-General himself took note of its views, while senior British officials who wished to introduce reforms contributed to its columns under pseudonymns. During the 1870s, the *Friend of India* was amalgamated with the *Statesman*, which today is recognised as the outstanding journal in the whole sub-continent. *The Bombay Times*, founded in 1838, later became *The Times of India*, predominant in Bombay and Western India.

The early vernacular press was an important means of shaping the new Hindi which was to assume such future importance. The Benares *Akbar* (Newspaper) which Raja Shiv Prasad started in 1844 was the principal means whereby he promoted his attempt to create a Hindi-Urdu synthesis in his Khichri Hindi; while the magazine *Kavi Vachan Sudha* (1867) and *Chandrika* (1874), published by Bharatendu Harishchandra, first popularised the literary style of Khari Boli Hindi which the Arya Samaj was to take up and convert into the speech of Hindu militancy. *Amrita Bazar Patrika*, most famous of all the nationalist papers, was launched in 1868 by the Ghose brothers as a Bengali journal, later being published in both Bengali and English editions. Some of the leading nationalist politicians owed a great part of their influence to being editors of newspapers. S. N. Banerjee, the 'king of Bengal', was editor for forty years of *The Bengalee* (which, despite its title, was an English-language paper). Bal Gangadhar Tilak, the protagonist of militancy edited *Kesari* (The Lion), the leading Marathi paper. In the 1920s, one of the principal Liberal politicians (a Minister in the U.P. government) was C. Y. Chintamani, editor of the Allahabad *Leader,* a paper which continued the tradition of Ram Mohan Ray in concerning public opinion with questions of social reform.

Writing to the Viceroy in 1876, Robert Knight, editor of *The Times of India,* observed: 'It seems to me that under the system of administration we have established in India the only right conception of the office of the press is that of Her Majesty's opposition.' This remained broadly the position right into the twentieth century. The only question was whether a paper chose to criticise the actions of the administration from the point of view of too much or too little, too fast or too slow. With some exceptions, the British-owned press in India was ultra-Tory. The public to which it directed its attention was the British business and planter class, and the 'respectable' Indian, the official or land-owner. Two examples of this type of paper, both showing a high standard of journalism, were the *Civil and Military Gazette* of Lahore, and the *Pioneer* of Allahabad (Rudyard Kipling was a cub reporter for both these papers).[1] Journals like these opposed all measures of political reform, and were highly critical of all government expenditure which might increase taxation.

With the founding of the Congress in 1885, most of the Indian-owned papers followed in its train. For example, *The Hindu* of Madras (which was published as an English-language daily from 1889) became a sturdy exponent of Congress policy. With the great expansion of Congress activity in the 1920s and '30s, came an increase in the number of pro-Congress journals. Motilal Nehru started the *Independent,* in 1919, but it only enjoyed a life of four years. Also in 1919, Gandhi began to edit *Young India* and in 1933 started *Harijan,* published in English, Hindi, and several other vernaculars. Jawaharlal Nehru, and other members of the Nehru family owned and directed the *National Herald* which first appeared in August 1938, as an official Congress organ. Because it was so frequently suppressed by the censorship, the *Herald* did not really begin to function effectively until 1945.

The growth of the Hindi movement was accompanied by an expansion of the Hindi press, especially in the Hindi heartland. *Aj* of Benares first appeared in 1920, edited by Sri Prakasa as a militant political daily; while *Pratap* of Cawnpore was another extremist Hindi paper. The Urdu press was mainly conservative, with a few journals promoting Islamic orthodoxy. From about 1930, the tone of the press became increasingly harsh; and comment on British policy in general, and on specific actions by British officials, became ever more wild and woolly. The historian who employs the Indian press of this period as a source, will need to distinguish carefully where factual reporting ends and speculative comment begins. Both the Hindu and the Muslim press helped to contribute to the growing atmosphere of communalism by giving the maximum publicity to any instance of worsening Hindu-Muslim relations. The Government of India found itself more divorced from contact with public opinion than ever before. It attempted to control the swelling chorus of hatred by assuming fresh powers; the Indian Press Emergency Powers Act of 1931, and the Emergency Powers Ordinances of 1932. These measures further defined objectionable subjects that might not be published, and gave magistrates further powers to act against periodicals before offending matter was actually published. The press responded to these attempts at restraint by increasing irresponsibility.

[1] The *Pioneer* moved to Lucknow in 1933.

The emergence of the Muslim League as a popular political force produced a need for a League organ. Being impressed by the writing of Altaf Hussain in the *Statesman*, Jinnah asked him to edit a League paper. Funds were provided by the Aga Khan and other wealthy Muslims. Altaf Hussain called his new paper *Dawn*, from the title of a literary journal he had previously produced. *Dawn* first appeared as a weekly in 1940, and was turned into a daily in 1946. An English-language journal, it soon established an all-India circulation.

Apart from the major nationalist papers, mentioned above, Indian journalism was bespattered by countless mushroom publications whose circulation was negligible and whose ethical standards were non-existent. The editors of these sheets were ready to sell their columns to any bidder, whether to promote a political stunt, to support a personal bid for gain, or merely to pay off a grudge. It was difficult to take action against such papers. A person who had been libelled knew that if he took action in the Courts he would not even recover his legal costs, for the paper's proprietor would turn out to be a man of straw; the only consequence would be to afford the paper publicity as a 'forum of free speech'. The value of such papers as means of providing even local news was limited by an inability to employ more than perhaps two reporters, who would be paid a coolie's wage, with perhaps some vague promise of commission. Straight news hardly ever appeared in their columns: only the fulminations necessitated by the current tortuous 'agitation'. Journals of this description made up perhaps three-quarters of the press of the sub-continent; the supply of a responsible service of news and comment was regarded as a public duty by perhaps one-tenth of the total number of newspapers.

The attainment of independence did not make for great changes. British ownership had already ceased to be a factor of any importance: the *Civil and Military Gazette*, and the *Pioneer*, for example, had already passed into Indian hands. Partition necessitated certain adjustments. *Dawn* moved from Delhi to Karachi, where it resumed publication as the official Muslim League organ. Such other pro-League papers as remained in India quietly changed their tunes. Some Hindu-owned papers in Pakistan, like the *Civil and Military Gazette*, ran into trouble; and some ceased publication. The principal change was that, overnight, the rôle of the press as 'His Majesty's opposition' was finished. The press ceased to abuse the British Government, and began to accord it a grudging goodwill, while—as was altogether natural—it gave a warm welcome to the new national governments. Criticism was no longer the fashion. When the editor of the *Statesman*, Ian Stephens, objected to certain features of the Indian take-over in Kashmir he found himself out of favour all round, and deemed it best to retire. The Indian Government only found it necessary to take action against certain sections of the press after the murder of Gandhi; otherwise the honeymoon atmosphere prevailed in the first years. By contrast, in Pakistan the central government felt compelled to proceed against seven Karachi papers in the first year after partition, banning four, and imposing censorship upon three.

Nevertheless, the general position of the press in both countries is broadly similar. Firstly, the circulation of newspapers remains small, relative to population. This is partly because of continuing illiteracy (more than four out of every five adults still cannot read) and partly because of the limitations on distribution. This, again, is partly due to poor communications, and partly to the nature of the distributive system in the sub-continent. Casual sales by bookstalls and newsvendors are on a very limited scale; most periodicals rely upon the regular subscriber, and in the rural areas, readers can only obtain their copies by post. These restrictions militate against any kind of sales campaign. In brief, only about one person in every hundred in the sub-continent buys a daily newspaper, and even if the paper is passed on to four or five other readers, this still remains a tiny section of the population which draws its news and views from the press.

Publication of daily papers is confined to the major cities: although middle-sized towns may have a population up to 100,000, they will not include a large leisured or retired group, drawn from the landowning and professional classes, nor a university population, these being the nucleus of the newspaper-reading public. The large city may support several daily papers: for example, Lucknow, the State capital of Uttar Pradesh (population, 1951: 496,861), possesses nine daily papers, of which two are in English, three in Hindi, and four in Urdu. When the local circulation position is analysed, it appears that the English-language papers come first. Of the 9,000 Lucknow subscribers to these papers, 56 per cent take the *Pioneer,* and 31 per cent the *National Herald*; 13 per cent only take Allahabad or Delhi papers, such as the *Statesman* or the *Leader.* The predominance of the local paper is obvious.

In make-up, language, and subject-matter, the English-language press has a distinctly Victorian air. Among the subjects considered news, sport (mainly football and cricket) and crime are given considerable space. Sex is conspicuously absent; except as an adjunct to crime, in which it is well-featured. Much attention is given to the comings and goings of local big-wigs; landlords, politicians, and senior officials. But pride of place is always given to politics. Politics mean, very largely, the debates in Parliament—both at Delhi and at Westminster—and in the state legislature. When editorial comment is made, it is delivered in the grand Delane style. Here is an example, taken quite at random, from the *Pioneer* for January 18, 1958, and headed, 'integrity in the Administration'.

> Nepotism and corruption are evils as old as the hills. They can be exorcised neither by exhortations nor admonitions. Only strong public opinion and resolute action of those in authority in the policy-making reaches can minimise these evils. Their total eradication is not possible, human nature being what it is, either in a totalitarian or a democratic Government. Prodded by public clamour for a cleaner administration several State Governments have taken measures—at least on paper— to keep a more effective watch on Government servants. . . . That in a democracy no one should be immune from public scrutiny in public interest has been further recognised. . . . It has been decided that allegations against Ministers will not go unnoticed. . . . This is a welcome and long overdue decision. . . . What is needed . . . is a certain ruthlessness to purge the administration of the twin evils—'sifarish' [favour] and graft —which have bitten deep into our democratic system.

The Old Lady of Printing House Square could not have done better herself.

The vernacular press presents a different picture. Circulation figures are much lower. The total daily circulation of the *Pioneer* is 10,411; of which 43 per cent is bought in Lucknow, and the remainder in surrounding districts. Total circulation of the *National Herald* is 9,609. The main Urdu paper published in Lucknow sells 2,870 copies: all other Urdu papers appearing in U.P. have a circulation of 1,000 or less. The main Hindi paper of Lucknow is *Swatantra Bharat,* with 4,847 copies printed daily. As we shall discover, there are larger vernacular papers published elsewhere, but these examples taken from one city are typical of the vernacular press at large; and we have not descended into the underworld of the poison-papers, where a circulation of three or four hundred (mainly distributed as 'complimentary' copies) is usual.

In gathering the news, the vernacular papers begin with one major disadvantage: all news coming from the agencies is in English. Not only do Reuters and Associated Press distribute their world-material in English, but also the Press Trust of India, and the United Press of India present their Indian coverage of news in English. Whereas the English-language papers can take material straight off the tape and put it into print, the vernacular papers are compelled to translate all their copy. In consequence, they are often very slow in getting a news-item into their columns, and most often they just do not make the effort to do more than follow the obvious big stories which are given on the radio. While the English-language papers can claim to offer a balanced coverage of the news, the vernacular coverage is distorted, and very weak on international or national events. The vernacular paper, with notable exceptions, is a local paper; interested in State politics, if it is published in the State capital, where the politicians may form a large proportion of its readership; but if located elsewhere, then mainly preoccupied with the politics of the district. If the vernacular press gains ground in the sub-continent, as appears likely, then the fissiparous forces of region and caste will have been substantially reinforced. After the riots in Assam in 1960 against the Bengali minority, an official statement declared that 'During the disturbances and afterwards, certain sections of the press, by instigating, fomenting and engendering a spirit of retaliation and revenge, and sometimes by giving publicity to false rumours or exaggerated accounts had endangered the peace of the State'. The outbreak of anti-Muslim feeling in U.P. in October 1961, which led to riots in a dozen towns, was similarly fanned by the emotionalism of the Hindu communal press. The politics of hatred is always news.

The average vernacular paper, then, will give a large space to local politics; usually presenting issues as 'agitations' of some kind. A high proportion of space will be taken up by advertisements. The large advertisements will be devoted to the local cinema, and branded goods of all kinds; the small advertisements will be mainly on the lines of 'B.A. with good prospects seeks bride, must have fair complexion'. The dependence of the small vernacular papers on advertising revenue is another limitation on their independence. In several instances, State governments have stifled incipient 'agitations' by notifying a paper that if it caused trouble it would no longer carry public notices. Only the more powerful English-language papers have been able to resist this not very subtle form of pressure. The vernacular paper usually only employs two or three reporters, and continues to pay them a pittance. In consequence, young men float through journalism, until they can find more attractive employment. Some will value journalistic experience because it brings them into contact with public men. They are unlikely to damage their standing by reporting in a critical style.

Altogether, the contribution of the press as a public watch-dog—or even in providing a reliable flow of information, is limited to a few exceptional papers. Partly because most of the old-established journals come within the Indian boundaries, but also because Indian public men have shown more regard for, at any rate, the formalities of press freedom, the press appears to be in a more healthy condition in India than in Pakistan.

According to the Registrar of Newspapers in India, the total circulation of the 212 daily papers is 2,460,000, of which 2,320,000 are actually sold (the rest are distributed free). The largest group, in terms of circulation, are the forty three English dailies, totalling 730,000. Hindi papers (forty-two) number 340,000; Gujarati (twenty-four) number 270,000; Marathi (twenty-two), 230,000; Tamil (eleven), 171,000; Malayalam (nine), 150,000; Urdu (nineteen), 120,000; and Kannada (eleven), 110,000. Of the ten top-selling dailies, five are in English, and only one in Hindi; the rest are in Tamil, Bengali, and other regional languages. This provides a measure of the popular reaction to the movement to make Hindi the national language. The *Indian Express* has emerged as the biggest paper in the sub-continent. It is, basically, one paper, though it is printed in four different centres; Bombay, Delhi, Madras, and Madurai. Its total daily sales have exceeded 200,000. The editor-in-chief is Frank Moraes, an independent-minded Indian Catholic. He has attempted to emancipate his papers from the Victorian pattern, but despite the choice of title, they still do not much resemble the British popular press. Moraes has taken a tough line on Chinese border invasions, and generally adopted a Rightist attitude. Among the other big English-language papers, the *Hindustan Times* is the voice of Rightwing Congress opinion. The *Statesman* (published in Delhi and Calcutta) and *The Times of India* contrive to appear somewhat detached, though generally supporting Nehru. The *Amrita Bazar Patrika*, as an English-language paper, has been printed at Allahabad since 1943, as well as in Calcutta. The Madras *Hindu* wears its Congress colours with a liberal, sometimes internationalist air. It is upon papers such as these that the maintenance of independent, responsible journalism in India mainly depends..

All these eminently respectable and responsible journals are owned, however, by powerful business interests, Marwari or Parsi. For example, the Birla chain has a controlling interest in eleven major papers; other outstanding press barons are Goenka and Dalmia, who like Birla are Marwaris.

Partly because they patently subordinate news to propaganda, the avowedly party journals do not possess either large circulations or influence. The Communists have dailies in Bengali, Telugu, and Malayalam. The best-known Communist publication, *New Age,* is published from Delhi and Madras. Its circulation figures are unknown, but probably do not exceed 10,000. The Socialists have a few small weeklies, and the Ganatantra Parishad has its own Oriya daily. The spectacular rise of the Tamil Separatist party, Dravida Munnetra Kazhagam, in Madras may owe something to its two weeklies—one in Tamil, and one in English.

The position of the press in Pakistan provides a striking instance of the problems which arise in the attempt to create one nation out of two culturally separated areas. First, there is the technical problem of establishing a national press when the two wings are 1,000 miles apart. Because Pakistan International Airways fly an overnight service between Karachi and Dacca, and Lahore and Dacca, all through the week, it is possible to distribute the principal western papers in Dacca on the morning after they are printed; but circulation outside the eastern capital area is impossible.

The press in West Pakistan caters mainly for the small, Westernised urban group. *Dawn* retains much of the prestige of the name of Jinnah (which it still carries at the head of its cover-page). Its Delhi offices were wrecked at the time of partition, but the editor and some of the staff escaped to Karachi, where Jinnah persuaded the Haroon family to begin publishing a new *Dawn* on their printing-presses. The paper continued in broad support of the League, until the military take-over; it continues to offer support to Ayub, though it urges the need for greater flexibility in relations with the Communist bloc. A Gujarati edition of *Dawn* is also issued from Karachi. The *Pakistan Times* was the mouthpiece of Mian Iftikharuddin, the crypto-Communist politician, until October 1958. The military then compelled Iftikharuddin to sell his paper to owners more acceptable to the new régime. Published simultaneously from Lahore and Rawalpindi, the *Pakistan Times* maintains a definite standard of journalistic competence. The other Lahore English-language journal, the *Civil and Military Gazette,* survives largely on its past reputation for responsible conservatism. The *Morning News* is published in Karachi, and also in Dacca; it has a Right-wing, non-Bengali policy.

Jang (War) owned by Khalilur Rahman is probably the outstanding Urdu paper. Formerly a Delhi paper, it has a wide popularity both in West and East Pakistan. *Nawa-e-Waqt,* published in Lahore, continued to pursue an independent policy under its editor, Hamid Nizami, during the military régime. Nizami continued to urge President Ayub to restore democracy; unfortunately he died, early in 1962, after a heart attack. Other notable western Urdu journals are *Imroz* (the vernacular counterpart of *Pakistan Times*), *Anjam, Kohistan, Shahbaz,* and *Afaq.*

The transfer of the capital from Karachi to Rawalpindi, pending the building of Islamabad has posed problems for the western press. A paper such as *Dawn* would prefer to print an edition for the capital, in order to reach an influential readership; but Rawalpindi cannot provide the necessary advertising revenue, so vital to newspapers in the sub-continent (and, presumably, everywhere else); so it appears probable that the administrative capital of Pakistan will be without a proper daily press. The tendency towards absolutism in the executive will remain unchecked.

East Pakistan, with more of a literate middle class, and a more highly developed political tradition has a more flourishing press. Two morning English-language papers appear in Dacca; the *Morning News,* and the *Pakistan Observer.* The latter is owned by a former Minister and lieutenant of Fazl-ul-Haq, Hamidul Haq Chowdhury, against whom PRODA proceedings were instituted in 1956. The *Observer,* then, is Bengali and somewhat hostile to officialdom in its tone. The army has started the *Daily Mail* as an evening paper to represent the views of the régime. Chittagong's *Eastern Observer* completes the English-language press. The Bengali press is, naturally, the most flourishing. *Azad* claims a circulation in the region of 15,000; this was formerly the official League organ, controlled by Maulana Akram Khan; it gives support to the present régime. *Ittefaq,* as the medium of the Awami League, adopted a more radical, and frequently anti-West Pakistan line. *Sangbad,* at one time a League paper, became a journal of the far Left, adopting a strongly militant attitude over the rôle of Bengali as a national language.

The Pakistan press has operated, both under the politicians and under the army, in the shadow of censorship and penal repression. The editors of both *Ittefaq* and *Sangbad* have gone to prison for adopting attitudes unwelcome to the administration. Papers have been suppressed, fines levied, and a system of precensorship has operated. It is true that many have been (in the words of a highly-qualified observer) 'wildly irresponsible and malicious'.[1] Freedom and responsibility must go together; if one is lacking, the other will also disappear.

[1] Keith Callard, 'Pakistan', in *Major Governments of Asia,* Ed. G. M. Kahin, Cornell University Press, 1958, p. 449.

IX

THE SILENT PEOPLE

THIS analysis of power and influence has at several points descended to
the level of the ordinary people, but it has dwelt much more among the
rulers than the ruled. Looking at the politics of language and caste, we
noticed how the Westernised, urbane all-Indian leader is being replaced
by the local political boss: yet we also saw how the new politics is creating its own Establishment. Although the new politician is compelled to
woo the mass electorate, he still manipulates the politics of a super-
imposed system; he is not really required to sound, or interpret the will
of those he purports to serve. Perhaps this is inevitable in any political
situation: it has been called the iron law of oligarchy. In his poem 'the
Secret People' (which helped to suggest the title of this chapter), G. K.
Chesterton observed how the rulers of England, even when pretending
to express the people's will, were supporting the interests of an Establishment. Yet Chesterton leaves the rulers with a warning:

> Smile at us, pay us, pass us; but do not quite forget;
> For we are the people of England, that have never spoken yet.

Some might say that since that poem was composed the people of England have indeed spoken; to their rulers' astonishment. But the people of
India and Pakistan still 'have not spoken yet'. Today's masters are very
different from the Mughals and the British of yesterday: but they are
masters yet. The District Magistrate may (it is possible) be the son of a
trader or a schoolmaster; but he still retains the aura of aloof pomp and
unpredictable power which pertained to his Mughal predecessor. The
politician is a new man indeed, and his speech is full of phrases about the
'national struggle' and 'freedom fighters'. But his motives seem to be the

same as those of ambitious men throughout time: the exploitation of power for profit. In olden days, officials were said to 'eat' the revenues of the districts they ruled. Today's Minister is a hearty eater: many State Ministers in India are directors of thirty companies, or more.

Both in India and Pakistan, political planners concerned with the problem of the concentration and abuse of power within a narrow circle of leadership have sought a remedy in decentralisation. In India this is called 'democratic decentralisation', and in Pakistan 'basic democracy', but in both the goal is to awaken a spirit of responsibility and initiative among the village people. This philosophy is surprisingly similar to that which influenced British policy in the earliest phase of the national awakening; the idea of training the ordinary people in political responsibility through local self-government.

In the 1880s, Lord Ripon mooted the notion of setting up village councils, as a conscious attempt to build upon the panchayat, but it was not until the 1920s that village councils were promoted to any significant extent. During the Dyarchy period, most of the provinces introduced legislation to give statutory powers to these bodies. A division emerged between those provinces which sought to equate the unit with the actual village (in imitation of the legendary village panchayat) and those who established units which were, in effect, the basis of a system of rural local government. Probably the most effective in this class were the Union Boards set up in Bengal; they covered, on average, an area of eleven square miles, and 8,000 inhabitants.

While the Bengal union boards were linked with the superstructure of rural local government, the new panchayats were mainly expected to function in isolation, apart from the sporadic supervision of the district officer and his staff. This reflected the widely accepted theory of the 'self-sufficient Indian village' as providing the historic pattern of rural life. We have had occasion to notice how caste marriage ties and jajmani create a web of petty inter-village relationships; but all this was ignored. Left to themselves, the panchayats registered only very limited achievements; although particularly enterprising villages could and did bring about important changes. One of the most far-reaching innovations was the creation of petty Courts to dispose of petty cases. In the administrative sphere, the panchayats were restricted; both in their resources—amounting only to a few rupees—and in their functions, confined to the upkeep of a few dirt roads, the provision of a few oil lamps, and the employment of a few sanitary sweepers.

The panchayat experiment, because it did not yield tangible results in a short time, was largely brushed aside in favour of rural uplift, or rural reconstruction. This began as the individual enthusiasm of a few British officials, of whom F. L. Brayne and M. L. Darling are probably the best known. Sir Malcolm Darling's approach was mainly economic; he placed great emphasis upon co-operatives; as agencies for agricultural credit, for the improvement of farming techniques, and for improved marketing. He and his school argued that if the peasant was shown how he could raise his standard of living by better techniques, then he would, as a natural consequence, adopt ideas which were socially desirable. Brayne's approach was more or less the reverse; he preached that first the peasant must be led to see how custom was dragging him down; when he had got rid of the filth, sent his daughters to school, and otherwise liberated himself from the slough—only then would he be capable of becoming more progressive in the economic field. It would be wrong to present the methods of Darling and Brayne as entirely opposed: but an argument in chicken or egg terms has largely dominated this field down to the present. Brayne's intention was to stimulate village initiative, and he set up 'village guides', drawn from among the more enterprising leaders, to act as intermediaries between the village folk and authority. But undoubtedly he forced the pace; he was impatient of the slowness of natural change, and imposed his will, rather than wait patiently for the village people to make up their own minds. Darling's appeal to the economic motive met with a more immediate response, and before independence a flourishing co-operative movement had been established.

In striking contrast to these officially-inspired movements was the Gandhian village cult. Gandhi made his political impact by appealing to the masses, and in a land where four out of five people live in the countryside, this meant an appeal to village India. When Gandhi began upon his first rural operation, in Champaran District in 1917, he had been absent from India for many years, and he viewed the Indian village through spectacles borrowed from Ruskin, Tolstoy, and Kropotkin. Strange mixture of mystic, and calculating lawyer-politician that he was, Gandhi contrived to see a community that was shaped as he wanted it to be. He saw the 'self-sufficient village community'; marred by a spirit of selfishness and materialism perhaps, as a result of Western influences, but still continuing in essence. By the revival of village crafts and industries, and the removal of the dark satanic mills of Western capitalism the old community spirit would be revitalised. With village life reborn, all the apparatus of the centralised, Westernised state could be discarded. India would then be a federation of village republics; the British Raj would have been replaced by Panchayat Raj.

The Gandhian vision appeared in the Indian constitution in attenuated form. Article 40 provided for the formation of village panchayats 'as units of self government'. Most State governments introduced legislation to implement this directive, but once again there was a clash of views on the size of the new bodies, between big and small panchayats. The small units were more closely related to the actual communities they incorporated; the large units would have larger resources and could be given wider powers. Once again, the concept of 'self-sufficiency' led to these panchayats functioning as autonomous and isolated bodies.

Amid the stress of rapid social and political change which characterises independent India, the panchayats served mainly as a forum for conflict. The Balvantray Team in their report of 1957, declared that 'the number of panchayats which were torn by factions or in which squabbles are rampant is large. In fact in some States they are in a majority. . . . Panchayat elections have resulted in creating or aggravating factional rivalries in about one-third of the villages in which there was a contest'.[1]

Political theorists sought a remedy for this situation in sarvodaya. 'It is this principle of unanimity which was the soul of panchayats in ancient India, and it requires revivification', urged a committee of the Congress convened by S. N. Agarwal, a leading Gandhian ideologue. Speaking less from theory, the Minister for Local Self-Government in U.P. observed that the panchayats 'suffered more from poverty than from any other evil or disease'. The panchayats were endowed with powers to raise taxes, but most preferred not to apply them. Even those taxes which they were compelled by law to levy were not collected: average collections amounted to under 50 per cent, and panchayat members figure prominently among the defaulters. The majority of panchayats (including the 'big' panchayats) have a total annual income of less than Rs. 500 (say £40, or $100), and over half their budget is spent on the salary of the secretary, and other working costs. A survey of sixty panchayats at work revealed that only about twenty made provision for lighting, or street cleaning, while 'their rôle in economic development is negligible'.

Faced with evidence of the short-term failure of the panchayat experiment, those in authority behaved exactly like their predecessors in the 1920s and '30s: they abandoned one nostrum and took up another. Once again, the remedy was sought in rural reconstruction, now called community development. Soon after independence, a number of 'pilot projects' were launched, the best-publicised being the Etawah Project, whose

---

[1] This quotation, and those that follow, will be found in the author's 'Authority and Community in Village India', *Pacific Affairs*, December, 1959.

presiding genius was Albert Mayer, an American architect and town planner.

Mayer tackled community development as a problem in 'social engineering', a question of bringing together administrative skill and technical know-how from outside, united with the local feeling and effort of the rustic folk, in order to achieve a physical and mental transformation in the village milieu. Mayer placed great emphasis upon realising the 'felt needs' of the people. He insisted that community development must be a co-operative effort between the government and the people. In fostering a team-spirit he placed great emphasis on the village level worker (V.L.W.) who could act as a catalyst, inducing the village folk to realise their aspirations and, through his elementary knowledge of agricultural and public health techniques, demonstrating what could be done. The V.L.W., unlike Brayne's village guides, was not drawn from the village itself; he would almost certainly be a countryman, but from another area. His Hindi title, *Gram Sevak*, 'servant of the village community', had a Gandhian echo; but the rôle of the V.L.W. soon emerged as a representative of the administration, not as a social service worker. Despite Mayer's emphasis on teamwork, the V.L.W. soon became the lowest member of the new development administrative hierarchy, stretching up to the district officer. The Etawah Project was undoubtedly a success; but this derived less from the spontaneous response of the rural people than from the single-minded leadership of Mayer and his able colleagues.

The Etawah Project was merged into a nation-wide programme, launched in October 1952. In the beginning there were fifteen pilot projects, based upon the 'block' covering between sixty and 100 villages; the block being divided into circles of five or six villages, each under the superintendence of a Gram Sevak. By 1962 there were 3,100 blocks covering about 370,000 villages with a population of 200,000,000 (about three-fifths of rural India). Yet this immense achievement was accompanied by an ever increasing volume of criticism. The Balvantray Report, which appeared in November 1957, brought this to a head, insisting that the programme was right off its course. It had been intended to kindle a new spirit of community, and to assist in launching the 'take off' in agricultural development; but instead it had been diverted into an officially-controlled 'bricks and mortar' programme of public works, lacking almost any popular dynamic. All the drive was provided by the administration, yet the District Officer, the lynch-pin of the system, could not devote more than half his time to development. The actual head of activities in the field was the Block Development Officer. There were supposed to be advisory committees, representing the countryfolk, both at district and block level, but these had only a shadowy existence. Meetings were called only rarely, and then attendance averaged a little over 50 per cent. The village representatives were uneasily aware that the officials remained firmly in control, and so they were constrained to 'play it safe' to defer to official proposals. The element of self-help and voluntary service which was supposed to distinguish community development flagged. All the village folk were expected to contribute voluntary labour which, in imitation of Bhave's bhoodan, was called shramdan, or work-gift. From many villagers came the complaint that the new shramdan was exactly the same as the old begar; compulsory labour, which was levied in former times by Mughal officials and landlords.

Faced with evidence that, despite all the publicity extolling the 'people's participation', the community development programme showed 'excessive dependence on continued government initiative', the Balvantray team made radical proposals for devolution and popular control. Their Report recognised that they were recommending 'an act of faith in democracy', for up till then there was little solid evidence of the readiness of rustic leaders to take over responsibility for the community development programme. They stressed that 'It is not theory or dogma which is impelling us to make these recommendations but practical considerations. Democracy has to function through certain executive machinery', such machinery must be devised to 'appreciate local needs and circumstances'. Accordingly, the main responsibility for economic and social activity should in future be entrusted to a local representative council at the level of the block, to be called a Panchayat Samiti. Within the block, the villages and hamlets would be grouped in circles and for this basic area a Gram Panchayat would be elected by the people. The Gram Panchayat members would choose, from among their own number, representatives to sit on the Panchayat Samiti. Where 5 per cent or more of the population belonged to the Scheduled Castes or Tribes, they would send a representative to the block council. The presidents of all Panchayat Samitis in a district, together with the local M.Ps and M.L.As, and the heads of the various departments, were to meet together in the Zila Parishad or district council. This would replace the former institutions of local self-government, but would not inherit their executive powers; it was supposed to be a co-ordinating body only.

This revolutionary proposal—aimed at liquidating the autocratic district system, which had served Mughals and British alike—was accepted by most of the States. The new order was called *Panchayati Raj*, no longer *Panchayat Raj;* instead of village government, government of the

villages. The distinction cannot be relegated to the realm of semantics
—there is a genuine difference; the 'self-sufficient village' concept was
finally relinquished. Henceforth, the village merged into the neighbourhood, and the neighbourhood into the district. Moreover, the adoption
of a system of indirect election—sometimes called 'functional representation'—for the higher councils, was a departure from standard Anglo-
Saxon notions of election. The attempt to lower the level of decision-
making from the district to the block, was a reversal of the centralising
pressures of the first years of independence.

Balvantray G. Mehta is a hard-headed Gujarati business man and as
former Secretary General of the Congress Party a tough, realistic politician; yet his community development scheme showed a remarkable
resemblance to *A Plea for Reconstruction of Indian Polity*, drafted by
Jayaprakash Narayan, who is usually characterised in the foreign press
as an idealist and a dreamer. Jayaprakash wishes to replace the present
'centralism' in India by a 'communitarian society'. His goal is *gram
dharma*. 'The function of dharma is to hold together harmoniously the
social order', he says; it is law rooted in social custom, or social ethics.
Jayaprakash looks to a federation of villages as the future Indian polity,
but he sees further than Gandhi in setting the village within a broader
context. He expects associated villages (which he calls the 'regional
community') to provide the main focus for his communitarian society:
'As we proceed from the inner to the outer circles of communal life and
organisation, there is less and less to do . . . so that when we reach the
circle of the National Community it has only a few matters to attend to,
such as defence, foreign policy, currency.' The present vast responsibilities of the Centre in the economic and social field would be dissolved:
'Planning would begin from the primary community and therefrom fan
outwards. In our scheme of things the . . . plan of the regional community
would be the pivotal plan. This would mean the regional plan—and not
the village plan which would be too small for the purpose—would be the
unit out of which the whole national plan would have to be constructed.'
The first draft of Jayaprakash Narayan's *Reconstruction* appeared in
1959, and formed the most cogent statement among many appearing at
this time of the new concept of democracy, based on the community,
rather than stemming from the individual voter.[1] Almost at the same
moment, the President of Pakistan—a statesman who at almost every
point differs from Jayaprakash—came out with his Basic Democracy

[1] His ideas bear a close relationship to those of Salvador de Madariaga as
expressed in his *De l'angoisse à la liberté* (Paris, 1953), subsequently published
in English under the title *Democracy versus Liberty?* (London, 1958).

proposals, also designed to change the unit of political choice from the individual voter (who had been 'driven like cattle to the polling station', as Ayub was later to say) to the broader, more solid basis of the rural community.

Community development in Pakistan was launched on a more restricted scale, and at a later date than in India. It was called Village AID (its full title being Village Agricultural and Industrial Development) and emphasis was mainly upon improved farming as the key to social awakening. Whereas the Indian programme was mainly conceived in terms of Brayne's philosophy of social uplift and regeneration, Pakistan followed Darling (who had left the stamp of his ideas all over Punjab officialdom) in building up the peasant's confidence by showing him he could raise his living standards by his own efforts. Initiated in 1954, the programme was designed to penetrate one-quarter of the villages within five years. The development structure was roughly similar to that in India (which, indeed, forms a more or less standard pattern in South and East Asia). A senior and farsighted Pakistani official emphasised that, in this new venture, 'the true rôle of the district officer is that of a guide, friend and philosopher and not that of a local despot'. Among the tough peasantry of West Pakistan, this was not easy to apply: they respect the strong man and despise the weakling, and where strength and domineering had for so long been equated, this new relationship of equality between rulers and ruled was hard to grasp. However, where the scheme was thoroughly worked out, there were solid results in terms of economic improvement. In terms of social change, the consequences were negligible. Like most development programmes, that in Pakistan did not attain the initial targets. By March 1959, development covered 18,456 villages, with a population of 1,269,800 out of a total rural population in Pakistan (1951 Census) of 68,000,000. Roughly two-thirds of the developed area was in the western wing: yet another example of how the east lags behind in economic progress. Of the techniques applied by the Village AID personnel, Brigadier Gulzar Ahmad (who assumed charge of Village AID when it was renamed the National Development Organisation) commented: 'We have become increasingly aware of the discrepancy between the theories taught in the classroom and the problems which must be met in the field.' As in India, an invisible line separates dogma and practice. The development officials are fully conversant with the doctrines enunciated by the American experts on 'group participation' and 'realisation of felt needs', but these same officials will often prove indifferent to the actual demands in the development areas, concentrating on 'development mathematics'—in the words of the Chief

Administrator of the National Development Organisation of Pakistan. By 'development mathematics', the Chief Administrator, Masih-uz-Zaman, means the paraphernalia of targets, plans, statistics, reports and graphs with which the administrators and the American experts have embellished the programme, in both Pakistan and India. Masih-uz-Zaman finds an even more fundamental reason why theory and practice have often been in conflict.

> It is one of the inner contradictions of community develop-
> ment that the people directing the programme represent the
> interests and classes which stand to lose their status, privilege
> and power if the programme succeeds. Today, political and
> economic power is concentrated in the hands of the westernised
> élite, and specially the Government servants. Democratisation
> of the society is bound to reduce this power. . . . It is therefore
> not surprising that the community development workers some-
> times fail to practise what they teach.[1]

However, encouraging experience in the Village AID programme was one of the factors in the decision by President Ayub and his advisers to launch the Basic Democracies. The new system bore a striking resemblance to the structure for community development proposed by Balvantray Mehta, though there is no evidence of actual borrowing. The basic unit, the Union Council, covered a somewhat larger area than the Gram Panchayat in India, as did the next 'tier', the Tahsil or Thana Council. There were also District Councils, Divisional Councils, and a Provincial Development Council for each wing. The members of the Union Councils (who are known as 'Basic Democrats') are directly elected by the village folk, but all the upper tiers are formed by indirect election from the inferior councils, together with officials sitting ex-officio. The District Council and the tiers above are so heavily weighted by the official membership that they have hardly any representative character. Unlike the Balvantray scheme, which gives the second level the main executive responsibility, the Basic Democracies' main activity is envisaged at the primary level. The Union Councils in East Pakistan are virtually a replacement for the Union Boards; they cover much the same area and population—about 10,500 souls. In the West, there had been no local authorities beneath the District Boards, and it was necessary to chalk out the whole scheme anew; because the population is generally more scattered, the Union population was fixed at 8,000. Whereas in

---

[1] Reproduced in *Village AID; Some Articles and Reports*, West Pakistan Government, Lahore, 1960, p. 176.

India *Panchayati Raj* was gradually introduced, State by State, Basic Democracy came into being throughout Pakistan at the same time. Elections were completed in West Pakistan by January 9, 1960, and in the East by February 14, 1960. All the Basic Democracies were 'inducted' by the end of February.

The President has claimed that (with minor exceptions) the Basic Democrats are all 'persons of substance in the community'. Information coming forward seems to show that traditional leaders have obtained most seats; former politicians are poorly represented; and a small movement has begun among the under-privileged to obtain a voice in affairs. In East Pakistan, members included traders, contractors, lawyers, maulvis and other religious leaders, and of course, farmers. A few persons of real eminence were elected, such as a retired Judge, and a former Principal of a medical college. About 10 per cent of the Basic Democrats were matriculates, and 98 per cent claimed to be literate. A survey of the Chairmen of the Union Councils in the East established that 20 per cent had 'a political background', and that 15 per cent belonged to the upper middle class, 50 per cent to the middle class, and 35 per cent to the lower middle class. In short, in East Pakistan the new Union Councils were broadly similar in composition to the old Union Boards. The apparently scant success of the Hindu minority in obtaining only 12 per cent of the seats, when they comprise 30 per cent of the total population, was, in fact, a tribute to the tenacity with which they have clung to their place in commerce, the professions and public life. The new West Pakistan Basic Democrats came from a wider social range. Nearly one-third were illiterate, and under 10 per cent were matriculates. A large majority were new to public life, and many came from the lower classes. The landlord-politicians, though excluded from directly entering the contest, appear to have promoted their nominees from behind well-concealed vantage points. Thus, in Sarghoda District, the former rivalry between the Noon family and Daultana simmered on through their nominees upon the new councils. Throughout much of Punjab, the retired Honorary Lieutenants and Honorary Captains, whom Ayub would clearly wish to come forward, have been elected in impressive numbers.[1] Yet it must be acknowledged that the President has succeeded in drawing upon a much wider pool of leadership than ever the former régime included.

The promotion of Basic Democracy cast a shadow over the Village AID programme, which was renamed the National Development

[1] Examples taken from Khalid Bin Sayeed, 'Pakistan's Basic Democracy', *Middle East Journal*, Washington, Summer 1961.

Organisation, and placed, with Basic Democracy, under the control of a Ministry of National Reconstruction. We have seen how, under British rule, in the rural setting 'political education' and 'economic development' could never co-exist; one was always outpaced by the other. From 1960, community development was regarded as ancillary to Basic Democracy. It was assigned the rôle of technical advice and service; its training academies were required to provide 'orientation' and training to officials and chairmen of the Basic Democracies. Because there were inadequate funds and resources, Basic Democracy regarded with some envy the allocation which Development had secured, under American patronage. Basic Democracy was backed by a particularly dynamic military man, Brigadier F. R. Khan, and included a sizeable proportion of army officers in its organisation. All the signs indicate that it is likely to swallow the development organisation as it gains strength.

The object of both these institutions is summarised in this quotation from the report of a study group of officials: 'From minor welfare work they were being called upon to take part in the national development effort.... The local effort instead of being an effort in isolation was now to beome a part of the integrated whole.' In the process of integration, would the popular, grass-roots character of village development be swallowed up by the exertions of the benevolent despots? This is the dilemma which attends Ayub's great experiment; his people must be trained to govern themselves, to take initiative; but they must also take part in the rapid modernisation of the economy, if Pakistan is not to slip back into stagnation. Will the one prejudice the other? After only two years' working, it is dangerous to generalise about the direction in which the Union Councils are heading; the following can only be a very tentative analysis. In East Pakistan, the Union Councils continue to act very much on the lines of their predecessors. They exhibit a noticeable reluctance to raise taxation, particularly to introduce graduated taxes upon the middle classes, the traders, contractors, and professional people. In consequence, their activities are still very limited; inadequate primary schools, inadequate health services and a few marginal social services. Only where there is exceptionally enlightened leadership is there any significant change. In Noakhali District, the centre of Islamic orthodoxy, the Municipal committee (now a side-shoot of the Basic Democracies structure) has introduced a marriage tax, designed to curb polygamy. For the first wife, the rate is Rs. 2, for the second additional wife, Rs. 50, and for the third, Rs. 500. There are other signs in the East that the ordinary peasant is prepared to take part in social change, when he understands its purpose; the history of recent attempts to take literacy to

Muslim women has seen, initially, intense opposition—followed by gradual approval, when the benefits of female literacy are understood. The Union Councils in the West, untrammelled by established notions of local government, have shown more enterprise. New taxes have been widely introduced, and quite frequently members of the less well regarded clans, like the Gujars, have stood up against the rural gentry. The ordinary people have to overcome many disadvantages; illiteracy, in the conditions of today, almost disarms a rustic who attempts to take a stand against a town man, or a petty official. The former may succeed in carrying the Council with him; but the latter can use the regulations, and their ability to communicate with higher officials to checkmate the rustics.

At all levels of consultation above the Union Council, the rural members are placed at a disadvantage by the tendency of officials and experts to communicate in English. It is argued that legal or technical matters can only be adequately considered in English. This is a genuine dilemma, which can only be solved by genuine compromise.

While this vast experiment was being launched in Pakistan, India was implementing the Balvantray Report: a similar solution to the problem of awakening a dynamic spirit among the country people, and gradually adjusting the rôle of the higher civil service from ruling to advising.

Rajasthan was the first State to initiate Panchayati Raj—in October 1959. Andhra, Madras, and Punjab followed soon after; while almost all the States in the Union passed legislation to enable them to adopt the new system. When the Gram Panchayats were constituted, considerable pressure was exerted from above to eliminate elections. Jayaprakash in his *Reconstruction* urged that the selection of panches should be reached 'by general agreement or by drawing lots' (the latter method is supposed to have been followed in antiquity, and is employed in the Bhoodan movement for the distribution of lands). Tangible inducements were offered to villages which were able to demonstrate their 'harmony' by dispensing with elections. In Punjab, for example, much higher grants were allotted to such villages; nevertheless, only about a quarter of the councils came into being without elections; a smaller figure than among English Rural District Councils, where apathy rather than ideology militates against elections.

A rather long period elapsed between the inauguration of Panchayati Raj and its effective introduction, in most States. Rajasthan did not hold elections until December 1960, when (despite the political backwardness of this State) considerable party activity took place. This was noticeable especially in the selection of the Chairman or Sarpanch of the Gram Panchayat. These men would form the major element in the next layer, the block Panchayat Samiti, and would choose the Pradhan or Chairman; the key figure in the new situation. Congress was most active in the elections, and the post-election deals. As at the national level, Congress politicians seem to equate the concept of sarvodaya with Congress Raj. If a Congress chairman is elected, this demonstrates the virtues of political harmony; if another party succeeds in installing its man, then this demonstrates the evils of "fifty-one per cent democracy" and factionalism. In Rajasthan, the Congress brought in many outsiders as candidates for the key post of Pradhan; most were old hands in politics; many were townspeople, with lawyers well-represented. A survey disclosed that two-thirds of the Pradhans were Congress-men; a much higher proportion than the party commanded in the State legislature.

First reports from Rajasthan and Andhra indicate that the new system, placing substantial funds and other resources in the control of the block councils, has considerably raised the temperature of local politics. In Andhra and Madras (another early beginner on the new system) the District Officer has succeeded in preserving a position as *Deus ex Machina* in local affairs; but in Rajasthan, where there was no I.C.S. tradition, Panchayati Raj and its considerable resources are at the absolute disposal of the new political bosses. They are discovering that, as in the United States, the ward boss must look after his supporters. The politics of the pork barrel is being learnt fast. In the first phase of Panchayati Raj, as in State politics, the principal beneficiaries are the middle castes; especially the prosperous farmers—and to some extent the quasi-farmers who have been created by land reform legislation out of the former absentee landlord classes. These are the people who know their way around the labyrinth of rural power and influence, and who, having obtained a firm footing in the new councils, will reap a substantial share of the benefits now accruing. In time, it may be expected that numbers will begin to count, and the less prosperous sections of the rural community will acquire the needful political literacy that will enable them to exert pressure from within the councils. But that day has not yet come; and meanwhile the rural masses seek a champion in the Congress Party and in Nehru. Their faith that Nehru and the Congress will raise them up, lay behind the continuing support they gave to the ruling party in the 1962 elections.

Is there any prospect of Panchayati Raj being extended upward, as Basic Democracy ascends to the provincial level? Addressing Parliament on May 13, 1961, S. K. Dey, Minister for Community Development declared: 'It is hoped in future some sort of functional representation will be provided by Zila Parishads, both in the State legislature and, maybe, indirectly in the Parliament.' At the same time, Dey announced the appointment of Jayaprakash Narayan as chairman of a Study Team on community development. When the revolutionary consequences of the last inquiry by a Study Team are recalled (the Balvantray reforms) then it is not impossible that Jayaprakash will initiate a further root and branch reform.

Should another major step be taken away from an electoral system based on 'one man, one vote' towards a 'communitarian society', this will indicate a real shift in political values. It may be that the latter will prove more democratic, in the context of South Asia; but it will mean abandoning one of the fundamental features of Western liberal democracy; the belief in the autonomy of the individual. The masses in South Asia, so far as their conscious opinions are known, appear to believe that they can only raise themselves up by a mass movement. Dr. Ambedkar, although he appeared in his lifetime to have failed, may be seen as a prototype of the proletarian politics of the future. Should the masses of South Asia succeed in attaining a higher status, they may eventually turn again to a form of politics rooted less in class (as the erstwhile 'working people' of Britain appear to be doing). But this will not happen for a long time yet.

Meanwhile, the Basic Democracies and the Gram Panchayats provide a forum in which the ordinary people may learn to speak. When the peasants and the labourers step forward in their own right, South Asia will see a transformation, compared to which the transfer of power in 1947 will appear to comprise only a prelude or overture.

X

FUTURE INDICATIVE

THE main thoroughfare between the city and the civil lines at Lahore is called the Mall—like all the principal roads in the cantonments throughout the sub-continent. An Englishman who knew the Lahore Mall in former times would find it much the same today. The Lawrence Gardens—renamed Jinnah Gardens—still provide a green shade. The tongas with their wiry ponies still clop down the Mall, and rustic Punjabi accents are sometimes overpowered by the harsh gutturals of Pashtu, as a reminder that central Asia begins here. That relic of the Afghan invader, the great cannon Zam-Zammah, still stands opposite the Lahore Museum on the gun-carriage designed by a former Curator, Rudyard Kipling's father. One landmark the returning Englishman would look for in vain: the striking statue of the first Lieutenant-Governor, John Lawrence. Islamic respect for the Third Commandment has caused this graven image to be moved from its plinth. The statue was taken down before 1958, but one who did not know might readily assume that its removal had been ordered by the military régime. For this was a statue with a message. The burly figure of the pro-consul was represented as standing four-square, holding in one hand a sheathed sabre and in the other, uplifted, a quill pen. Echoing Pope's asseveration that 'The pen is mightier than the sword', John Lawrence was supposed to be challenging the people of Punjab: 'Will ye be governed by the pen or the sword? Choose!'

Can the people of Pakistan be said to have deliberately chosen the rule of the sword? And what if this challenge were repeated in India—say, in western U.P., where Lawrence first learnt to govern? Far better to have this statue out of the way than face the anxious question 'Will ye be governed by the pen or the sword?' The final answer given by the ordinary people of south Asia—if they are afforded the opportunity for a free choice—will affect the whole future of Asia, and probably that of the world.

Whatever machinery were devised to register the choice of the people of Pakistan for a leader today, there can be little serious doubt that Field Marshal Ayub Khan would obtain an overwhelming popular mandate. But while there may be general confidence in his honesty and goodwill, this does not necessarily mean that the politically literate are altogether enthusiastic about his plans. They are proud of their army—which they regard as second to none. But they do not really want military rule. How can this dilemma be resolved? In the past, the Indian Muslims looked to Turkey for political leadership, and Pakistan today feels more affinity to Turkey than to any other country. Yet the Turkish experience demonstrates all too aptly how difficult it is for a quasi-military, quasi-dictatorial régime to transform itself into a democracy; even though that be its purpose. Kemal Ataturk put his faith in education, and one senses that President Ayub is looking to youth—particularly to the youngsters from both West and East Pakistan who are being educated together in the establishments modelled on English public schools at Sarghoda, Hassan Abdal, and elsewhere—to provide the future leadership of the country. Meanwhile, it seems probable that Ayub will remain in power. At his right hand stands General Azam Khan, who relinquished his post as Governor of East Pakistan in April 1962, but who is regarded as a man of political ambition. Here is a successor, if successor be needed; though in Pakistan, the question is not often posed.

In India, the question is constantly propounded. Following the third general election, the conundrum of who will succeed Nehru, and how, and when, remains as baffling as ever. A would-be political prophet can only review the alternatives. First, will Nehru, like Mr. Gladstone (to whom a comparison was earlier made), cling to power too long? Gladstone, it may be argued, in his declining years split his party, spoilt the opportunity to establish a worthy successor, and blurred the issue so that his party failed to evolve a forward-looking programme. Nehru could quite easily do the same. Equally, he may, like Winston Churchill, sense the appropriate moment to retire; and so consolidate his party in office and confirm his own standing at the bar of history. Nehru has been compared to the great banyan tree, which gives shelter and protection to the many, but which prevents the growth of any sapling under its spreading branches. No politician can 'succeed' Nehru in the true sense; he can only follow him. If Nehru has indicated any intention in this matter, it is a secret in which the present writer does not share. Many regard Krishna Menon as Nehru's choice. The two men have almost everything in common: theosophy, science, socialism (bordering, in the 1930s on communism), internationalism, secularism, rationalism, and a deep sense of the holism of India. Krishna Menon has undoubtedly increased his political stature since the third general election. His position—well to the Left of Congress—would be an admirable one for forming a Leftist coalition. He cannot be overlooked: and yet, his accession to the premiership would be against the run of probability. Because he is, intellectually, a man of the West, and because he has spent so much of his life in England, Menon stands apart from the rank and file of Congress. Although he can display great courtesy, and his conversation is a stimulant, Menon's personality is his greatest drawback. Rudeness, rage, and sulkiness are overlooked in Nehru, because he is Panditji. But Krishna Menon is not Panditji; and there are few persons in public life who do not bear him a grudge. Finally, with every year that passes, Menon's age becomes a disability. Nehru was born in 1889; Menon in 1897. Nehru became Prime Minister at the age of 56; Menon would be over 65 on taking office. It is scarcely conceivable that he could be a candidate when he has passed the age of 70.[1]

Possibly, Nehru would turn to one of 'the managers' to follow him; Lal Bahadur Shastri is known to be close to the Prime Minister. But this could only happen in circumstances of internal and external stability. As Indian politics becomes less like the unified politics of Britain, and more like the locally-based politics of North America, so leadership may go to a man who has demonstrated his political expertise by the successful management of a State political machine. Such men are not drawn to New Delhi while Nehru remains supreme: there is room for only one boss at New Delhi. But afterwards—what more natural than that, in a system of machine politics, an expert be called in to control the biggest of the machines? Nehru is known to have a warm corner in his heart for Bijoyanand Patnaik of Orissa; and Mr. Patnaik has shown, in various ways, that he is a man of some vision. However, just as in the United States it is becoming ever more important for a Presidential candidate to come from a key State like New York or California, so ability to control a sizeable block of votes in the Lok Sabha may become more and more necessary for an Indian Prime Minister. In this

[1] Possibly, the election of Dr. Radhakrishnan as President in May 1962 might prejudice the selection of another southerner as Prime Minister. Dr. Radhakrishnan would be ultra-scrupulous in observance of constitutional proprieties.

respect, Y. B. Chavan, the energetic Chief Minister of Maharashra may have the edge on Patnaik.

However, it may be that, in the end, the prize will go to an outsider. In a situation where thoughtful people are increasingly tired of the politics of the machine, of manipulation, and nepotism, they may well turn to the *deus ex machina*, the man who has clean hands. It was in a situation such as this (when the original leadership of Congress was carried off by death) that Gandhi, newly returned from South Africa, stepped unexpectedly into command of the Nationalist movement. To-day, the most distinguished leader—outside of the arena of party politics, yet recognised as an outstanding politician—is Jayaprakash Narayan. The Western press is apt to depict Jayaprakash as a Dr. Pangloss; and it is true that there is a vague and somewhat theoretical side to his political outlook. However, in Indian eyes he is a man apart, dedicated, and uncontaminated. A recent public opinion poll organised by the *Statesman* asked the simple question: who would you like to be the next Prime Minister of India? The choice of a majority of those interviewed fell upon Jayaprakash Narayan.

These men who may inherit the problems, though not the prestige of Nehru symbolise the different possible courses which India may choose to take. The leadership of Krishna Menon would be directed towards a policy of more comprehensive, and perhaps more ruthless national planning. Neither big business nor the superior official would receive such freedom as they have hitherto enjoyed. Hostility to Pakistan would be intensified, and co-operation with the United States and a Conservative Britain would not be made easy. Bijoyanand Patnaik might be expected to move in quite a different direction. Planning would give way to a more pragmatic economic policy in which industrialists of an enterprising and progressive character would be encouraged. India's relations with the United States might become more cordial, while hostility to the Communist world would increase. Should Jayaprakash Narayan, the man with clean hands be called upon, there might be a genuine return to the Gandhian ideal. The great administrative ant-hills of New Delhi would be tumbled down, and an attempt made to re-discover the soul of India in the immemorial countryside. In international relations, Jayaprakash might be expected to look with favour on the Commonwealth and to promote other institutions of international co-operation, with a renewed emphasis upon Afro-Asianism.

It may be that the successor to Nehru will be unable to hold together the fissiparous forces within the Congress, and that disintegration will follow, whether soon or late. Then, national leadership may devolve upon a Prime Minister from within the Communist Party. The decisions taken by the C.P.I. at the end of April 1962 may have far-reaching consequences. In an attempt to secure agreement between the two factions, supreme power was divided, by a special amendment of the Party constitution, between E. M. S. Namboodiripad, former Chief Minister of Kerala, and S. A. Dange, leader of the Communist group in the Lok Sabha until his defeat in the 1962 general election. Namboodiripad took over the post of general secretary, vacant since the death of A. K. Ghosh, and Dange was given the newly-created office of chairman. In an internal tussle for power, both these men would be doughty fighters, but Namboodiripad is likely to have the edge over his rival; and it is not impossible that one day he will be seen attending a Commonwealth Prime Ministers' conference.

The alternatives before Pakistan cannot be related so neatly to the alternatives of political leadership. The most probable course would seem to be a long period of apprenticeship under quasi-military tutelage, terminating in the emergence of the 'sound, vigorous, progressive and powerful state' of Ayub's hope. But all this depends upon the creation of a dynamic economy in place of the present stagnation; the promotion of a genuine spirit of service within the élite of the community, instead of the present truculent 'the world owes me a living' attitude; and an adaptation of Islamic values to the principles of democracy. The poet Iqbal, who strove to achieve an intellectual synthesis of Western philosophy and Islamic faith once wrote: 'I do not know what will be the final fate of the national idea in Islam. Whether Islam will assimilate and transform it, as it has assimilated and transformed before ... or whether it will allow a radical transformation of its own structure by this idea, is hard to predict.' So far it is difficult to detect any interaction of the beliefs of Islam and of liberal democracy in Pakistan. As the Muslim religion is the one tie which binds East to West Pakistan, it is unlikely to be reduced in scale to that of a private, personal faith, as Jinnah envisaged in his inaugural speech to the constituent assembly. Most of the countries of the near and middle East have abandoned the search for a synthesis between religion and the modern, secular state. But Pakistan (whose citizens equal in number the inhabitants of the middle Eastern countries) was created as an expression of the Islamic spirit. As Maulana Maudoodi has trenchantly observed: 'If a secular and Godless, instead of Islamic constitution was to be introduced ... what was the sense in all this struggle for a separate Muslim homeland? We could have had it all without that.' Yet, to a majority of the politically literate in Pakistan, Islam is at best a spiritual inspiration, at worst an outworn shibboleth. The search for an Islamic solution helped to bring about the collapse of parliamentary government in 1958 (though only as one cause among many). It may dog the path of the present régime in its search for progress. Pakistan's leaders, baulked of other solutions, may turn to the maulvis and the mullahs. Pakistan is a land where the leaders and the led desperately want certainty and security; an overall solution to their apparently insoluble problems. Communism purports to offer such a solution. To avoid these latter alternatives, Pakistan must develop an *élan* such as hitherto has eluded its leaders.

'Will ye be governed by the pen or the sword?' It was a turbulent land into which men like John and Henry Lawrence introduced the novelty of law and order. For a time, their Indian subjects were so impressed by the contrast with the old *gardi-ka-waqt* or time of trouble that they regarded British rule as evidence of Divine providence. This attitude faded, within two or three generations, and before they departed the British were to hear Gandhi and Nehru speak of their 'Satanic government'. As the years pass, British rule is seen as an interlude, an *entr'acte*. Much that was confidently regarded as part of the British legacy has already disappeared; dismantled as quickly as the statues of Queen Victoria and her captains and governors which were the lapidary evidence of British rule. How much will survive, and how much will be replaced by institutions evolved out of the experience of independence, we shall see in time. The British were fond of comparing their empire in Asia with the empire of the Romans. When Mr. Macmillan visited India at the beginning of 1958, he is supposed to have murmured: 'I wonder if the Romans ever went back?' Whether or not any did return to Britain after 442 A.D. the Roman spirit never entirely departed from British shores. Will the thousands of young Indians and Pakistanis who today go to Britain and the United States for higher education carry back enough of the joint culture of those whom Carlyle called 'the subjects of King Shakespeare' to mingle with the ideas and beliefs of their own ancient land to create a living spirit of liberty and social justice? A spirit that, perhaps, will have something to teach the Anglo-Saxons when they flag on the way.

APPENDIX: KASHMIR AND THE BORDERLANDS

THE addition of a tailpiece dealing with frontier and external questions to a work on politics can be readily justified. When in 1784, the British in India first established a department to handle foreign affairs, it was called the 'Secret and Political Department', and a 'Political' was the recognised cognomen of an official dealing with border matters right down to independence. A constant preoccupation with the frontiers and the bare mountains beyond has been a feature of high policy both before and since independence. Lord Curzon summed the problem up in one of his evocative literary passages:

> India is like a fortress, with the vast moat of the sea on two of her faces, and with the mountains for her walls on the remainder; but beyond these walls which are sometimes of by no means insuperable height and admit of being easily penetrated extends a glacis of varying breadth and dimension. We do not want to occupy it, but we also cannot afford to see it occupied by our foes. We are quite content to let it remain in the hands of our allies and friends, but if rivals and unfriendly influences creep up to it, and lodge themselves right under our walls, we are compelled to intervene. . . . He would be a short-sighted commander who merely manned his ramparts in India and did not look beyond.[1]

Before Curzon's day, the 'Great Game' had been played out in central Asia. The names of lonely British officers, like Eldred Pottinger, are

[1] Quoted by C. S. Venkatachar in ' Sea Power in the Indian Ocean '; see also his ' Geographical Realities of India ', both published in the *Eastern Economist Pamphlets* series, edited by E. P. W. da Costa.

remembered by a few; but those of valiant Indian agents who observed and reported are forgotten—recalled only by the slightly comic figure of Kipling's Hurree Chunder Mookerjee. While these British and Indian agents precariously sought to extend the influence of the Raj amongst the Amirs and Khans and Lamas, Russian armies moved relentlessly forward. When Curzon became Viceroy, he decided to strike back, and the Younghusband expedition was despatched to Lhasa, to plant the Union Jack on the Roof of the World. Curzon's policy of looking beyond the fortress walls of India led to a more vigorous frontier policy. With Nepal, the most important of the border kingdoms, Britain had traditionally followed a policy of friendship and non-intervention, while recruiting twenty battalions of Gurkhas for the Indian Army. This policy continued, but elsewhere on the frontiers British influence was intensified. In 1910, the ruler of the Buddhist state of Bhutan signed an agreement, transferring conduct of foreign relations to British India, in return for an annual subsidy. The collapse of the Imperial régime in China, and the withdrawal of the Chinese residents and their guards from Tibet, provided the occasion for bringing Tibet into a closer relationship with India. Surveys were made of the remote frontier areas stretching from Ladakh or 'Little Tibet' in the west, along the watershed with Assam, towards the Burma border. Negotiations took place at Simla, 1913-14, which led to an agreement between the Government of India and Tibet, recognising the line laid down by Sir A. H. McMahon as the joint frontier, and permitting the British to establish certain agencies in Tibet to facilitate trade. This agreement was initialled by a Chinese diplomatic representative as third party, but he was subsequently instructed by his government not to sign a treaty.

This represented the high-water mark of the Curzon policy of security through outward influence. In 1919, the Amir of Afghanistan, who had previously conducted his foreign policy through the Government of India, secured recognition as King with a free hand in foreign affairs. The first phase of the Russian revolution saw a temporary collapse of Russian power in central Asia, but despite revolts (the last was in 1937) Communist domination was effectively imposed. Chinese weakness prevented any reassertion of authority in Tibet, though Chiang Kai-shek's political testament, *China's Destiny*, reiterates Chinese rights in Tibet.

After independence, the relations of the Indian Republic with its small Himalayan neighbours closely followed those of the British: for three years, the representative of India at Lhasa was a British official, Hugh Richardson. Sikkim, the state which had been most closely linked with British India, signed a new agreement in 1950. Article 2 states that

'Sikkim shall continue to be a Protectorate of India'. Indian troops may be stationed in the state, and Sikkim undertakes to conduct all its foreign relations through India. A Political Officer is resident at Gangtok, the capital, while the Dewan or Prime Minister is also an Indian official appointed by Delhi. Bhutan negotiated a new treaty in 1949. India undertakes not to interfere in the internal administration of the state; Bhutan agrees 'to be guided by the advice of the Government of India in regard to its external relations'. India allows Bhutan to import arms and warlike stores through Indian territory, while Bhutan agrees not to export such arms across its boundaries. While the treaty did not give India such complete control as that with Sikkim, it confirmed the special relationship between the two parties.

The treaty negotiated between India and Nepal in 1950 was quite different. Article 1 lays down that 'The two Governments agree mutually to acknowledge and respect the complete sovereignty, territorial integrity and independence of each other'. Yet, despite these declarations, India soon came to play a vital part in the internal politics of Nepal. For over 100 years, the Government of Nepal had been in the hands of the Rana family. The Ranas were Prime Ministers and Commanders-in-Chief; all actual power was in their hands. The kings were semi-sacred remote figureheads. The despotic rule of the Ranas was widely resented, and the germ of a democratic movement began among young Nepalis educated in Indian universities. A Nepali National Congress was founded in January 1947 at a meeting in Calcutta, and a civil disobedience movement in 1948 led to small political concessions. Early in 1949, the Democratic Congress was started in Calcutta by a member of the Royal Family of Nepal. The two movements coalesced, and launched a campaign to end Rana rule, with the secret support of the king, Tribhuvana. The Ranas discovered his leanings, and in November 1950 Tribhuvana took refuge in the Indian embassy at Kathmandu. He was flown in an Indian military plane to Delhi and the Nepali Congress launched an uprising from Indian territory. Indian diplomatic pressure induced the Ranas to come to an agreement with the king, at Delhi in January 1951; a coalition government, including the Ranas and the Nepali Congress, would be formed. The most prominent figures in Nepali politics were now the Koirala brothers. A number of governments followed, and a national election was held in February 1959, which resulted in B. P. Koirala becoming Prime Minister. Tribhuvana had been succeeded in 1955 by his son, Mahendra, and the young king did not approve of the chaotic methods of the elected government. Early in 1961 he dissolved parliament and dismissed Koirala, returning to a semi-autocratic form of government. This provoked militant resistance, including attempts on the king's life.

Meanwhile, Nepal was becoming a vital sector in the cold war. By 1960, in order to gain Nepal's amity, foreign aid had been forthcoming to the tune of £23,000,000 from India, £12,000,000 from China, £9,000,000 from the United States, and £4,000,000 from the Soviet Union. The Indian build-up was becoming more evident, military roads were built, and instructors trained the Nepal Army; all this led to resentment against Indian 'Imperialism'. Despite Chinese claims to Mount Everest, there was less feeling about China, and when in October 1961 a treaty was negotiated in Peking which recognised Everest as within Nepal, relations were placed on a cordial footing.

The background to these events was, of course, the deteriorating relations between India and China. When in 1949 the Communists consolidated their hold on China, they were able (as the Kuo Min-tang never could) to re-assert historical claims to the border territories. In May 1951, Tibet recognised China's suzerainty in return for national regional autonomy, after ineffectual attempts had been made to mobilise international support against Chinese penetration. India played a leading part in this arrangement, and in April 1954 a treaty was concluded between India and China which recognised Chinese sovereignty in Tibet; the agreement was to span a period of eight years, and covered India's trading relations with Tibet. The special political agencies built up as a result of the Curzon forward policy were now liquidated. The preamble to the agreement enunciated for the first time, the Five Principles of Peaceful Co-existence. There was criticism in the Lok Sabha of the weakness of Indian policy, but Nehru regarded the agreement as a demonstration of the dynamic of neutralism, and looked forward to perpetual peace and co-operation with China.

Almost immediately, there were indications that China regarded the 1954 agreement as a first step towards readjustment of the Himalayan border to conform with the claims of the past. Chinese activity was marked in two areas, both at the extreme limits of the Indian border. One was Longju, in the high hills to the north of Assam. This area had long been shown on British maps as falling within the boundary of India, but no attempt was made to provide even a skeleton administration until after the second World War when a North-East Frontier Agency was formed to provide a framework for a loose administration. The Agency comes under the Ministry of External Affairs in its 'Political' capacity; this Ministry also controls the Assam Rifles, the military police who maintain watch and ward on the border. The Governor of Assam as 'Agent' for the President exercises the local functions of the Ministry. The other area which was to become a focus of Chinese attention was Ladakh, a remote Buddhist principality which was conquered between 1834 and 1840 by Gulab Singh, who later became Maharaja of Kashmir. British officers made a settlement of the border with Chinese officials in 1842, but the most remote corner was left undemarcated. The signing of a Cease Fire agreement between India and Pakistan in December 1948 left the Republic of India in possession of Ladakh, and Pakistan in occupation of the other frontier dependencies of the Kashmir Darbar, Baltistan and Gilgit. At this point we may conveniently review the main features of the Kashmir dispute from 1949 onward.

At the instance of India, the question had been taken before the Security Council of the United Nations, which proceeded to appoint a series of mediators to attempt to find a solution to the dispute. Successive proposals made by General McNaughton of Canada, Sir Owen Dixon of Australia, and Dr. Graham of the United States were all rejected by India, which took the line that Kashmir had acceded to India, and therefore the only acceptable course was for the complete withdrawal of all Pakistan forces. India gave conditional assent to the holding of a plebiscite (which, indeed, Lord Mountbatten had laid down as a condition for Kashmir's original accession to India) but would not accept any of the many suggestions for plebiscite proceedings. Admiral Nimitz of the United States was appointed plebiscite administrator, but Indian objections led to his resignation from a task he could not hope to discharge.

The unresolved dispute produced endless repercussions. Pakistan's resentment and frustration at India's refusal to negotiate led to a growing association with the United States as a military ally. Pakistan subscribed to the Manila Treaty (SEATO) and to the Baghdad Pact (later CENTO), mainly out of a desire to find international support in the quarrel with India. India, in turn, viewed all such arrangements with suspicion, although the SEATO Council under pressure from Pakistan, went no further than to urge 'an early settlement of the Kashmir question' (March 1956). When the matter was again brought before the Security Council in January 1957, India found herself in complete isolation. Even the Soviet Union, usually to be relied upon to support the Indian case, remained studiously aloof. Krishna Menon attempted to postpone consideration of the matter by a dramatic eight-hour peroration, which terminated in a heart attack. Even this could not prevent the adoption of a motion which amounted to a rejection of the Indian case. Dr. Graham again busied himself in an attempt to devise a formula acceptable to India, but once more his proposals were rejected by the Indian Government.

The internal politics of Kashmir reached a similar deadlock. As Prime Minister, Sheikh Abdullah was the power in the land, and he arranged for elections to be held in September and October 1951 in order to create a constituent assembly. As the number of candidates exactly equalled the number of seats there were no contests: and this fortunate situation has prevailed at every subsequent election. The constitution which Sheikh Abdullah envisaged provided for a certain degree of internal independence, and in India the suspicion grew that the Sheikh was really working towards separation. In August 1953, Abdullah was placed under arrest, and the premiership was given to Bakshi Ghulam Mohammad; demonstrations demanding the release of Abdullah had to be repressed by force. The new Prime Minister proceeded, in February 1954, to complete the full accession of Kashmir to India, and the Indian Constitution was extended to take in Kashmir. Despite the systematic distribution of Indian largesse, the Ghulam Mohammad régime was unable to attain genuine popularity. The incarceration of Sheikh Abdullah cannot have rested easily on the conscience of Nehru, his former friend, and in January 1958 Abdullah was released. Immediately he began a campaign in favour of holding a plebiscite; three months later he was re-arrested; at the time of writing he is still in jail.

This was the uneasy background to the India-China border imbroglio. From 1950, China began to construct a road across the Aksai Chin area, the undemarcated portion of the Ladakh boundary. In 1958 Chinese troops clashed with Indian border patrols, and Indian soldiers were arrested. The whole question was given a more dangerous twist when, in March 1959, the Dalai Lama fled from Lhasa and entered the North-East Frontier Agency, together with thousands of his followers, to claim political sanctuary. Indian opinion came out very strongly in his support, and in condemnation of Chinese violation of Tibetan rights. From the Chinese point of view, this was a departure from the Five Principles of Co-existence, and a hostile note entered into their dealings with India. There were attacks on Indian garrisons in Longju, and in October 1959, an Indian patrol in Ladakh was attacked; nine men were killed and the rest taken prisoner.

An explosive situation now prevailed: Chou En-lai blandly proposed that both sides should withdraw their forces twenty kilometres, leaving the civil administration in charge of existing positions, pending negotiations. This of course would have left China in control of areas recently occupied. Nehru replied by proposing that both parties should withdraw from the territory claimed by the other, but this was not acceptable either.

In the crisis, President Ayub attempted to effect a *rapprochement*. He emphasised the need for India and Pakistan to combine in the event of a Communist threat, and he pointed out that Kashmir was the one issue which really divided the two neighbours. Setting aside the argument that Kashmir should join Pakistan because of its mainly Muslim population as one that Nehru could not accept, Ayub pointed out how West Pakistan depended on Kashmir as the source of the rivers which fed her canal system: the economic argument might, perhaps, prevail where the religious argument had failed. But these advances also met with no success.

Further discussions between India and China led to a joint investigation and the publication in February 1961 of a joint report. This, however, only underlined the fundamental nature of the disagreement between the two countries. Furthermore, the Chinese refused to discuss with India the boundary to the west of the Karakorum Pass: that is to say, Baltistan, the region under the occupation of Pakistan. Independently, China and Pakistan proceeded to demarcate the 300 miles of frontier which lay between them, concerning which no serious difference is revealed.

In this unsatisfactory state the whole situation uneasily remains suspended, with China (according to Indian claims) in occupation of 12,000 square miles of Indian territory and with India and Pakistan no nearer to agreement on the future of Kashmir.

By comparison, Pakistan's dispute with Afghanistan has a cardboard quality despite its serious inferences. Pakistan acquiesced in the territorial delimitation of the sub-continent, although convinced that both wings had been compelled, unfairly, to surrender pockets of Muslim population to India. A small enclave, the port of Gwadur, which belonged to the Sultan of Oman in Arabia was transferred, by agreement to Pakistan in 1958. Only Kashmir—and in particular, the Vale of Kashmir—was regarded as *terra irredenta*. But, as we have seen, Afghanistan promoted the Pakhtoonistan demand as an artificial territorial issue.[1]

After independence, the Pakistan Army withdrew from the Pathan tribal areas, leaving watch and ward to locally recruited militia. This represented a remarkable demonstration of faith in Islamic solidarity. The British had believed a strong military *présence* essential, and even at the crisis of the war with Japan had kept fifty-seven infantry battalions

[1] See Chapter VI, pp. 142

and four armoured regiments on the North-West Frontier. Now, the great cantonments of Razmak and Wana were abandoned; the tribesmen were to be trusted. Afghanistan attempted to overthrow this trust; the Faqir of Ipi, the bane of British commanders in the 1930s, was persuaded to stir things up again. The Pakistan Air Force was able to disperse concentrations of raiders, and in general the tribes remained well disposed to Pakistan. Attempts by Afghan diplomatic representatives at Peshawar and elsewhere to cause trouble led to the closure of Afghan consulates. In retaliation, Afghanistan refused to accept goods despatched through West Pakistan to Afghanistan; this somewhat pointless boycott mainly affected American supplies of Aid. In addition, there were attempts to launch tribal raids with a stiffening of regular Afghan troops. Mr. Nehru chose to contribute fuel to this quarrel by hinting (in September 1961) that the Durand Line as a British-imposed border was of doubtful international validity; as India's case in the dispute with China rested entirely upon British claims, especially that of the McMahon Line, this was a curiously shortsighted gesture. The Pakhtoonistan claim would only become a serious threat should Russia choose to offer strong support to Afghanistan; a development that does not appear likely.

Meanwhile, the Kashmir question and the problem of China's intentions on the border remain, to encourage India and Pakistan to concentrate on military preparedness. Over 60 per cent of the Indian budget, and about 75 per cent of Pakistan's budget are absorbed by defence expenditure. The political implications of this concentration of resources do not require spelling out in detail.

A GUIDE TO FURTHER READING

This bibliography has been prepared on an analytical, chapter-by-chapter basis for the assistance of those who intend to study particular subjects in greater detail. Even so, this list does little more than dip a bucket into a pond. The size of the pond can be ascertained by reference to *Government and Politics of India and Pakistan, 1885–1955: A Bibliography of Works in Western Languages*, compiled and edited by Patrick Wilson, and published by the University of California, Berkeley, in 1956.

The reader who comes to the whole subject without previous reading is recommended to begin with the general works. Where one particular book is outstanding in its field, this is indicated by an asterisk.

GENERAL

Moon, Penderel. *Strangers in India.* London: Faber & Faber, 1944.

Moreland, W. H., and Chatterjee, A. C. *A Short History of India.* (4th ed.) New York: Longmans, Green & Co., 1957.

Schuster, George, and Wint, Guy. *India and Democracy.* London: Macmillan & Co., 1941.

Spear, T. G. P. *India, Pakistan, and the West.* (3rd ed.) New York: Oxford University Press, 1958.

Literary works can often afford a deeper insight into the mind and mood of a society than political or sociological analyses. The following are specially valuable.

AUTOBIOGRAPHY

Chaudhuri, N. C. *The Autobiography of an Unknown Indian.* New York: The Macmillan Co., 1951.

Forster, E. M. *The Hill of Devi.* New York: Harcourt Brace, 1953.

Gandhi, M. *The Story of My Experiments with Truth: An Autobiography.* London: Phoenix Press, 1949.

Nehru, Jawarhalal. *Toward Freedom.* New York: John Day, 1941.

NOVELS

There are a great many second- and third-rate novels which may entertain but do not enlarge one's experience. Among English-language novelists of the Indian scene, R. K. Narayan stands supreme (*Mr. Sampath, The Financial Expert, The Guide, Waiting for the Mahatma,* etc.). His technique is deceptively simple, but revealing. Ahmed Ali (*Twilight in Delhi*), Mulk Raj Anand (*Coolie, Across the Black Waters*), Dennis Kincaid (*Durbar, Their Ways Divide*), Khushwant

Singh (*Night Train to Pakistan*), Philip Woodruff (*Call the Next Witness, Wild Sweet Witch*), all have something valid to say. Rudyard Kipling should not be dismissed as a period writer; see especially *Kim*, and "The Miracle of Purun Bhagat" in *The Second Jungle Book*. In Anglo-Indian literature, Flora Annie Steel's *The Face of the Waters* is one of the earliest and best.

CHAPTER I

DE BARY, W. T. *Sources of Indian Tradition*. New York: Columbia University Press, 1958.

BASHAM, A. L. *The Wonder That Was India*. New York: The Macmillan Co., 1955.

BROWN, D. M. *The White Umbrella: Indian Political Thought from Manu to Gandhi*. Berkeley, Calif.: University of California Press, 1953.

GARRATT, G. T. *The Legacy of India*. New York and London: Oxford University Press, 1937.

RAWLINSON, H. G. *India: A Short Cultural History*. New York: Frederick A. Praeger, 1952.

CHAPTER II

AZAD, ABUL KALAM. *India Wins Freedom*. New York: Longmans, Green & Co., 1959.

GOPAL, S. *The Viceroyalty of Lord Irwin*. New York: Oxford University Press, 1957.

*MASANI, R. P. *Britain in India*. Bombay: Oxford University Press, 1960.

MENON, V. P. *The Transfer of Power in India*. Princeton, N. J.: Princeton University Press, 1957.

MOON, PENDEREL. *Divide and Quit*. London: Faber & Faber, 1961.

CHAPTER III

BRECHER, MICHAEL. *Nehru: A Political Biography*. New York and London: Oxford University Press, 1959.

GRIFFITHS, PERCIVAL. *Modern India*. New York: Frederick A. Praeger, 1957.

MORAES, FRANK. *India Today*. New York: The Macmillan Co., 1960.

MORRIS-JONES, W. H. *Parliament in India*. Philadelphia, Pa.: University of Pennsylvania Press, 1956.

PARK, R. L., and TINKER, I. (eds.). *Leadership and Political Institutions in India*. Princeton, N. J.: Princeton University Press, 1959.

CHAPTER IV

BINDER, LEONARD. *Religion and Politics in Pakistan*. Berkeley, Calif.: University of California Press, 1961.

CALLARD, KEITH. *Pakistan: A Political Study*. New York: The Macmillan Co., 1958.

CHOWDHURY, G. W. *Constitutional Development in Pakistan*. New York: Institute of Pacific Relations, 1959.

*SAYEED, KHALID BIN. *Pakistan: The Formative Phase*. New York: Institute of Pacific Relations, 1960.

SYMONDS, RICHARD. *The Making of Pakistan*. London: Faber & Faber, 1950.

CHAPTER V

As for Chapters III and IV. In addition:

OVERSTREET, G. D., and WINDMILLER, M. *Communism in India*. Berkeley, Calif.: University of California Press, 1959.

QURESHI, I. H. "Islamic Elements in the Political Thought of Pakistan," in R. BRAIBANTI, and J. J. SPENGLER (eds.), *Tradition, Values, and Socio-Economic Development*. Durham, N.C.: Duke University Press, 1961.

ROSE, SAUL. *Socialism in Southern Asia*. New York and London: Oxford University Press, 1959.

WEINER, MYRON. *Party Politics in India*. Princeton, N. J.: Princeton University Press, 1960.

CHAPTER VI

BAILEY, F. G. *The Broker in Politics; Orissa in 1959*. (Forthcoming.)

CHATTERJI, S. K. *Languages and the Linguistic Problem*. ("Oxford Pamphlets on Indian Affairs," 11.) Madras: Oxford University Press, 1943.

DESAI, M. P. *Our Language Problem*. Ahmadabad: Navajivan Publishing House, 1956.

*HARRISON, SELIG. *India: The Most Dangerous Decades*. Princeton, N. J.: Princeton University Press, 1960.

SINGH, KHUSHWANT. *The Sikhs*. London: George Allen & Unwin, 1953.

CHAPTER VII

For the Army:

BIRDWOOD, LORD. *A Continent Decides*. London: Robert Hale, 1953.

For the Civil Services:

BLUNT, EDWARD. *The I.C.S.: The Indian Civil Service*. London: Faber & Faber, 1937.

BRAIBANTI, RALPH. *The Civil Service of Pakistan*. ("Duke University Commonwealth Studies Reprint Series.") Durham, N.C.: Duke University Press, 1959.

CHANDA, ASOK. *Indian Administration*. New York: The Macmillan Co., 1959.

GORWALA, A. D. "The Public Services and Democracy," in R. L. PARK and I. TINKER (eds.), *Leadership and Political Institutions in India.* Princeton, N. J.: Princeton University Press, 1959.

*WOODRUFF, PHILIP. *The Men Who Ruled India.* New York: St Martins Press, 1954, 1955.

CHAPTER VIII

For the Judicial Process:

GLEDHILL, ALAN. *The Republic of India: The Development of its Laws and Constitution.* London: Stevens & Sons, 1952.

———. *Pakistan: The Development of its Laws and Constitution.* London: Stevens & Sons, 1957.

LINDSAY, BENJAMIN. "Law," in L. S. S. O'MALLEY (ed.), *Modern India and the West.* London: Oxford University Press, 1941.

For the Press:

WOLSELEY, R. E. *Journalism in Modern India.* Bombay: Asia Publishing House, 1953.

WORDSWORTH, W. C. "The Press," in L. S. S. O'MALLEY (ed.), *Modern India and the West.* London: Oxford University Press, 1941.

CHAPTER IX

DUBE, S. C. *India's Changing Villages.* Ithaca, N.Y.: Cornell University Press, 1955.

MARRIOTT, McKIM (ed.). *Village India: Studies in the Little Community.* Chicago: Chicago University Press, 1955.

TENNYSON, HALLAM. *Saint on the March: The Story of Vinoba Bhave.* London: Victor Gollancz, 1955.

TINKER, HUGH. *The Foundations of Local Self-Government in India, Pakistan, and Burma.* London: The Athlone Press, 1954.

———. "The Village in the Framework of Development," in R. BRAIBANTI and J. J. SPENGLER (eds.), *Administration and Development in India.* Durham, N.C.: Duke University Press, 1962.

INDEX

Abdullah, Sheikh, 44, 214
Adibasis, 145
Administration, 12-13, 15-17, 53, 62, 70, 85, 151-8, 165-7, 183
Advisory Council of Islamic Ideology, 92, 177
Afaq, 186
Afghans, 11, 16, 75
Afghanistan, 142, 210, 215-16
Aga Khan, 24, 181
Agarwal, S.N., 191
Agra, 125
Ahimsa, 28, 43
Ahirs, 128
Ahmad, Brigadier Gulzar, 195
Ahmad, Z. A., 106
Ahmadabad, 137
Ahmadiyya movement, 76, 119, 177
Ahrar movement, 76, 119
Ain-i-Akbari, 16
Aj, 180
Ajlat, 131
Akalis, 42, 132
Akali Dal, 55, 138-9
Akbar, Emperor, 16, 20, 158
Akbar of Allahabad, 20
Akbar (newspaper), 179
Aksai Chin, 214
Alamgir, Emperor (Aurangzeb), 20, 22
Alexander, A. V. (Lord Alexander), 35
Ali, Mrs. Aruna Asaf, 111
Ali, Maulana Athar, 119
Ali, Justice Fazl, 134, 173
Ali, Chaudri Mohammad, 79-81, 89, 105
Ali, Muhammad (of Bogra), 76-9
Aligarh Muslim University, 20, 78 n.1
Allahabad, 66, 173 n.1, 179, 180, 185
All-India Kisan Sabha, 112-13
All-India Progressive Writers' Association, 111
All-India Trades Union Congress, 111-13
All-Pakistan Confederation of Labour, 118
Ambedkar, Dr. B. R., 46-7, 50, 54, 97, 131-3, 201
Amrita Bazar Patrika, 179, 185
Amritsar, 27, 41-2, 138
Anand, Mulk Raj, 111

Anandamath, 126
Anjam, 186
Andhra Pradhesh, 47, 57, 58, 67, 107-8, 113, 127, 135, 145-9, 199-200
Anjuman-i-Shabal-Muslimeen, 119
Antar Bhasha, 126
Arabic, 12, 124, 127, 141
Army, 12, 13, 25, 33, 37-9; and Pakistan, 72-3, 76, 84, 87-8, 97-8, 141; professional rôle, 151-8, 210, 215-16
Arnold, Dr. Thomas, 158
Arya Samaj, 18, 20, 126, 131, 179
Aryan languages, 11, 124
Ashraf, 131
Assam, 22, 33, 38, 139, 173 n.1, 184, 210, 212-13
Assam Rifles, 213
Assamese language, 124, 133 n.1, 135
Associated Press, 183
Ataturk, Mustapha Kemal, 28, 127, 203
Attlee, Clement (Lord Attlee), 36
Auchinleck, Field Marshal, 38
Aurobindo, Sri, 18
Australia, 49, 173 n.1, 213
Awadhi, 125
Awami League, 77, 79, 81-3, 121, 187
Awans, 128
Ayyangar, M. A., 122
Azad, 187
Azad, Abul Kalam, 35 n.1, 50, 102
Azad Kashmir, 44, 72
Azad Pakistan Party, 107

Bahawalpur, 39, 73, 77, 91
Baidyas, 143
Bailey, Dr. F. G., 130, 144
Baltistan, 44, 213, 215
Baluchi language, 124, 142
Baluchistan, 73, 77, 91
Balvantray Report, 61, 191-3, 199, 201
Bande Mataram, 32, 126
Banerjee, S. N., 179
Bangalore, 62
Bardoli, 29
Basic Democracy, 86-91, 93, 189 194-9, 201
Begar, 15, 193
Benares, 45, 180

221